PEORIA HEIGHTS PUBLIC LIB

296
.442
DAV

10644320

WI ... y?

"As a family thera... ...oved this book. Judy Davis is the first writer I know to take the best ideas from family therapy and weave them into a ceremony of ordinary life. The bar/bat mitzvah is usually seen as a rite of passage for the adolescent. Here it becomes a magical interlude of healing for the whole family and a beautiful example of how a life-cycle ritual can be used to transcend the hurts and differences that arise in any group. Judy has braided a challah of hope for everyone."

—Lynn Hoffman, author of *Foundations of Family Therapy*

"This book is both an indispensable tool and a precious gift for every bar and bat mitzvah family. It is required reading. At last we have a manual for lay people detailing in easy and engaging language what every religious professional has known all along: that the dynamics of our extended families are the primary source not only of our joy and anxiety but also our best hope."

—Rabbi Lawrence Kushner, author of *Invisible Lines of Connection*

"Thoughtful, helpful, and wise, *Whose Bar/Bat Mitzvah Is This, Anyway?* gives parents the great gift of perspective. Judith Davis writes about the emotional and developmental dimensions of this old-yet-new coming-of-age ritual that is ultimately all about 'enacting our best selves.'"

—Anita Diamant, author of *The New Jewish Wedding* and *Choosing a Jewish Life*

"I have read *Whose Bar/Bat Mitzvah Is This, Anyway?* with great pleasure—with laughter one minute, tears the next. The greatest strength of the book lies in its numerous anecdotes, each of which has an important lesson to impart. I have always said that parents can learn the most from other parents' experiences, and this book will be the proof of that."

—Cantor Helen Leneman

Whose
Bar/Bat Mitzvah
Is This,
Anyway?

Whose
Bar/Bat Mitzvah
Is This,
Anyway?

PEORIA HEIGHTS PUBLIC LIBRARY

A Guide for Parents Through
a Family Rite of Passage

Judith Davis, Ed.D.

St. Martin's Griffin
New York

WHOSE BAR/BAT MITZVAH IS THIS, ANYWAY?: A GUIDE FOR PARENTS THROUGH A FAMILY RIGHT OF PASSAGE. Copyright © 1998 by Judith Davis, Ed.D. All rights reserved. Printed in the United States of America. No part of this book may be used or reproduced in any manner whatsoever without written permission except in the case of brief quotations embodied in critical articles or reviews. For information, address St. Martin's Press, 175 Fifth Avenue, New York, N.Y. 10010.

Design by Nancy Resnick

Grateful acknowledgment is given for use of the following material:

The poem by Elie Wiesel in Chapter 8 is from *Souls on Fire: Portraits and Legends of Hasidic Masters.* Copyright © 1972, 1993 by Elie Wiesel. Reprinted by permission of Georges Borchardt Inc. for the author.

Some of the material by Judith Davis has been previously published as follows:

A version of Chapter 3 originally appeared in *Bar/Bat Mitzvah Basics: A Practical Family Guide to Coming of Age Together,* edited by Cantor Helen Leneman. Copyright © 1996 by Cantor Helen Leneman. Permission granted by Jewish Lights Publishing Company, P.O. Box 327, Woodstock, VT 05091.

A version of "The Bar Mitzvah Triangle" in Chapter 5 originally appeared in the *Family Therapy Networker,* July-August 1989. Reprinted by permission.

A version of "The Bar/Bat Mitzvah Balabustah: Mother's Role in the Family's Rite of Passage" in Chapter 6 originally appeared in *Active Voices: Women in Jewish Culture,* edited by Maurie Sacks. Copyright © 1995 by the Board of Trustees of the University of Illinois. Used with permission of the University of Illinois Press.

Library of Congress Cataloging-in-Publication Data

Davis, Judith, Ed.D.
    Whose bar/bat mitzvah is this anyway? : a guide for parents through
a family rite of passage / Judith Davis.
        p. cm.
    ISBN 0-312-18197-3
    1. Bar mitzvah.   2. Bat mitzvah.   3. Jewish families—Religious life.
    BM707.D38   1998
    296.4'424—dc21   97-36420
                                                                  CIP

JUL 0 8 1998

First St. Martin's Griffin Edition: April 1998

10   9   8   7   6   5   4   3   2   1

In memory of
my mother,
who was there
in my tears,

and

in appreciation for
the families
who opened their doors
and their hearts.
Thank you.

If ritual is about opening up space,
may you find treasures
in the clearing.

Contents

Acknowledgments

In addition to the families who shared their stories with me, I have many families to thank and it's hard to know with which to begin—my family of teachers, my family of coworkers, my friends who feel like family, my family at home . . .

The families whose stories appear here, of course, come to mind first. I hope that as they recognize themselves on these pages they will sense my respect and my appreciation. To the extent that this book is useful, these families deserve great credit.

My teachers come next. From Evan Imber Black, my first professor of family therapy, and my original dissertation committee members, Ted Slovin, Charlotte Rahaim, and Janine Roberts who coached me through the process, to Lynn Hoffman, my current teacher, mentor and friend who continues to inspire me, I have been a very lucky student.

And then there are my teachers in the publishing world. From Michael Sanders who first put me on the right track, to

Jane Chelius, Hope Dellon, and Deborah Pugh, who have worked to keep me there, my good fortune continues. Thanks for all the instruction and patient support.

Next are my family of friends. Not only am I lucky; I am blessed. Deep thanks to Carol Rundberg and Renée Spring, my old friends with the recipes and the love, who were there for me when I myself was the bar mitzvah mother (and thanks, Renée, for the book's title); to Hannah Kliger and Rachmiel Peltz, who are there for me always; to Rabbi Shiela Weinberg, who shares with me her experience and insights; to Sally Freeman and my colleagues at the Counseling and Assessment Center, whose support and encouragement go way back; to Barbara Hanson, whose creativity always comes through for me; to Barbara Little, whose kindness and hard work at the Center have no limits; to Grant Ingle at the Office of Human Relations, who shouldered my work as well as his own through many intensive dissertation periods; to Jayne Pearl, who convinced me "it was a book already"; and finally to Cindy Hardy, without whose good-humored typing through pages and pages of indescribable chicken scratch this volume could not have materialized. Thank you all from the bottom of my heart.

And with heart comes my family at home (where for long periods I often wasn't). To Louie, whose bar mitzvah so many years ago began my own rite of passage, to Eric, whose close reading at the end gave me such energy, and finally, to Allen, whose own journey since Louie's bar mitzvah has been so profound, your love is my anchor. Thank you.

Author's Note

My Story: How I Became a Bar/Bat Mitzvah Junkie

Whenever there's a bar or bat mitzvah in my vicinity, I go to it. Whether I am invited or not, whether I even know the family or not. And before anyone else in the congregation—even before the parents or grandparents—I begin to cry. I don't sob or anything like that, I just get choked up, a tear or two spilling out occasionally. Just enough to streak my makeup. Nothing conspicuous, but inevitable.

I wasn't always like this. I used to attend these things like a normal person, just watching the performance on the *bimah* (stage) and feeling the usual skepticism about its meaning. I knew the family wasn't religious. I knew the kid would be quitting Hebrew school as soon as he could. And I knew that the parents who were looking so thrilled with it all had been fighting about one thing or another up to the last minute. Sure, I'd get choked up a little seeing the frail old grandfather being helped up for his *aliyah* (the honor of reciting the blessings before and after the Torah reading), or by the child's shining little face next to the huge, velvet-covered Torah, or by something in the Rabbi's speech to the family. But for the most part, I'd just sit there with my doubts about the bar mitzvah and my worries about the future of the Jewish people.

That was before my own son's bar mitzvah, before I became a family therapist, and before I began studying ritual and its relationship to family.

In 1980, two things happened. The first is that we survived our eldest child's bar mitzvah, an experience that ended up having a profound and completely unexpected impact on my marriage. To make a long story short, it forced my husband, Allen, and me to grow up and allowed all kinds of changes to follow. In particular, it allowed us to give up some of our rigidly held differences about Jewish ritual. Ever since we had met and married fourteen years earlier, I had always been the good daughter trying to keep my kitchen kosher, while he played the rational humanist denouncing "antiquated superstition" wherever he saw it. You could set your Jewish calendar by our fights about each holiday. They had become a regular part of our routine—until the bar mitzvah, that is. Preparation for this event—an event that would be, after all, our family's first public statement about our relationship to Judaism—changed our dynamics forever. What started happening to our son, as he began practicing his Haftarah, forced us all into new ways of being. I won't go into it here—the whole story is in Chapter 5—but Louie's response to our conflict and the way we responded to *his* response somehow allowed something in our dynamics to shift. In ways that we couldn't begin to understand at the time, Allen and I were somehow able to become less attached to our old ways of interacting around Jewish practice, and this new flexibility let Louie off the hook of divided loyalties. The change between us ultimately allowed our son to climb down from the tightrope he'd been walking between us ever since he *could* walk. The change was fundamental, and its reverberations continue to this day.

The second thing that happened, a few months afterward, was that I began training as a family therapist. Here I was part of a team experimenting with what were then cutting-edge ideas about healing and therapeutic rituals (paradoxical tasks prescribed to disrupt problematic behavior). By practicing these rituals, it was thought, the family could begin interrupting the "dysfunctional" patterns that were keeping them "stuck." The team would do things like having a family meet together each night to thank the ten-year-old for wetting his bed because his "symptom" helped the rest of them avoid dealing with more difficult things—Sister's potential learning disability, Mom's grief over her mother's recent death, the unspoken conflict between the parents. Or, in the case of a feuding couple, we prescribed that when the fighting was about to begin, they stop their interaction and go out to visit the site where they had ceremoniously buried their list of grievances about the affair that happened early in their marriage.

You get the idea. These tasks were designed to work paradoxically in that they directed the family to do what it was already doing, but in a particular and ritualized way that changed the meaning of what they were doing just enough so that they couldn't continue to do it as before.

One day as I sat with a family I was working with, struggling to present the elaborate ritual my supervisor had devised, I kept thinking about the real-life bar mitzvah ritual I had just gone through and wondered about possible connections. Had our experience been completely idiosyncratic, simply a function of my family's particular *mishugass,* or was there something more? Was it possible that I could learn something from naturally occurring cultural and religious rituals that would actually be useful in helping families stay healthy and not need to go into therapy and be given rituals that were artificial?

This question became the basis of my graduate research. For the next five years, I read everything I could get my hands on about ritual, about how families change, about adolescence, and about bar/bat mitzvah. From this reading, I came to two major conclusions: (1) There are, in fact, some fundamental connections between cultural ritual and family health; and (2) no one was looking at them. In particular, no one was looking, from this perspective, at the ritual of bar/bat mitzvah.

For the most part, sociologists had dismissed the bar/bat mitzvah as a nostalgic, if not regressive, remnant of an earlier age; novelists mocked it; and anthropologists ignored it altogether. Even Jewish educators were conflicted about its value. The only psychological literature I could find at that time focused solely on the child and explained the phenomenon simply as oedipal drama. Even the proverbial fountain pen, the quintessential bar mitzvah gift, was sexualized. For psychoanalysts, it became the immigrant family's version of the phallic sword! Not too helpful. In fact, it was missing the point (so to speak) entirely.

In contrast, I decided, my research would look *not* just at the child, but at the entire family; *not* just at the ceremony, but at the entire year surrounding it; and *not* just at the religious meaning of the event, but at its psychological and social potential for the evolution of the family. Ultimately I did a study in which I followed four very different families for six months, while they were planning, experiencing, and reflecting on their first child's bar mitzvah. Not only did I do interviews, but I also attended all of the bar mitzvahs—"researcher as guest," a new category.

Throughout the process I was constantly exploring what

family therapist Karl Tomm calls the *circular connections* between who the families were, what they were doing, and what it all meant to them. It was an incredible experience. The first family was a divorced couple in which the new stepmother—who wasn't Jewish—became pregnant three months before the bar mitzvah. How's that for a little stress? In the second family, the two sets of grandparents hadn't met since their children's wedding fifteen years earlier—a day remembered as "extremely tense, to put it mildly." The next meeting was scheduled to happen at the bar mitzvah. And by the way, this was a family in which this was to be the first bar mitzvah in three generations. The third family was an immigrant family with a single mother whose son's bris had been held in Russia—in secret. The doctor was a friend and had promised not to report it. And the fourth was a Hasidic family with five generations of Rabbis on both sides. This ritual, according to the father, was "a mere blip" in a life of almost constant ritual. What an array of perspectives! And yet what a surprising similarity of experiences.

I came away from this thesis not only with a diploma, but also with an enormous respect for the power of ritual and with a completely new view of the value of bar and bat mitzvah in the lives of contemporary American Jews.

I also came away with this crying condition. Somehow, I can't look at a bar/bat mitzvah family now without imagining all that it took to get these people to this place in their lives—and what this place symbolizes for their future—whether they're conscious of it or not. The poignancy of the moment always fills me with tears.

But my new way of seeing the bar/bat mitzvah has led me to more than just a few good cries. It has taken me on an unanticipated journey that is still very much in progress. At the beginning of my research, I was almost embarrassed to answer people who asked me what I was studying because they would inevitably start snickering and tell me to hook up with a band and a caterer and go into business. Who ever heard of doing research on bar mitzvahs? Who, really, took the event seriously?

Things are different today. Now when I say I've written a book to help bar/bat mitzvah families through the process, I feel proud, and no one is making jokes. Not only has the idea of ritual become decidedly more respectable, but it is clear to me that my first son's bar mitzvah—so many years ago—was, in fact, the start of my own coming of age. It is a fitting example of the idea that our child's rite of passage is as much a family milestone as it is our child's.

But I'm getting ahead of myself. As I said, the conclusions I drew from my research surprised me. I hadn't expected to come away from the study with so positive a view of a ritual that I had previously found so hollow. As a therapist, what impressed me most dramatically was the potential of the process to promote family healing and growth. The ritual's classic capacity to help participants change and remain stable at the same time—precisely the function of therapy—fascinated me.

When I was asked to write a chapter about my findings in a professional book entitled *Rituals in Families and Family Therapy*, I did so eagerly. It was, I thought, a perfect way to share my ideas with other therapists. It was also, I thought, a perfect way to be finished writing and thinking about bar and bat mitzvahs so I could start thinking about something else. The Bar Mitzvah Lady moves on!

But then the Rabbi of a local synagogue asked me to talk to a group of parents whose children would be celebrating their bar/bat mitzvahs in the next six to twelve months. That talk went very well—so well, in fact, that it led to many more talks with many more groups of parents—and lots more thinking. Wherever I went, the feedback was the same: There is much more going on for families engaged in the process of planning a bar/bat mitzvah than anyone acknowledges, and the amount of sheer emotion, if not anxiety, is profound. Parents in all kinds of configurations and at all levels of Jewish practice— from those who were Orthodox, to those who rarely set foot in a synagogue, to those who were actively conflicted—were hungry to talk about what they were feeling, and universally grateful for ideas that helped them make sense of those feelings. From parents who were worried that they were becoming over-whelmed with anxiety, to parents who were worried that they weren't worried enough, the message was the same: "You should write a book!"

So here it is, a book that contains the ideas, stories, and suggestions I've been collecting in the course of my journey. I am indebted to all who encouraged me to translate my "the-ory" into practical application, and I am especially grateful for their support while I struggled to find a voice for this transla-tion.

A NOTE ON THE PHRASES *BAR MITZVAH* and *BAT MITZVAH*

The phrase *bar mitzvah* or *bat mitzvah* is a noun, not a verb. It is the name of the celebrant and (in current usage) the name of the ceremony. Translated literally from the Aramaic and the Hebrew, it means "son of" or "daughter of" or "subject to the commandments."

We say that we are planning our child's bar or bat mitzvah, and we say that our child is becoming a Bar or a Bat Mitzvah. (The plural is *B'nai Mitzvah* when it is a group of males or of males and females. It is *B'not Mitzvah* when it is a group of females.) We do not say our child is "being bar or bat mitz-vahed." Yes, I know we *say* it, but grammatically we shouldn't. Philosophically we shouldn't either. "Being bar/bat mitzvahed" implies that something is being done to a passive celebrant. "Becoming" a Bar/Bat Mitzvah describes what is happening much more accurately as an active, evolutionary process.

In this book I will use *bar* and *bat mitzvah* in the lower case to refer to the event or the child (as in *bar mitzvah boy* or *bat mitzvah girl*). I will use the upper case, *Bar* or *Bat Mitzvah,* when I refer to the celebrant without using the word *girl* or *boy.*

Introduction

Today I Am a Basket Case

"You know the joke about how the child is supposed to say 'Today I am a man'?" Sandra* asks.

"Yes." I nod tentatively.

"Well, for me it's going to be 'Today I am a basket case!' " she says, eyes welling with tears. Sandra has come to my office to talk about the anxiety overwhelming her as she is planning her son's bar mitzvah. "I just can't imagine it . . . standing up there on the bimah and talking to Joey about what this all means to me. I can't imagine even getting to that day with all that has to be done and all that's going on."

Sandra's husband, Don, it seems, has some real reservations about the meaning of bar mitzvahs. His own had left him with a bad taste and he is being "totally uncooperative." Every time she goes to him for help with something on her "to do" list, they end up fighting. She is fighting with her son also. Joey

---

*All names and enough descriptive details have been changed to protect confidentiality.

isn't studying regularly enough, and Sandra can't see how he is going to learn his Haftarah in time. On top of that, he is starting to give her trouble about his curfew. "You know, Mom," he yelled at her one night, "I'm not a kid anymore. You can't keep telling me what to do and when to do it all the time!" It is so unlike him.

But Sandra has something bigger to worry about than arguments or curfews: Her father's emphysema. It is getting worse. How is he going to make it to the bar mitzvah? But he has to. As he'd told her so often on the phone, he is "living for this day."

By now Sandra is sobbing.

Sound familiar?

If you are in the process of planning your child's bar or bat mitzvah (and especially if it is your first), I have no doubt that something in Sandra's story strikes a chord. Though the details may be different, I am sure that you, like Sandra, are dealing with unanticipated issues that are threatening the joy of this "joyous occasion."

Maybe you're divorced and you and your ex are fighting over how much this is all going to cost, never mind how you're going to handle all of the public awkwardness you already foresee.

Or maybe your spouse is not Jewish and the whole question of religious meaning is coming up all over again.

Or maybe you're worrying about your relatives' disapproval. They're from the city, and your plans for an informal party in the backyard will never meet their expectations.

Whatever the details, the distress is always the same. "What's wrong with me?" I can almost hear you asking. "What's wrong with my husband/wife, our child, our marriage, our family? The bar/bat mitzvah is supposed to be wonderful. How come I feel so miserable?"

There is nothing wrong with you, your child, or your family. You are simply in the thick of an extremely complex and pressured moment in your life. Sandwiched between the needs of your emerging teenager and your aging parents, and dealing with your own issues about being old enough to be the parent of a Bar/Bat Mitzvah (you were always the kid at these affairs, weren't you?), you and your family are caught up in the inexorable process of developmental change. All of the family's biological clocks are ticking: Susie's growing up, Grandma's getting sicker, you're getting slower. And in the midst of all that ticking, you are planning one of life's major public dramas. You are in the process of orchestrating your child's formal coming of age in the Jewish community. What would be crazy is if you *weren't* feeling stressed.

For over a decade, I have been studying the meaning of bar/bat mitzvah in the lives of contemporary American Jewish families. As a family therapist and educator, I have been meeting and talking with hundreds of bar and bat mitzvah families—religious families and secular families, families who live together, and families who don't. I have counseled single-parent families, gay families, interfaith and interracial families, families with lots of money, and those with little. I have seen families with bar mitzvah traditions going back hundreds of years, and families for whom this is all brand new. From all of this experience, a few fairly simple—but very clear—observations have emerged.

The first is that *we underestimate the complexity and power of this event.* The bar/bat mitzvah is not simply a religious ritual and a big birthday party. Nor is it just another developmental milestone along the child's road to adulthood. It is, instead, a major transitional event in the life of the entire family: the child, the parents, and the grandparents. It is a rite of passage that reverberates throughout the entire extended family as well.

If you don't believe me, when was the last time you heard so much from Great-Aunt Doris on your mother's side?

The second observation is that, for most of us, *it is a time not only of great joy, but of great turmoil as well.* To begin with, yours is a family entering a new—and some would say particularly challenging—life stage. Most obviously, or maybe most confusingly, your baby is growing up. Between Barbies and bras or Weebelos and wet dreams, your head is spinning.

Mirroring your child's changes are your own transitions. You are maturing, and your relationship with your spouse or partner must also mature. Like it or not, still married or not, the two of you are having to find new ways of dealing with each other and with your differences over this upcoming rite of passage, this initiation into Jewish responsibility, and your child's transition into adolescence.

And finally, your parents aren't getting any younger, either. With their aging increasingly apparent, you are beginning to worry about them in new ways. If the inevitable caretaking reversals haven't yet begun, they are fast approaching. No wonder you're anxious. You are dealing with change in relation to your child, your parents, your partner, and your self.

With these stresses, your hands are full enough . . . but there's more. As a family, you have chosen to celebrate your child's thirteenth (or twelfth) birthday with a religious ritual that has a long history and lots of expectations around it. You have thus taken on the challenge of organizing—not to mention paying for—what is, no matter how you do it, the biggest, costliest, most emotion-filled event you've ever been responsible for. Think about it. The last event of this magnitude and importance was probably your wedding, and that your parents may have managed.

Never before have you, as an adult, brought together all of the people who are important to you in your life and in your child's life to meet at a single event at once so personal and so public. For the first time, you will be encountering *with one face* all of your relatives, neighbors, colleagues, and friends from over the years. This is a huge emotional, as well as logistical, undertaking.

And that's still not all. Unless you are an observant Jew or one who has evolved an alternative connection to Jewish tradition with which you feel totally comfortable, you are probably at least ambivalent—if not altogether conflicted—about the spiritual meaning of what you are doing and what you are asking your child to do. This is especially true for many of us who grew up in the God-Is-Dead sixties and seventies, a time when we rejected religious ritual as hollow and meaningless. If you are like me, every time you read or hear something critical or ridiculing about today's bar and bat mitzvahs, you probably wince with recognition if not self-blame.

The third observation, you will be happy to hear, is not about more stress, but about the way the bar/bat mitzvah helps us make use of the stress. In the context of these life-cycle changes and these pressures of preparation, *the bar/bat mitzvah works therapeutically to help us heal and grow*. Like a lightning rod, it draws out in dramatic relief whatever is important or difficult in the family and pushes us to deal with it—in one fashion or another—through the event and its preparation. The bar/bat mitzvah, like all life-cycle rituals (weddings, circumcisions, baby namings, funerals), focuses the family's attention on exactly those developmental issues it needs to be addressing.

How the Bar/Bat Mitzvah Works Therapeutically

The bar/bat mitzvah works therapeutically in many different but complementary ways. Most basically, it works by providing us with a familiar format; a safe, protected structure for making and marking transitions. It gives us a powerful vehicle for expressing both our grief and our joy as we, our children, and our parents move into new phases of our lives. With its rhythmic symbols and ceremony, the ritual guides us almost hypnotically into new territory. It makes our journeys public and positive.

And it makes us cry. We cry with love and pride as our child soars, and we cry for all of the losses that come with that achievement. Our tears are as traditional as the Torah. And in that moment, surrounded by those who love us, our tears are healing. Whether Sandra's father is there in his wheelchair or there only in words and in prayer, her sorrow will be understood and shared by all. The people we have brought together for the bar/bat mitzvah ritual become our community, amplifying our happiness and cushioning our grief. This is what communities have done throughout the ages. This is what communities—and rituals—are for.

The bar/bat mitzvah ritual also has potential for healing in the way it works symbolically to mark boundaries and make connections. Yes, the bar/bat mitzvah is the child's proclamation of growing maturity and eventual independence, but it is a proclamation being made in the embrace of the family and in the center of its tradition. It is a proclamation of increasing distance, yet paradoxically also one of connection and continuity. "Yes," the child is saying, "I am growing up and away (and you can't tell me what to do), but I will always be connected to my family, its culture, and its tradition." In this ceremonial performance, the ties between the generation before Sandra's and the one that follows hers are strengthened.

Through the bar/bat mitzvah, the child enters the pivotal teenage years not only with an act of accomplishment that enhances his or her sense of pride and self-confidence, but with an expression of both separation and connection that is developmentally perfect. It is perfect because it represents exactly the shifting boundaries between closeness and distance that emerging adolescents need to be working on as they evolve their self-stories, their ideas about themselves as young people "getting ready" to become adults. And given that their stories and their parents' stories are so interwoven, the bar/bat mitzvah's capacity to help with these shifting stories is developmentally perfect for us too. Just as the experience helps our children develop confidence in themselves, it helps us have confidence in them—and in our own ability to know how much to hold on and how much to let go—not only as parents, but as partners and as children ourselves.

In a highly charged and dramatic way, the bar/bat mitzvah itself is a kind of story—a story that the family enacts about the child's growing up. It is in this enactment that the child—the central character—gets to portray his or her unique version of the evolution, and the parents and grandparents—the other members of the cast—get to enact their versions of support. The invited family and friends, who have gathered as audience, witness and celebrate the enacted changes.

The bar/bat mitzvah works to promote growth and healing in yet another way as well. This "work" is much more prosaic, almost accidental, and generally unnoticed. It happens during the planning period, the months before the event when we are immersed in the nitty-gritty decisions about whom to invite, where to house them, what to feed them, where to seat them, what kind of party to have, what kind of music to play, etc.

These pragmatic decisions are, of course, about managing the size, shape, and feel of the event, but they are also about much more than that. Whether we consciously notice their potential or not, these decisions and the manner in which we make them often turn out to be opportunities for evolving new ways of relating to each other—new ways that our new life stages demand. For instance, how we negotiate whose names will be on the invitation when there has been a remarriage can help estranged parents reach a new level of compromise and understanding. Such a shift could begin changing old patterns that have kept our child painfully choosing between us for years. Allowing the bat mitzvah girl to wear the party dress we'd thought too grown-up could be an important message acknowledging her increasing maturity and our acceptance of it. Our choice to house both sides of the family in the same hotel, despite the still-painful misunderstanding at the last family gathering, becomes an opportunity for reconciliation that would have been impossible with continued distance. At the very least, it is a message about our expectations that such movement is possible. Our decision to invite Aunt Rosie, who's been cut off from the family since Uncle Ben died, could begin healing wounds throughout that generation, many of which we aren't even aware of. *Our decisions about everything, from prayers to parties, guest lists to thank-you notes, are really decisions about relationships.* They are the therapeutic opportunities hidden in the ritual's details, the "work" that occurs as we outgrow old roles and take on new ones.

"So you mean I'm not the only one walking around crying all the time," Sandra said with relief as I shared some of these ideas in response to her story. "No, you are not alone," I told her, as I now tell those of you who may also be crying. There is a lot going on in your lives at this moment, and only some of it is obvious.

This book, I hope, will help you with the part that is not so obvious: the part that goes on behind the scenes and below the surfaces, the part that no one prepares us for. If I have learned anything in my work with bar/bat mitzvah families (and in fact, with all families), it is that when we begin to understand that our anxieties are not automatically a sign of "hypocrisy," "pathology," or "dysfunction," we begin to feel better about what we are experiencing. When we see how our feelings make sense—and in fact can be useful—we want to know more about what we are feeling. When we understand that life-cycle rituals work on many different levels at once, we want to find ways of making the experience as useful as possible on as many levels as possible. This book, I hope, will help you to do this. It is a book for those of you who are as upset as Sandra, for those of you who are upset about *not* being upset ("How come this isn't touching me the way it seems to be touching others?"), and for those of you who are simply interested in learning what you can about the bar/bat mitzvah experience.

It is intended to offer a new perspective on what might be going on for you and your family as you plan and live through this rite of passage. It is a view that is different from, but complementary to, the more familiar perspective of the Rabbi and Jewish educator. Whereas their focus is on the religious and spiritual aspects of the experience and on the bar/bat mitzvah's potential to help us and our children become more connected to Judaism, this book focuses on the family dynamics involved in the process, the bar/bat mitzvah's potential to help us evolve through the interlocking cycles of our lives.

The traditional concern is to make the experience as *religiously* meaningful as possible. My concern in this book is about making the experience as *developmentally* useful as possible. The views are different, but intrinsically related. To the extent that we absorb our culture and traditions through the family, whatever enhances our family's health and well-being also enhances our ability to pass on its values and its tradition. Similarly, that which enhances our ability to connect our spiritual past and our future, enhances our potential for health in turn.

*　　*　　*

A word of warning: Some of what you will read here might make you feel more stressed—at least at first. Given that I am putting into words much of what is rarely mentioned when we talk about bar and bat mitzvah, I am bringing to the surface a lot that is—in the short run at least—easier to not think about. But hang in. After the initial gulp, the usefulness of this way of thinking becomes apparent—and comforting.

My hope is that this book will give you not only a greater appreciation for the richness and importance of what you are going through, but also provide some new ways of thinking and talking about it with each other that will help you take advantage of the opportunities embedded in the process. Although this is clearly not a recipe book—*101 Steps to a Better Bar/Bat Mitzvah*—it does contain lots of practical suggestions that flow out of this way of looking at the ritual. They are suggestions for how to use the bar/bat mitzvah to enhance relationships, foster maturity, solidify connections, heal old wounds, enrich traditions, and celebrate strengths. They are ideas for helping the bar/bat mitzvah process do more of what it does naturally.

The word *naturally* here is key. Life-cycle rituals are our original form of therapy. They work their magic *naturally. The suggestions in this book are meant only to enhance the bar/bat mitzvah's intrinsic power. They are not prescriptions that must be followed before proceeding.* In fact, just reading about them might be enough to enrich what is already happening, or help get you through a place where you feel stuck. They are ideas to stimulate your own thinking. They are not tasks to add to your list of things to worry about.

The truth is that, in general, if you do nothing more than plan the event and live through it, the process will leave you feeling profoundly moved, and in a way you might not even notice at first, somehow changed. The sense of pride and accomplishment most families experience—even (or maybe especially) those who thought they'd never get through it—is enormous. On so many levels, it is not only the child but the whole family who mounts the bimah, passes through the ordeal (and it *is* an ordeal or it wouldn't be an achievement), and moves forward in life. And the family accomplishes this feat, with whatever imperfections, surrounded by an almost mesmerizing atmosphere of love and goodwill. No matter what the tensions or disharmonies, with the whole clan gathered to witness, nurture, and celebrate the journey, the power of the process is extraordinary and universal. One bat mitzvah mother described the experience as being "love-bombed." Every time she turned and took a peek at the sea of friends and family seated behind her in the synagogue, she felt overwhelmed. "They were smiling at me, nodding at me, winking, crying. It just filled me with love."

My hope is that the ideas in this book will add to your experience of this love. I am honored to be joining you on your journey, and I hope that my presence will be useful. But before I get too choked up imagining it all, let me wish you and your whole family a heartfelt, anticipatory "Mazel tov!"

Part I

The Issues

Chapter 1

The Bar/Bat Mitzvah
"Stress Syndrome"

THE MEANING OF *MAZEL TOV*

All my adult life I've hardly ever been able to say the words *mazel tov* without getting a lump in my throat. Something in that phrase would get to me, but for years I had no explanation. Then I figured it out. I came across a definition that explained the intensity.

According to Leo Rosten in his book *The Joys of Yiddish*, this phrase (which translates literally as *good luck,* but is used as "congratulations") is spoken by an individual not only as an individual, but implicitly *as a representative of the community.* It is used as an acknowledgment that the person being addressed has just done something hard or has gone through something dangerous.

Now it made sense. This little Yiddish phrase—used so often it's almost English—is actually packed with meaning. It not only conjures up the power of the whole community, but it amplifies all of the effort and risk involved in what the recipient has just been through. No wonder it is so moving. And no wonder it is shouted out immediately after the bar/bat mitzvah child completes the Haftarah and the blessing. The "ordeal" is over and these words express not only our great joy, but our great relief as well.

STRESS AND THE STEINS

Ever since the bris, the Steins had been looking forward to Barry's bar mitzvah. But now that it was less than six months away, they were miserable. Always a loving, communicative couple, they were suddenly finding themselves unable to talk to each other. According to Sharon, Jerry wasn't doing enough to make the bar mitzvah (and the family) more spiritual, and according to Jerry, Sharon was going overboard in her need for "visible manifestations of faith." Wasn't it enough that they'd started lighting Sabbath candles, going to the synagogue on Friday nights, and having a seder each year? Not according to Sharon. She believed the family needed more, and she felt they should be figuring out what "more" was together. "I resent being the only one coming up with innovative ways of involving the children in Jewish holidays and rituals," she would say repeatedly. In response, Jerry was feeling increasingly punished for not being more creative.

Both of them were shocked at how badly they were feeling and frightened by how difficult it was for them to talk about it.

Stress and the Bar/Bat Mitzvah

Bar/bat mitzvah stress, like cholesterol, comes in two kinds: healthy and unhealthy.

Healthy Stress

Healthy stress is the kind that is inherent in all life-cycle rituals. It comes from the pressure of our biological clocks and the pressures of the performance.

By definition, big changes are happening and not just for your child. As your son or daughter matures into adolescence, you and your parents are also changing, and those changes are all connected in complicated, important, and sometimes painful ways. A big test is being set up, and it's not just your child who is going to go through it. Your child is responsible for learning his or her Haftarah, but you are responsible for organizing and managing the event at which that learning (and all that it symbolizes) will be demonstrated and celebrated. Your child's ordeal (what psychoanalyst J. Arlow calls a "trial by recitation") is public. Yours is behind the scenes, private, and probably more than you'd bargained for.

The third source of natural pressure comes, not with all life-cycle rituals, but only those that are connected to our religious or cultural identities. For most of us, preparation for a religious or cultural ceremony brings up all of the unresolved spiritual questions and issues we carry. "What do I really believe about all of this, and what do I want my child to believe?" What *are* my values?

These stresses of change and of preparation are normal, necessary, and useful. Believe it or not, in combination with each other they work to help us get through this transitional time in our lives. Preparing for the event forces us to deal—literally and symbolically—with whatever is difficult or important for us and our families (aging, divorce, illness, estrangement, loss of faith, death). And the event, in turn, provides a structure for those who love us to witness and support our efforts. It is in these ways that the stresses are helpful. They help us move from the known to the unknown, from the familiar role of being a child to the uncharted territory of being a teenager, from the familiar role of being a parent of a child, to the new world of parenting a teenager. These are necessary pressures that assist in our whole family's evolution. They are so much a part of our everyday experience in this stage of life that we hardly take notice of them—much less appreciate their impact or value.

Unhealthy Stress

The unhealthy stress, on the other hand, is not inherent in the process, but comes from the myths and doubts we carry around in our heads about the bar/bat mitzvah. The myths are the unspoken assumptions about right and wrong ways to "do" a bar/bat mitzvah. They are the *shoulds* we keep measuring ourselves against: This *should* be easier; this *should* be harder; we *should* be more religious; our child *should* be more enthusiastic; we *should* be making a different kind of party; our parents *should* be more supportive; and so on and so on.

The doubts come from the ridicule and the criticism we have absorbed over the years about today's version of bar and bat mitzvah. Between the comedians' mockery, the Rabbis' exhortations, and our family's idiosyncratic expectations, it's hard not to feel confused or embarrassed—and sometimes even panicked—because we are too busy to take time out to deal with any of these feelings. What *are* we doing all this for, anyway?

These stresses are further complicated by the fact that there are at least two of us involved in the planning. We and our spouses (and our ex-spouses and our new spouses) all have different histories and needs in relation to this child's coming-of-age in the Jewish community. Each of us brings our own issues and confusions into the process, and conflict is often hard to avoid.

But because one of the myths we hold on to is that there shouldn't be stress, confusion, or conflict (and if there is, there's something wrong with us), we feel doubly bad about how we're handling this whole thing. No one prepares us for the complexity of what we are experiencing, and so we think we're the only ones finding it all so difficult. We feel overwhelmed and fall silent. We don't talk to each other, to our parents, to our children, or to other bar/bat mitzvah parents about what is really going on for us. Shame exacerbates the natural pressures of this period and makes even the simple tasks—not to mention the really difficult ones—huge hurdles. The pattern I'm describing is what those who give such things labels might call the bar/bat mitzvah "stress syndrome."

But before I make this sound worse than it is, let's go back to the Steins.

THE STEINS, CONTINUED

When we left the Steins, tensions were mounting and every little planning decision was becoming a potential source of pain. The more tense they became, the more silent and resentful they were with each other. And the more silent and resentful, the more difficult it was to agree on even the most minor of details. The pressure was building, and they felt powerless to stop it.

Sharon and Jerry were walking on eggshells with each other, and the kids were clearly feeling the cracks. Barry was getting headaches every time he had to go to Hebrew school, and eight-year-old Becky was beginning to wake up regularly with the nightmares she hadn't had since she was five. By the time they came to a workshop for bar/bat mitzvah parents that I was leading at their synagogue, they weren't sure they were going to get through the ordeal at all.

Surprisingly, it didn't take much to make a difference for the Steins. Just hearing about the complexity of the bar/bat mitzvah process, and the pressures inherent in the experience, seemed to be enough for something new to begin happening. It was as if a valve had been opened and the built-up steam released. "You mean we're not the only ones feeling like this?" they said. "You mean other 'happily married' couples are also having problems?" The relief was palpable as they and the other parents started sharing their stories and discovering common patterns.

What had the most impact for the Steins was learning that conflict between partners over the bar/bat mitzvah can often be connected to unresolved issues with their own parents. Hearing this seemed to be transforming. It was as if the idea gave them a kind of permission that was liberating. Over the next few weeks, they found themselves talking with each other in ways they hadn't for years. It was as if they were meeting each other for the first time and telling stories about their childhoods and histories that were new to themselves as well as to each other. As each began exploring what they thought this bar mitzvah—and the way they were planning to do it— would mean to their parents, new worlds of understanding and empathy seemed to open to them. They were feeling closer and more intimate than they had for years.

Jerry's parents were Holocaust survivors, and for them the bar mitzvah could never be Jewish enough. They'd never forgiven their son for moving out of the neighborhood and away from their Orthodox world. Nothing their son could do would make up for this "betrayal." For Sharon, on the other hand, whose parents had long ago rejected Jewish tradition in favor of more "progressive" causes, her return to ritual was regressive and unfathomable, if not altogether disloyal. As far as they were concerned, she was going off the deep end.

It was fascinating, the Steins told me, to think about how differently (and similarly) each set of parents was responding. It was even more fascinating, they went on, to see how intensely and characteristically each of them was responding to their parents' responses. And it was most fascinating of all to see how their individual reactions were interacting with each other's. Suddenly their conflict had a whole new meaning—one that was much less threatening and shameful. "This is really about ourselves growing up," Sharon said in amazement. "About dealing with our parents as adults!" added Jerry. "No wonder this has been so hard!"

When I saw Sharon and Jerry a month or two after that workshop, they talked about how helpful it had been to hear that their stress was normal in relation to what they were experiencing and not necessarily a sign that their marriage was deteriorating. They talked also about how differently they were talking to each other these days, let alone whether they were talking differently to their parents. Of course, there was still plenty of stress and plenty about which they disagreed, but now, somehow, they had a much less threatening understanding about their differences. Rather than fighting with each other about what they were or were not doing, they were talking about the meaning of their anxieties. Rather than silence and shame, there was talk and curiosity. Nothing about their circumstances had changed, but the atmosphere was different.

And it was a difference that the children could feel too. Both the headaches and the nightmares had disappeared. Now Barry was talking to his parents not only about how scared he was about performing in public, but about the ambivalence he was feeling about the whole thing. More significantly, Jerry and Sharon were talking honestly with their son about their own thoughts and feelings, and about what meaning the bar mitzvah held for each of them and their families. Barry's doubts became something he could talk about without shame, and his parents could help him deal with them by talking about their own.

GOOD STRESS AND THE STEINS

As their first child was entering adolescence, Sharon and Jerry were also maturing. As preparation for their child's bar mitzvah was forcing each of them to confront their changing relationship to Jewish ritual, it was also forcing them to confront their changing relationships to their parents. These changes were necessary, but understandably difficult. As they were preparing for their child's process of letting go, Jerry and Sharon were engaged in their own letting go. They were growing up. Jerry was no longer needing to be so haunted by (yet rejecting of) his parents' painful history in order to stay loyal to them. They would simply have to accept the fact that the ceremony—and their son—would be "less religious" than they would have wanted. And for her part, Sharon was no longer needing to agree (or disagree) so adamantly with her mother's forceful ideas in order to remain a good daughter. Her parents would simply have to accept the fact that the ceremony—and Sharon—would be "more religious" than they would have wanted.

These were big shifts in Sharon's and Jerry's identities as children of their own parents, but they were more than that. As we mature in relation to our parents, we mature in relation to our partners and our own children as well. In preparing for life-cycle rituals, a kind of emotional echo chamber gets set up, and shifts in one generation reverberate throughout the others. This is difficult but important work. It is exactly what the good kind of stress helps us with. When this rite of passage is working, it forces us to grow.

BAD STRESS AND THE STEINS

As their child was changing, so were Sharon and Jerry changing, and the upcoming ritual was forcing them to confront these changes. Not realizing any of this, all Sharon and Jerry knew was that they were fighting and feeling terrible about it. This fighting was bad enough, but what made it worse was that it was in direct contrast to the love and joy they had expected to feel during this moment in their lives—a moment they had been looking forward to for so long. The contrast was shocking and scary. Their response, not surprisingly, was to blame themselves, each other, and their son who "wasn't practicing enough." Increasingly they were becoming less and less able to talk about what was happening. Instead of being joyful, talk about the bar mitzvah had become toxic. Their level of bad stress was in the danger zone.

The Steins began reducing the stress when they started looking at it from a new perspective. Once they began to see more of what was really going on for them below the surface of the details, the more the tensions made sense and the more they were able to talk about them. As they talked, they were able to separate issues between them as a couple from issues between them and *their* parents that had nothing to do with their marriage, but nonetheless affected it dramatically. Without the silence that had acted like a petri dish in which their fears and resentments flourished, they were able to use their son's upcoming bar mitzvah as catalyst for their own coming of age.

You and the Stress:
Taking Your Family's Pulse

As you read about the Steins, I'm sure pieces of your own story are running through your head and taking shape. What parts of the Steins' experience resonate with yours? What feels very different? What new thoughts come to you as you read about them and the ideas about good and bad stress?

Here are some questions that might be useful in thinking about your own story. They are the kinds of questions I'd ask if you and I were talking in my office.

- As you prepare for your child's bar/bat mitzvah, what are the areas of stress you are aware of? For yourself, your partner, ex-partner, the bar/bat mitzvah child, other siblings, your parents?
- What are some areas of stress you might not be aware of but that others might be? (It sounds like a crazy question, but think about it.) What do you think your husband/wife/child/parent would say is stressing you and what about that is stressing them?
- What do you know about how you've dealt successfully with stress in the past that can be helpful in this situation (beyond the usual prescriptions to take a breath, take a nap, and take a hike)? What do you want to make sure you do and what do you want to make sure you avoid doing regarding this stress? Another way of asking this question is: In what ways have you, in the past, succeeded in resisting stress's power to debilitate?
- Who in your family or among your friends is aware of the stress you are experiencing? Who would be most surprised to hear about what you are feeling? Who would be least surprised?

- What might be different if you shared some of what you are feeling, thinking about, hoping for with your partner, your parents, your child, your sibling, your friend?
- How might you begin?

If this kind of activity appeals to you (some people hate these questionnaire formats), jot down some of what fits for you. Then notice in what ways you can turn the bad stress into good.

Good Stress

Example:

Sometimes I feel like I'm losing it with Jessie. One minute I can't believe how competent she is and the next I'm treating her like an eight-year-old.

_____

_____

_____

Bad Stress

Example:

Everyone loved cousin Paul's daughter's "black-tie optional" bat mitzvah party in Connecticut. What will the family think when they see the informal party we're planning to make?

_____

_____

_____

Bad Stress Made Good

Example:

In what ways can I change worrying about my family thinking that I am not financially successful enough, to thinking about how this kind of party reinforces the way *I* want to live? In what ways can I use this as an opportunity to talk with my child, my parents, my siblings about what's become important to me at this stage in my life?

_____

_____

_____

Putting It on Paper: A Strategy for Stress

Journals

For some parents, writing about what they are thinking and feeling can be very useful. In fact, many parents begin keeping a bar/bat mitzvah journal at this time. This journal—not to be confused with the "to do" list—often comes to be the place where they can take some time out to capture what they are experiencing and to think about it in new ways. By putting feelings into words on paper, we often get new perspectives that are helpful. These new perspectives might also give you some new ways to think about sharing what your are thinking with those in your life with whom such sharing might be useful. Your answers to the stress inventory could be a way to begin.

Letters

Writing in journals can often lead to writing letters. Although we usually think of journal writing as writing to ourselves, what we often discover in them are ideas and feelings that we want others to hear.

As you read what you've written in your journal, you might want to think about how to turn some of your thoughts into letters. What ideas, needs, or feelings come up for you as you think about your child's rite of passage that you want, for instance, *your* mother to know about? Which of these could you convey more easily in a letter than in a face-to-face conversation? How could this letter help make way for such a conversation? What thoughts and feelings could you share more easily with your child in the form of a special letter to her than in another "heart-to-heart"?

Here's what two women did with this idea:

LENA'S LETTERS

Letters can be useful even if they aren't or can't be sent. One bat mitzvah mother whose own mother died when she was thirteen knew that the intense sadness she was experiencing preparing for her daughter's celebration was not about the upcoming event but about her own loss. Still, she couldn't shake her sadness. She was worried that the grief she thought she had always been able to contain would now spill out and spoil her daughter's *simcha*, her joyous event. Through her tears, Lena wrote in her journal about the anger she felt toward her mother for having left her, and in the process began expressing a level of compassion for her mother—and for herself—that she had never before been able to feel. It took only my casual suggestion that she might turn her journal thoughts into a letter to her mother for Lena to take off with ideas of her own.

Not only did she write to her mother (a letter that she keeps in her drawer of private treasures), but she wrote two more as well. The second was to herself as the thirteen year old who'd suffered alone and in silence. As an adult woman, she wrote to acknowledge the child's loss and console her grief. This letter too went into the special drawer. The third letter was to her bat mitzvah daughter about the strength, compassion, and ability to express emotions that she so admired in her and that she felt so proud to have fostered. This letter also went into the drawer—but only after it was copied and read aloud to her daughter on the day of her bat mitzvah.

The act of writing had proved liberating. Once the letters were completed, Lena began planning her daughter's celebration with an energy and spirit she'd never thought possible. Once her ideas were to become part of the public praise (for her daughter and for herself), they became a resource on which both she and her daughter could continue to build.

REVA'S DREAMS

One mother I know began keeping a list entitled "Dreams I Had for You When You Were Born." It was in a separate section in the loose-leaf book she'd put together to keep the planning details organized. Whenever she began doubting herself or the appropriateness of even going through with the bar mitzvah at all (her husband was not Jewish and she herself had grown up with almost no Jewish practice), she would go back to this list and remember how it *did* fit with her hopes and her dreams. What also became clear from the list was how she wanted her son to know about that fit. The letter to him that she eventually turned this list into became—as in Lena's case—not only a family treasure, but the basis of her words to him on the bimah.

Chapter 2

Bar/Bat Mitzvah Myths:
Debunking the Unexamined "Shoulds"

Whether we recognize them or not, all of us carry around myths about bar/bat mitzvah that we've absorbed over the years. These are the unexamined "shoulds" that silently shape our actions and the meanings we make of our experience. Here are a few that I hear most commonly—and how I've come to respond to them. I've also included an occasional story to illustrate what I'm talking about.

The bar/bat mitzvah should be joyous. *So how come I feel more fear than joy?*

Yes, it *is* joyous, but it is not simple. Much more than celebrating is going on. The effort involves lots of complicated changes, competing needs, hard work, and often even pain. And no one prepares us for this complexity. Everything we've ever heard or read related to bar and bat mitzvah has been about the child's needs, or the family's level of religious observance, or about how to deal with the caterer. No one talks specifically about what's going on emotionally for us as parents, so we assume that that's somehow not very important. It's no wonder then that we're left with the idea that our feeling confused or upset is simply proof of what we've always suspected: That we are, at best, unusual, and at worst, dysfunctional.

We should know what is expected and how to organize everything perfectly. *So how come I'm feeling so incompetent?*

Why should you know what's expected and how to do it? Have you ever been in this place in your life before? Especially if this is your first child, it wouldn't be surprising if your general level of anxiety is edging off the charts. Not only have you never organized a religious/public/family event like this, you've never had a child becoming an adolescent like this. Child-development experts say that it is the first child in the family who takes us over our "learning edge." Absolutely everything is new and uncharted. And even if you already have one bar or bat mitzvah under your belt, this is not only a different child with different strengths, needs, and relationships, but a different family—maybe smaller, maybe larger, definitely older, hopefully wiser.

No matter what your family's circumstances, the number of decisions you have to make can feel staggering. Beyond whatever structure the rabbi and the synagogue impose on the service and the child's "requirements," everything else is left to your discretion. Depending on the synagogue, there are still lots of choices to be made regarding even the service (like who gets the aliyahs, who presents the tallit, who makes speeches, who reads additional prayers, etc.). And in terms of the festivities after the service, the whole thing is usually up for grabs.

Whether the celebration will be big or small, formal or informal, limited to the day of the service or spread out over a long weekend, the choices are completely open and each choice leads to yet another tier of choices. And all of our choices have repercussions—most often *emotional* repercussions. It is no wonder that we sometimes feel overwhelmed.

Our focus should be on the spiritual and religious aspects of the event. *So how come we're spending all our time worrying about petty details and logistics?*

Of course the religious and spiritual aspects of the bar/bat mitzvah are important; indeed central. After all, this is not just another birthday party. It is a religious ceremony proclaiming your child's identity as an emerging Jewish adult. But the plans and logistics that you focus on during the months before the event are also important. They are, in many ways—some more directly than others—very much connected to the religious and spiritual aspects of the event.

Most obviously, without our doing the organizing, our child's bar/bat mitzvah wouldn't be happening. Simply making the decision to mark your child's twelfth or thirteenth year with this Jewish ceremony is, in itself, a statement of values and identification. In making all of the decisions about such things as time, place, invitations, food, housing, honors, and music, we are also determining the size, and shape, and "feel" of the event through which our child and our family will be experiencing and expressing who we are and what is important to us. Everything from who gets the aliyahs to where we house the out-of-town guests says something about what we value and what messages we want to transmit to our children. Even the most seemingly pragmatic decisions can have larger meanings. It's probably not for nothing that you are worried about what your mother is going to say about which caterer you chose. Whether the chef's specialty is shrimp or strudel can have important emotional meaning.

Even the choice of date can have such meaning.

BUBBIE'S FEET

One day when I asked a family how they had chosen the date for the bar mitzvah—what I thought was an innocuous query to ease into an interview—the question was met by silence and puzzled looks all around. It was hard to remember such a detail so far back. Then suddenly, Donnie, the bar mitzvah boy, piped up with a smile: "It's because of Bubbie's feet!" "Bubbie's feet?" I asked. "Yeah, my grandmother lives in Florida and she has bad feet. So we had to make my bar mitzvah in May instead of in February when my birthday really is, so it wouldn't snow and Bubbie could wear open shoes."

With this one small detail, a whole world of meaning emerged. Donnie's parents were not only being pragmatic, they were doing important emotional work: honoring the past, solidifying connections between generations, and modeling the way children should care about parents. They were also, it turned out, engaging in a process of healing. For as long as he could remember, Donnie's father, Mark, had been in conflict with his own parents. As a young man, Mark had dramatically rejected their "smothering" old-world demands and had kept himself emotionally as well as physically distant. At some unspoken level, his son's upcoming bar mitzvah was Mark's message to his parents about love and about reconnection. Zayda, Donnie's grandfather, had died years ago. Bubbie just *had* to be there.

This next story illustrates another way in which details can be useful.

DETAILS AND DISTRACTION

Both Sarah and David Bergman are Jewish educators. Few parents could be more committed to, and creative about, fostering a solid Jewish identity in their children. So when their first child began studying for her bat mitzvah they were thrilled. They were looking forward to the whole process with great joy and anticipation.

But when I met them a month before the event, they didn't look so joyful. Almost in a whisper, they confided that they were not at all happy with how things were going. "Instead of concentrating on what is really important," they said with embarrassment, they were "drowning in a thousand and one details" that they felt were "in and of themselves unimportant, but at this point, unavoidable." What they were worried about was that the event had become too big and too complicated and that they were losing sight of the real meaning of what they were doing.

By the time I met them again, it was three weeks after the bat mitzvah and they were not only feeling better, but actually radiant with pride and happiness. "It was more than we could ever have hoped for," they said ecstatically. "Despite how prepared we thought we were for what this 'coming of age' ritual was all about, we were totally unprepared for what it felt like standing up there with Tanya in front of everyone. The emotional release just hit us in the face."

What the Bergmans were struggling to describe was the meaning of their experience. "It was as if our earlier distraction with the logistics had forced us to hold off on the feelings until that exactly perfect moment. . . . I don't really understand it," Dave continued, "but I do feel there's some connection here."

The child should choose freely whether or not to have a bar/bat mitzvah. *So how come we acted like Benjamin's bar mitzvah was a given? Did he ever really have a choice?*

It is not possible for a twelve-year-old child to make a decision of this kind independently. Such decisions are always a reflection of his or her parents' choices; whether those choices are expressed explicitly or implicitly, singly or jointly.

In families where both parents are clear and unconflicted about their identification with Judaism and its ritual practices, it is rare that a child will even question the idea of becoming a Bar/Bat Mitzvah. In families where either or both of the parents have doubts about Jewish ritual in general or this ritual in particular, the child is very likely to reflect similar doubts and ambivalence. In families where there is actual conflict between the parents over whether or not there should be a bar/bat mitzvah or how it should be approached, the child is caught in the impossible position of having to choose between parents, an absolutely untenable position. It is at this point not a spiritual or religious decision, but a decision to side with one parent and to figure out how least to reject the other. Most children find creative or creatively problematic compromises. They find ways of doing it and not doing it at the same time—practicing, but practicing reluctantly; participating, but being sick, sullen, or rebellious.

MY OWN SON'S CHOICES

My son, Louie, bridged the abyss between his parents on matters of ritual quite ingeniously. Although both of us are Jewish and in fact first generation Jews, Allen and I had diametrically opposed ideas about Jewish tradition and practice. Louie's usual way of managing our differences was to act like me and think like his father. He did what I told him to do, but questioned and mocked it the way Allen did. He attended Hebrew school, but told me that he thought that religions divide people. He didn't drink milk with his hamburger, but ridiculed kashrut as irrational. He studied his Haftarah, but stopped doing his public school homework. Our son had found some uniquely creative solutions to the problem of staying loyal to both of his parents. It was not until these solutions became problematic enough (the call from his English teacher was the last straw) that Allen and I were forced to come together in new ways on this topic of ritual practice. (See "The Bar Mitzvah Triangle" on p. 107).

In retrospect, our situation was easy compared to others I've heard about since then. The following stands out in particular.

DIVORCED AND FURIOUS

Cindy and her ex-husband were in pitched battle over whether or not their son would have a bar mitzvah at all. Cindy's ex was not Jewish. When they first married, neither she nor Jack were interested in religion and they'd never really talked about how they would raise their son. It was only after the divorce, five years later, that Cindy became interested in her Jewish identity and in fostering that identity in her son. When Jack found out that Matt was in Hebrew school preparing to become a Bar Mitzvah, he grew furious. Sure, Cindy had custody, but he had some say in his son's upbringing too, didn't he? Jack was adamantly opposed to his child's participating in this "archaic Jewish ritual."

Needless to say, Matt was in a terrible position. He didn't know what to do, and every time his mother asked him what he preferred because she "didn't want to force anything on him," he simply shrugged his shoulders and withdrew. As the time to start studying his Haftarah approached, Matt became more and more withdrawn, and Cindy more and more worried.

It was not until she heard other families' stories at a workshop in her synagogue that Cindy knew what to do. She told her son that *she* had decided that he would have a bar mitzvah, and that he did not have a choice. She had taken Matt out of the middle of his parents' battle and relieved him of the responsibility of having to choose between them. The relief, Cindy said, "you could actually feel." As soon as Matt knew he didn't have to choose between his parents, he was able to join his fellow students wholeheartedly in their preparations and able to learn his Haftarah with ease. Cindy was thrilled with the progress Matt was making, and determinedly found ways of dealing with her ex-husband on her own.

Our relatives should be thrilled and supportive. *But if my father-in-law makes one more sarcastic remark, I'm going to tell him to stay home.*

People approach the bar/bat mitzvah the way they approach life in general, only more so. The helpfulness of those family members who are usually supportive will probably intensify as the event draws nearer. On the other hand, we can expect the criticism, backbiting, and general unhelpfulness of those who usually relate to us in these ways to escalate similarly. Two metaphors come to mind. The first is that preparation for the bar/bat mitzvah acts like some forms of therapy that deliberately escalate the family's level of interaction and emotion in order to make the patterns more visible and thereby more available for change—as when the family is instructed to eat a meal together during the therapy session and the differences between the ways Mother and Father deal with their anorexic daughter's refusal to eat is highlighted and examined.

Another way of thinking about this intensification process is in terms of a lightning rod: The process of planning the event attracts and brings into sharp relief whatever issues are salient in the family, and in one way or another pushes us toward dealing with them (thus making them less dangerous). Examples here include a loss that was never grieved, a conflict that's never been resolved, a pain that's never been acknowledged, a new family member who has never really been accepted.

Hearing the bar/bat mitzvah described in terms of therapy or lightning, can, I know, be frightening. But this kind of thinking can also be comforting. There is a difference between intensity that is predictable and expected, and intensity that comes out of the blue—with no warning and precisely at a time when we are anticipating nothing but sweetness and light. Like the intensity that becomes useful in therapy, and the electricity that gets channeled and made safe through the lightning rod, the intensity we can anticipate and then use during the bar/bat mitzvah process can be experienced as helpful rather than dangerous. Knowing ahead of time that the process of planning our child's bar/bat mitzvah is likely to bring up intense emotions—within us and between us—allows us the opportunity to make use of those emotions. It gives us some space to think about alternative ways of responding to the emotional currents; ways that are different from those in which we have previously been trapped.

SUSAN AND HER SISTER

Susan and her sister had never gotten along. As the younger of the two, Susan had always been labeled the good daughter in contrast to Arlene, who'd been "difficult" since birth. Needless to say, the more Susan's goodness was pointed out in the family, the more Arlene had to be the opposite and the more the tension between them grew. By the time they were young adults they'd learned to make their fights less overt, but no less intense. As soon as they could, they moved away from the house and from each other. A fortuitous series of job relocations, however, ultimately landed them and their families in the same small town. Their children were in Hebrew school together.

As Susan's first child's bat mitzvah was approaching, Arlene found herself truly excited for her sister and wanted to help. She tried—and Susan let her try—but they were soon arguing in ways they hadn't since childhood. For every decision Susan made, Arlene had some objection or some better idea. Their tension was becoming a real source of worry and sadness for Susan. She was increasingly afraid that their "old stuff" would spill and spoil the simcha.

From one of my articles that a friend had sent to her, Susan read about how the bar/bat mitzvah can be used to interrupt emotionally painful patterns. She decided to try it with her sister. The way things were deteriorating, what did she have to lose? She became determined not to get "hooked" into lashing back the next time Arlene said something critical or sarcastic. What she found was that when she didn't respond with her usual defensiveness, Arlene's next remark would be more palatable and her own response would be more acceptable to Arlene in turn.

The cycle of escalation was interrupted, and with this progress, Susan found herself feeling even more courageous. One day when they were out shopping together, Susan talked to her sister about the pain she'd felt as a child in being cast as the angel while her sister was being cast as the demon. This candor and compassion opened up a flood of feelings between the two sisters. They talked for hours—about themselves, about their parents, about what each thought the other had been thinking. In an indirect but very real way, this talk changed the bat mitzvah talk. Not only could Susan now hear her sister's suggestions differently, but even the suggestions themselves seemed different.

This is the most important birthday in my child's life. The party should be exactly how she or he wants it. *So how come we're not hiring that hip-hop band?*

Yes, king or queen for the day. Yes, hero or heroine of the story. But it's not only the child's day and not only the child's party. It is a day for the entire family and a party to celebrate everyone who is part of and connected to that family. It needs to be a party they can all enjoy, and hip-hop—no matter how cool—probably won't fit the bill.

As parents, it is up to us to set limits and teach values, to use the opportunity to continue promoting our child's moral and social development. In the process of negotiating the party's details, we are teaching all kinds of lessons. Lessons about taste, about money, about the importance of celebration and pleasure, but also lessons about empathy, consideration, and respect.

Engaging our child in a discussion about how we can make sure Aunt Gertie and Uncle Morris, who traveled so far to be with us, can feel comfortable, implicitly teaches a lesson very much connected to what the bar/bat mitzvah is all about. It is a great opportunity to talk about and demonstrate what it means to care for others' needs and comfort. Developmentally it is a perfect time to be helping our children move from the self-centeredness of childhood to the self-awareness of young adulthood. By emphasizing the balance between the child's pleasure and the pleasure others also need to experience, we are teaching very important lessons. We'll just have to keep looking for a band that can play some freilach as well as some funk.

If we don't make a bar/bat mitzvah, our child will never be accepted as an adult in the Jewish community. *But we've never had anything to do with a synagogue or with religious rituals. We're Jewish, but such an event seems totally alien to our family.*

Where is it written that someone needs to have a bar/bat mitzvah in order to be a Jewish adult? Nowhere. There is nothing in the Bible about having a bar or bat mitzvah. The term bar/bat mitzvah refers to a legal status, a status to which every Jewish person—at least thirteen years and one day of age—is entitled. (For girls, it's twelve and one day.) It is a status that defines the person as responsible for his or her own moral actions and able to be counted in the *minyan* (quorum needed for public prayer). No special ceremony whatsoever is required.

The bar/bat mitzvah ceremony as we know it today is a folk custom that began in the fourteenth or fifteenth century. It was originally a minor marking of the first time a boy was called up to bless the Torah. (A girl blessing the Torah wasn't conceivable until the twentieth century.) The bar mitzvah was never meant as a significant turning point in a person's life, much less in the family's life. The "event" usually happened during a regular Thursday morning service (one of the three days of the week when the Torah is read) and the boy went back to *cheder* (school) immediately afterward. Or it might have happened on Saturday morning as a little extra during the Sabbath service. If the family or shul could afford it, there was maybe a little schnapps and herring afterward, but that was it.

The bar mitzvah didn't become a major event until the twentieth century when American synagogues needed to find ways to make sure that first- and second-generation Jews would join, send their children to Hebrew school, and pay dues to keep up the building; when a big "affair" came to mean that the immigrant family had made it in America; and when kosher caterers became popular and Hallmark got wind of an opportunity.

The bar mitzvah waned in popularity during the late sixties and seventies when Americans of all persuasions were rejecting religion and religious ritual, but began growing in popularity again in the eighties. At this point in our evolution, the bar/bat mitzvah has become a phenomenally popular institution.

Indeed, even adults are now having them. With a general resurgence of interest in ethnic roots and ritual performance, many women and men who did not become B'nai Mitzvah as teenagers are choosing to do so as adults. With the vast number of interfaith marriages, and the growing number of converts who are also choosing to become B'nai Mitzvah, the number of these ceremonies is continually growing.

All this is to say that the bar/bat mitzvah is not a ritual written in stone. It is a flexible, evolving phenomenon that has a very different set of meanings for every era, for every celebrant, and for every family. Although a fixed age—thirteen—is a useful piece of clarity and connection in an era where most everything else seems so murky and individualistic, you need to do what is right for you and your family. If having a bar/bat mitzvah is not possible or appropriate at this time, don't beat yourself up. It can always be done later. And it can be done differently.

A TALLIT OF KENTE CLOTH

When their older child, Sal, was thirteen, he did not want a bar mitzvah. Good thing, because Amy and her husband, Troy, were not ready to make one for him. Amy was Jewish and Troy, African-American. Despite fifteen loving years of working to help themselves and their children embrace these two identities, they had not yet figured out how to create a coming of age ceremony in the synagogue that would meet Amy's needs but not ignore Troy's. It took a few more years and lots more talk and tears until they were able to move beyond this emotional impasse. By then, Sal's sister, Maya, was turning thirteen and very certain that she *did* want a coming of age ceremony.

What they created was an enormously powerful "family service" in which both children were able to demonstrate in their own unique ways what they had been learning with their Hebrew tutor and how they had integrated their learning as Jews *and* their learning as African-Americans. With parents and friends participating with them on the bimah, Sal and Maya talked about "not being half anything," but about being whole. They led prayers, chanted readings, gave talks, read poetry, and made music that movingly demonstrated their maturity, their values, and their pride in their heritages. They called what they had created "A Tallit of Kente Cloth: A Celebration of Family." All of us packed into the synagogue that night called it wonderful.

The bar/bat mitzvah should reflect our family and our level of ritual observance. *So how come the Rabbi is being so rigid—forcing Keith to attend a year of Saturday morning services and saying we should come with him despite how busy she knows we are?*

The kente cloth story is an example of a creative alternative to a traditional bar or bat mitzvah, but it was deliberately *not* called a bar/bat mitzvah. According to the rules of that family's synagogue, neither Sal nor Maya had fulfilled the educational requirements for becoming a Bar/Bat Mitzvah and so they had to call what they were doing something else. In this case it was called a "family celebration" and it suited the family's unique needs perfectly. But this is not the path most families could or would choose.

Most families who decide that their child will become a Bar or Bat Mitzvah in the more traditional sense discover that there are some very clear requirements established by their synagogue and enforced by the Rabbi—or Cantor or whoever works most closely with bar/bat mitzvah families. While these requirements vary from synagogue to synagogue and can appear at times arbitrary, the idea of "a set of requirements" is a very important part of the ritual process itself. Life-cycle rituals evolved over the ages in order to ease transitions, to make passages from one stage of life to another "safer." It is the very structure, the *requirements* of the ritual that ensures this safety. There is a beginning, middle, and end to this process and everyone is held by this inevitability.

Knowing that there is a clear sequence from beginning to end allows us to throw ourselves into the process without fearing that we might never get out of it. The logical sequence of preparation (first the guest list, then the invitations, then the . . .) and the prescribed steps of the performance (first the blessings, then the Haftarah, and then . . .) act as our road map through the journey. No matter how emotionally involved we become, we know implicitly that the event will not only happen but will eventually be behind us. One of the paradoxical truths about such rituals is that to the extent there is structure, we have freedom. By knowing the parameters of an experience, we can plumb its interior to whatever depth we choose. The structure or "rules" are our compass. Eventually we will get out of this forest.

By knowing what has to be accomplished both before and during the ceremony, we know when we have passed the test, when we have survived the ordeal. In light of this idea, the child who thinks she or he has conned the Rabbi into reducing the number of Haftarah lines or number of prayers she or he would have to learn is ultimately cheated out of the sense of accomplishment that might have been felt by "playing within the rules."

What's more, the rules you and your child are following are the same that all the other families and children in your congregation are following. This commonality of experience is an expression of shared community. That your child is going through the same experience as his or her Jewish classmates is part of what binds them together as a community. It will be a memory they share and on which they build.

To round out this description of classic ritual process, what you should know is that ritual has what is called "open" parts as well as the "closed" required parts. In contrast to all that is structured by the synagogue, Rabbi, and teachers, there is all the rest that you as the celebratory family get to determine for yourselves. Who will receive the aliyot, how you want to present the tallit, whether or not you want to speak to your child from the bimah, what you want the party to be like—these are the places where the event reflects your individuality and the customs of your local community. These are the open spaces that the closed parts make possible.

This should be something our child is thrilled about and looking forward to. *So how come he seems more bored than thrilled, more scared than excited?*

Although the number of children who express enthusiasm for the upcoming event is beginning to grow with improved bar/bat mitzvah programs in some Hebrew schools, most (especially boys) do not—at least directly. Even when they are clear that they definitely want to go through the experience and are proud they are doing it, enthusiasm about studying a lot and performing in public is not characteristic of most adolescents. The event *is* an ordeal, and since when is any twelve-year-old thrilled about ordeals? Of course they're excited about the party afterward and the presents and, for many, the idea of seeing cousins and friends who live far away, but first they have to live through "the torture."

Dennis was a child who put the archetypal torture into words. He seemed to understand the symbolic "death" inherent in all rituals of initiation.

THE EMERALD FOREST

After several heart-stopping pauses and an occasional grimace of unmistakable desperation, Dennis breathlessly chanted the last note of his Haftarah and the concluding prayers. With a huge sigh of relief and a very broad smile, he then went on to deliver his speech. In it he talked about what the process of preparing for his bar mitzvah had been like for him and what he'd learned through it. He began by talking about a movie he had seen recently. It was called *The Emerald Forest* and it included a tribal initiation ceremony.

"The line in that movie that best fits how I feel now is when the boy's father says, 'The boy must die.' When I first heard it, I thought it meant the boy would literally die. But as I watched, I realized it was a symbol of what that culture thought the torture would accomplish. It really meant that through the torture he would die as a boy because he was becoming a man. He will lose some things and gain others. Judaism has a similar torture—the Haftarah. I also am losing some things and gaining others."

Even though most B'nai Mitzvah will say afterward that they were happy and proud to have accomplished what they did, real appreciation for the bar or bat mitzvah is generally something that grows for the child in retrospect. It is generally not until young people approach the end of their teenage years that they are capable of looking back and beginning to value the experience on many levels. Even those for whom it really did feel torturous are usually able to admit years later to being glad that they'd been made to go through it. This really is one of those instances in which "they'll thank you (more) for it later."

If this is about coming of age, my child should be acting more maturely. *So how come she or he seems to be regressing these days?*

"One minute he seems to show such insight and the next, he's checking out kindergarten all over again." How many times have I heard this kind of lament!

Two thoughts come to mind in response to this expectation of maturity. One is that maybe our children do regress a bit—a last fling at feeling little before the pull toward getting bigger can no longer be avoided? A little backward spiraling in the service of pushing forward? A common reaction in the face of stress? Perhaps. Or maybe it just *seems* to us that our children are regressing. Just as likely, they are acting age appropriate, but it is our expectations that are changing too rapidly. As much as we may know that our twelve-year-old is still "only a child," the act of preparing for a bar/bat mitzvah emphasizes the fact that soon he or she won't be "only a child." As much as we know that this "ceremony of adulthood" does not mean our child is becoming an adult, we also know that it does mean that he or she is on the verge of a big transition. To the extent that we are on the lookout for "signs of this verge," our child's usual ways begin to feel incongruous. Like the dolls on Sarah's pillow.

BEDTIME BARBIES

The lineup of Barbies next to Sarah's pillow each night was so much a part of her bedtime routine that it had become almost invisible. It was not until she began practicing her Haftarah that her mother began to think seriously about all of the changes she and her daughter were about to experience. It was "as if I could actually see into the future," Mrs. Cohen said of that moment when she began noticing the dolls in new ways. "All of a sudden I loved those Barbies and wanted them to stay right where they were. In fact, I even found myself wanting a few more of the old-time baby tantrums I'd just been complaining about."

Uncovering Our Family's Myths: "Shoulds" We Should Know About

Family Questionnaire

Most of us don't even recognize that we have myths about the bar/bat mitzvah. Myths are by definition so pervasive that we hardly notice them. This questionnaire is an opportunity to begin to pay attention to the ideas we carry around with us about bar/bat mitzvahs—ideas we got from our parents, our Rabbis, stand-up comedians—and our own experience. Some myths are useful and serve as goals toward which we want to aim (e.g., the bar/bat mitzvah should be meaningful), but most do little more than put unnecessary pressure on us (e.g., the weekend should be flawless). To uncover what myths you and others in the family may hold, here is a questionnaire you can photocopy and pass around. After it's been completed you can exchange them and/or gather as a family to talk about them.

Name _____

My relationship to the Bar/Bat Mitzvah _____

End these sentences as many times as you can:

1. The bar/bat mitzvah ceremony
   should _____
   should _____
   should _____

2. My (child's, grandchild's, nephew's, etc.) bar/bat mitzvah
   should _____
   should _____
   should _____

3. At my bar/bat mitzvah, I
   should _____
   should _____
   should _____

4. At my (son's, niece's grandchild's) bar/bat mitzvah, I
   should _____
   should _____
   should _____

5. My Rabbi (Cantor, etc.) thinks I
   should _____
   should _____
   should _____

- Which of these "shoulds" are you glad you hold? Which would you like to give up?
- Are there some different "shoulds" you would like to adopt? Share your answers with each other.
- Who's carrying the most "shoulds"?
- From where in the family did each person's "shoulds" come?
- Which of your child's/parents'/parner's "shoulds" surprise you?
- Which of your "shoulds" surprise others?

Ideas About Our Ideas

Think about the most negative ideas you hold about bar/bat mitzvahs. How have these ideas affected your approach to preparing for your child's rite of passage? If you had different ideas about this event, what would be different now for you, your child, your partner, your parents? In what ways does thinking about having different ideas free you to actually have them?

A Final Myth That I Want to Be Sure This Book Doesn't Foster

It's the myth that other families—like the ones in this book, for instance—all do it better emotionally than yours. Most of the stories I've included in this collection are examples of families making good use of the emotional opportunities the bar/bat mitzvah experience offers. I chose them hoping they would be inspirational, *not* necessarily normative. They are meant as antidotes to the horror stories with which most of us are already too familiar—not as models against which to measure your family. In addition to the positive aspect of these families' stories I've highlighted, for most there is some other aspect that was less than ideal. Not everyone in every family rises to the occasion every time. Presented here are selected parts of selected experiences. No one piece is the whole story.

And while I'm on the subject of self-measurement, let me repeat what I said in the introduction: The ideas in this book are only ideas, *not* prescriptions. No one family could or should *possibly* do everything suggested here. These ideas are meant only to stimulate your thinking. If you were to take every idea or suggestion literally, you would drive yourself crazy thinking about "the deeper significance" of every move you—or anyone else in the family—makes. As much as possible, please try to read from a place of curiosity rather than anxiety. If you get nothing more from this book than a larger frame for understanding your experience or one new thought about one piece of your experience, that will have been enough. *Dayenu.*

Chapter 3

Ritual Magic and Family Drama: Finding New Meaning in an Old Story

Ritual Drama

Depending on how we look at it, the bar/bat mitzvah can be mundane or magical. From a mundane point of view, it is a special birthday event for which the child memorizes and performs a lot of Hebrew words and the parents organize and pay for a very big party to celebrate the memorization. The guests are family and friends who come from all over with gifts and good wishes. Everyone enjoys the chance to see each other and participate in the festivities. When it's over, the guests go home and family goes back to whatever it was doing before they'd begun preparing for the event.

On the face of it, this is probably an accurate description. But it is not an adequate description. It leaves out all of the magic, all of what makes the bar/bat mitzvah such a powerful event in most families' lives, even—or especially—for those who had not expected it to be. From this point of view, there is something very special, if not sacred, going on, yet it is hard to describe, and in this age of cynicism probably even more difficult for most of us to swallow.

This idea is certainly not something I would have believed before I'd gone through the experience myself and before I began actively studying the experience of others. But as a result of that experience and that study, I now can't help but see the bar/bat mitzvah in this more magical way. So, at the risk of overly romanticizing what most people see as a much more prosaic activity, let me share with you some of the ways in which this ritual works its magic, the ways in which it retains some of the mystery of the original tribal ceremonies whose rhythms it echoes.

To begin with, today's bar/bat mitzvah, even in its most contemporary form, has embedded in it a very ancient structure, makes use of very ancient symbols, and affects us in much the same ways that life-cycle rituals like it have affected participants throughout history. According to anthropological theory, rituals of transition (from child to adult, student to graduate, single persons to married couple, etc.) all have three parts. The first is the *breach*, the separation stage that includes the preparation for change. The second is the *transition*, the journey, the neither-here-nor-there part that includes the public act that manifests the change. And the third is the *reintegration*, the private consolidation of the change into everyday life. At the broadest level, the bar/bat mitzvah year incorporates these three stages.

The Ritual Year: A Magical Space

The months of planning and preparation, practice and anticipation, are the first stage of the ritual year. Once we and our child enter it, we are acknowledging that something is different. In a sense, we are enacting a change, a break from a time when we were not a family with a child getting ready to be a teenager, when we were not a family getting ready for a bar/bat mitzvah.

As the event gets closer, we and our child become increasingly focused. More and more of our time and energy are devoted to the upcoming performance. As "the bar/bat mitzvah family," we increasingly become known by others, and know ourselves, as special. We are getting ready to go through something out of the ordinary, and it is as if our own changed awareness acts as a protective cloak, an emotional tallit.

The bar/bat mitzvah weekend constitutes the second phase. Once the guests (the community) begin to arrive on Friday afternoon, the public part of the ritual has begun. The synagogue service is the centerpiece of the drama. It is here, surrounded by sacred symbols, caught up in ancient rhythms, and engaged in dramatic processions, that our child performs the transforming act of blessing the Torah for the first time. And it is here that the community witnesses—and affirms—the deed. In the context of this highly charged atmosphere, we and all who have come to be with us draw closer to one another, experiencing a profound sense of connectedness. It is as if the usual boundaries have momentarily melted. Anthropologists call this an experience of *communitas*.

This ceremony is followed by the celebratory feast that further extends and nurtures our feelings of warmth and happiness. Many bar/bat mitzvah families talk about the weekend almost as an out-of-body experience. "I felt like I was floating in air," said one parent. "Time evaporated," said another. "The next thing I knew—boom, it was over," said one bar mitzvah child, clearly still reeling from the experience.

The weeks and months following the weekend constitute the third phase, the phase of reintegration. Here, we and our child leave the sacred space and return to our more usual day-to-day concerns. We settle back into our former lives the same as we were before the magical space and time, but at some level subtly changed. We are the same because, *even though the bar/ bat mitzvah works magically, it doesn't work magic.* In our or-

dinary lives and our ordinary life issues, we are still dealing
with whatever problems and possibilities we were encountering
before the event: the fights about curfew, the negotiation of
custody schedules, the worries about jobs, health, money. The
bar/bat mitzvah doesn't make these things go away.

And yet the change, though subtle, is unmistakable. We return to our everyday worlds as a family that has accomplished
a major task, passed a difficult test, launched itself into a new
phase of life together. The meaning of that change and its repercussions will continue to unfold for years. At some level,
the experiences we have just been through together will have
an impact on all that is to come.

That is the sequence on the macro level. If we zoom-in on
the synagogue service itself, we can see the three-part drama
reiterated on a micro level in even more symbolic detail.

The Ritual Ceremony: A Magical Moment

The stage is set. The Torah is in its ark, the prayer books set
out, the flower arrangements adding their color and scent to
the scene. The public action is about to begin. The ritual per-
formers assemble early, taking their places in the center of the
ceremonial space. They are costumed carefully and appropriately for their parts: the bar mitzvah suit with the trousers
rehemmed at the last minute after another growth spurt, the
bat mitzvah dress finally agreed upon, the outfit Mother
shopped months for, and the new suit Father didn't really want
to buy. Together, the family watches anxiously and excitedly
as their guests arrive and prepare for the service to begin. "But
Uncle Sol isn't here yet! What if he's late for his aliyah?"

Act one begins as the Rabbi, the tribe's ritual leader, wel-
comes the assembled congregation and begins the first phase
of the three-part ceremony. The initial rites and prayers an-

nounce the "separation" between the service itself and everything that has come before it, between the normal workday worries and concerns, and the special ritual service about to begin. Implicitly, it is also an announcement of the end of one period in the family's life—the period in which it was a family with a child—and the beginning of a new era: an era in which it is a family with a child who has somehow passed beyond childhood.

The stage is set visually, kinesthetically, and emotionally for the increasing intensity to come. The prayers follow their familiar sequence and the ancient melodies wash over the congregation with a rhythmic quality that is almost hypnotic. To the extent that most of the guests do not understand Hebrew, the prayers hang in the air like mystical mantras. The child, already seated onstage or called up to it, looks very young, very intense, and very isolated. This is exactly how "the one who is in transition" is supposed to look.

In the second act, the middle part of the service, the activity and intensity increase on cue. The Torah, the central symbol of the Jewish people, is removed from its resting place in the holy ark and brought down—as if from Mt. Sinai—to the people. And again, as if at Sinai, the congregation reenacts its acceptance by singing the Shema, the fundamental prayer of faith. Increasingly the child and members of the family are drawn into the Torah's powerful aura by the ritual actions they perform: opening the ark, holding the scroll, carrying it around the congregation, uncovering it, lifting it for all to see, reading its words, kissing its letters, blessing it, dramatically passing it from grandparent to parent to child.

By now, the congregation has become emotionally aroused, enveloped by an air of growing expectancy and anticipation. It is precisely at this moment that the child is summoned to the center of the stage and the center of the family to bless the Torah for the first time, reading from it, chanting the Haftarah, delivering a speech explicating the readings and acknowledging the family's role in his or her having gotten to this place in life. It is as if the child has been summoned from the rites of preparation, the seclusion of study, and the security of protected childhood, to face the ritual test—to face it in much the same way all those who came before faced it. The child is summoned to demonstrate publicly that he or she has come of age and is ritually ready to join the community of elders.

Of the scores of bar/bat mitzvahs I have attended, one in particular brought this moment home to me most dramatically. Nathan, the little bar mitzvah boy (and he was little), came up to the bimah, and stood in front of the large, imposing, gold-inlaid ark. Wide-eyed and nervous, he looked heartbreakingly alone. But not for long. One by one, the old men of this Orthodox congregation, draped head to toe in their huge, ceremonial tallitot (prayer shawls) came up and stood in a semicircle around him. Then, as if on cue, they all lifted their arms and recited their priestly prayer. In that moment, the bar mitzvah boy literally disappeared from view, lost in the folds and the fringes of their symbolic embrace. In my mind's eye, the scene was transformed, and it was as if little Nathan had been whisked away to a hidden place where the secrets of the tribe were mysteriously being passed on to him.

But all bar/bat mitzvah ceremonies have drama. The child is up there standing alone before the world, his or her unique world, ready to chant the prophet's ancient text. The congregation is silent and intently focused. Will she remember the notes? Will his voice crack? Will she lose her place? You can hear a pin drop as everyone concentrates, willing the child to make it through the ordeal unscathed and with grace. The love, encouragement, and goodwill in the air are almost palpable. The sense of connectedness among those present is visible in every face locked in on the child in front of them. When it is over, when the last note of the Haftarah and its blessings has been voiced, the collective sigh of relief is loud and joyous. "Mazel tov! mazel tov!" the witnesses shout. Smiles and tears abound as the child grins and ducks to avoid the candies sailing through the air. And the tears continue as the parents make their speeches, pronouncing their words of love and praise for their child, their words of sadness for those not present, their words of promise for the future yet to be. The performance has now reached its peak and what is left is the winding down. In the final processional around the congregation, the Bar/Bat Mitzvah again carries the Torah, but this time without the parents following behind. This time we know he or she is capable of managing the honor alone.

In the third act, the phase of reintegration, the Torah is replaced, the child and family return to their seats, and the intensity rapidly dissipates. Acknowledgment of the transition begins immediately as the Rabbi pronounces blessings and congratulates the family. The synagogue's president continues the process with a welcoming-the-new-adult-into-the-community speech and with a presentation of the congregation's gift. Whether a wine goblet, a set of Sabbath candlesticks, or some other ritual object, the gift is a kind of trophy, a symbol of achievement and of promise.

Closing prayers and announcements about the week's upcoming secular events end the ritual drama and prepare participants for leaving the sacred space. With the smell of kugel and hot coffee beckoning, the celebrants and their witnesses file out of the temple and make their way to the feast. A profound sense of satisfaction and accomplishment prevails.

No, this has not been a tribal ritual in the bush with its physical dangers and primal terrors, but it has been an intensely dramatic moment in the lives of all those experiencing it. The power and magic cannot be denied.

From this perspective of magic, we see the contemporary bar/bat mitzvah as a transitional drama with unique risks and unique rewards. The child, risking embarrassment and ridicule, works harder than ever before, succeeds beyond expectations, and experiences a flood of approval and love from "everyone in the world." King or queen for the day, they will never forget this moment. The parents, taxing their deepest emotional, physical, and often financial resources, succeed beyond *their* expectations in pulling off an organizational feat that months earlier had seemed impossible. And in doing so, they experience the pleasure of both their child's accomplishment and their own. They have provided the means and the guidance for their child to grow and to shine, and in doing so have inadvertently grown themselves.

The parents have now witnessed their child standing separate from them—and triumphing. The child has now experienced the power of acting independently, of succeeding at something very hard that the parents—no matter how much they might have wanted to—could not have done for him or her. What intensifies the magic of this transforming moment is the way in which it is indelibly linked to the sights and sounds of the family, and of the Jewish people. Amid the swirl of symbol and song, the passing on "from generation to generation" has become more than just an idea. It has now been incorporated at the level of the body. The words and cadences of the prophets have now come through this child's breath. This child and these parents have now physically reenacted the handing down and the acceptance. *No matter how little they think consciously about the meaning of what they have just done, the unconscious meanings have been imprinted—and they are profound.*

Plots and Subplots: The Family's Drama

When I think about all the bar/bat mitzvah families I have known and studied, what comes to mind is a flood of stories and modern dramas, each one unique and powerful. But what strikes me most about these stories is how they are simultaneously both different and the same.

At the level of the main plot, the stories are all the same and the central character is always the bar/bat mitzvah child. It is, at its core, a drama about the child's growing up, of his or her coming of age in the Jewish community. All of the other family members are supporting players in this dramatic production. At the level of subplot, however, the supporting characters become the stars, and the stories here are all very different.

In one family, the major characters in the subplot are the divorced parents, and the dramatic tension comes from their struggle to contain their pain and hostility long enough to make their child's coming of age a positive experience.

In another family's drama, the mother and the grandmother become the major players. There the central issue is one of control. After having helped her single daughter for years to raise this bar mitzvah child, will it be grandmother or her daughter who is in charge of organizing the event? Will it be her sensibilities or her daughter's reflected in the luncheon? Tzimmes or sun-dried tomatoes? Farfel or focaccia? How will they compromise? How can their combined effort and love for this child and for each other be demonstrated?

In a third family, the drama takes on a larger cultural meaning. Alex was born in Soviet Russia. His bris had been held in secret. Being able to have her son's bar mitzvah in the U.S. felt to his mother like a miracle. She was going to make it as big and as showy as possible. What then would she make of the Rabbi's admonition? This bar mitzvah, he said, was a symbol for the entire immigrant community. Would it lead the way toward a life of Jewish observance, or would it merely be "a stepping-stone into the world of American consumerism"?

No matter their dramatic differences, the common theme in all of these stories is always family and the way in which the process of preparing for and living through the bar/bat mitzvah affects its members up and down the generational ladder.

Symbolically, the bar/bat mitzvah ceremony allows us to proclaim that as a family, we are changing and the changes are good. At the same time, it allows us to proclaim that as a family, we are stable and connected emotionally (even if, in many cases, no longer legally) to each other and to those who came before us. And what's so interesting is that *it is precisely this stability, these connections, that allow us to change.* To the extent that we feel stable and connected, we are capable of taking risks and of moving on. The ceremony allows our child to announce, "I am ready to be treated differently." And it allows us as parents and elders to announce—however ambivalently—"We are ready to treat you differently—no matter how hard it is to accept the idea that our baby is growing up and we will have less and less control." Through this ritual of continuity, we are proclaiming our changes. And through this proclamation, we are enhancing our stability. This is precisely what ritual's classic magic is all about: the ability to promote change and continuity simultaneously. It is a paradox, wonderful and very human.

Future Memories: Scripting Our Story

Part of what makes an intense situation difficult is that we are so completely immersed in it that we have no perspective, no way of seeing what we are going through differently. One way to get some perspective, some new view, is to imagine that we are characters in a story that *we* are writing. With this thought in mind, new ideas often emerge. If this way of thinking appeals to you, the following exercise in self-scripting might be very useful.

Imagining Our Story

Imagine it is three months after the bar/bat mitzvah and you are telling a new friend about it. What kind of story would you hope to be telling? How does the story begin, evolve, end? What were the emotional dimensions you would want to be able to talk about? What were the spiritual dimensions you would want to be feeling good about? If you were to give your story a title, what would it be? What title would your child give it? Your parents? Your partner?

Imagining Our Child's Story

Imagine a day in the future when your child is talking to his or her own thirteen-year-old child. What stories about the bar/bat mitzvah would you hope your grandchild would be hearing? What, if anything, might be done differently during *this* planning period to make those stories possible? With whom else in the family can you share these imaginings? How would the stories they would hope for be similar to, or different from, your own?

Part II

The Players

Chapter 4

The Bar/Bat Mitzvah Child: Change and No Change, Risk and Safety

It's not clear why thirteen was chosen as the age of responsibility, the age for bar/bat mitzvah. Was it because Abraham was thirteen when he shattered his father's idols, because Jacob received the firstborn's blessing at thirteen, or because the Rabbis felt that this was the age of physiological puberty, the age at which a boy was capable of growing two pubic hairs?

Whatever its origin, thirteen is probably the worst time to have a bar/bat mitzvah. It's probably also the best. From the child's point of view, a more awkward, embarrassing time couldn't be imagined. From the point of view of child development experts, it couldn't be better.

For the child with a body that's becoming unrecognizable, a voice that cannot be counted on, and a face that the "zit monster" has just begun calling home, being required to stand up and sing in front of everyone in the world—including your friends who are giggling and whispering out there in the back row—is nothing short of torture. Alternately, for the child development expert, the idea of a ritual that speaks precisely to the issues of change and continuity, of letting go and staying connected—the very issues that are at the heart of adolescent transition—the bar/bat mitzvah is a dream come true.

This chapter deals with how the bar/bat mitzvah "fits" developmentally and culturally, and how we, as parents, can help make the whole process as useful as possible. Specifically, this chapter will focus on the appropriateness of the event, the child's ambivalence—no matter how appropriate the event is—and about what you can do not only to minimize anxiety, but also to maximize emotional connectedness and growth.

Betwixt and Between: Developmental Fit

Adolescence, by definition, is an in-between stage. No longer child but not yet adult, the confusions abound. One mother's experience says it all:

PLAYTHINGS AND *PLAYBOY*S

Walking in to turn off the bedroom lights after her son—a month away from his bar mitzvah—had fallen asleep, Phyllis was touched to see that his old teddy bear was off the shelf and on the floor next to his bed. As she reached down to pick it up, she saw what else had fallen out of her son's hand—a *Playboy* magazine. It was a perfect representation of what she'd been experiencing with him lately—one minute close and loving, the next rude and rebelling, one minute wise beyond his years, the next "more infantile than his baby brother."

The bar/bat mitzvah, as a classic ritual of transition, speaks to this betwixt and betweenness at every turn. As we will see, although all three of the ceremony's defining elements—the aliyah (the central act of blessing the Torah), the *d'var Torah* (the speech interpreting the portion read), and the *seudat mitzvah* (the celebratory feast)—emphasize change, the subtext throughout is all about no change—that is, about continuity.

Through the first action—blessing the Torah—the child symbolically proclaims his or her growing maturity and independence. It is a ringing statement about change and about distance. "Today I am a man/woman"—or more accurately, "today I am no longer a child." Through the second action—presenting (i.e., "teaching") his or her own interpretation of the week's reading—the child is practicing the behavior of adult, of leader. It is a temporary role reversal that portends a future status. And finally, through the third action—participating in the party—the child gets to practice the maturing social skills this life stage invites. It is the last event in the ritual sequence and it highlights the move from preadolescence—where the child was when all of the preparation began—to full-blown adolescence, where the thirteen-year-old has arrived.

Yes, each element is a statement about growing up, about increased independence and individuation, but that is not all it is about. Just look at the setting, the context for these rites of transformation: Every aspect of this event is taking place in the bosom of the family and in the embrace of its tradition. These are statements about continuity and connection every bit as much as they are statements about leave-taking. It is precisely this both/and aspect of the process that is so useful developmentally.

Aunt Ethel and the Red Sea

Almost forty years after my bat mitzvah, I can still remember the scene. Standing up there, my knees literally knocking against each other and my heart pounding so loudly that I could barely hear what I was saying, I began my d'var Torah. I was supposed to start by saying, "I'm sure you're all familiar with the crossing of the Red Sea." Instead, what came out was, "I'm sure you're all familiar with the Red Cross." Oh, God! The terror, the humiliation. I wanted to die. But I didn't. I just grimaced, joined in with the chuckling, and started all over again. To this day, my aunt Ethel's face beaming up at me with love and pride and encouragement is engraved in my memory. The sense of connectedness, at precisely the moment I was announcing my eventual letting go, was profound. (I can't remember my parents' faces. They were in the first row and too close—in more ways than one—for me to have focused on.)

In order to move on and out in life, the child needs to feel safe, to feel anchored and connected—to the family, to its history, and to its future. *The bar/bat mitzvah is an act of anchoring. It is a ceremony about relationships.* Without a doubt, the child will forget the words memorized for the performance, but never the feeling. The sensation of being "love bombed" (even for those few seconds) stays with you.

It stayed with me.

Hurry Up and Wait: Cultural Fit

In our contemporary American society with its ambivalence—if not hostility—toward teenagers, a public performance that both *fosters* and *proclaims* the new teen's positive characteristics and sense of increasing competence is not only a great opportunity, but a rare one. As a society, we have very few, if any, positive makers of our children's entrance into teenagehood; very few, if any, opportunities for our adolescents to enact the ancient role of hero or heroine. Instead, our expectations about teenagers revolve around negative images of alcohol, drugs, sex, and violence. As a culture we hurry our children out of childhood and then make them wait a very long time (at *least* until after graduate school) before we treat them as adults. No wonder psychologists say that in adolescence symptoms erupt like acne on previously smooth skin.

The bar/bat mitzvah is an opportunity for the child and for us to counter the prevailing myths about adolescence. It is an opportunity for the child to demonstrate publicly that he or she is changing and that the changes are good. It is an opportunity for us as parents to demonstrate publicly our readiness to accept and nurture these changes, to demonstrate our faith that our emerging teenager is healthy, achieving, and capable of taking on new challenges. Symbolically (whether we know it or not), we are demonstrating our belief in our child's *yetzer hatov* (good inclination). For, as the Rabbis tell us, it is at the age of thirteen that the child develops the inclination for good as well as for bad (*yetzer hara*). The child is becoming old enough to make choices and be responsible for them. What we are doing with this ceremony is increasing the chances that the choices our child makes will be good ones. At this critical time we are contributing positively to the ongoing dialogue out of which our child's identity evolves.

Change, the experts tell us, is less likely to be traumatic if it is anticipated. The bar/bat mitzvah allows us not only to look ahead, but to look ahead and expect the best. It is those expectations that feed back and inform our child's sense of self and of his or her potential. In this context, the bar/bat mitzvah ritual serves many functions and the various names we have for it make sense. It is known not only as a rite of passage, but as a rite of initiation and a ceremony of definition. And, as mentioned earlier, as a trial (by recitation). Often the performance is so flawless that we lose sight of how much effort is actually involved. It is only when the child stumbles—loses the place, forgets the notes, begins to panic—that the congregation stops breathing and we are reminded of the difficulties and the dangers.

The Kiddish Cup

With these ideas of torture, tradition, and transition in mind, the synagogue's ritual gift, the wine goblet, seems especially appropriate. Presented usually by the synagogue's president, the goblet is first of all a symbol of welcome into the adult community. It represents the hope of all those gathered that this new adult's cup will run over—with good health and happiness, and that he or she will use it on many, many more joyous occasions—holidays, life-cycle celebrations, and countless Sabbaths. It is a statement about the child's future attachment to the past. It is a statement also about the child's transformation. Having gone through the tradition's initiation requirements, the child is now being entrusted with the adult privilege of drinking wine. In this context, the wine itself has also been transformed. It is here not the symbol of danger associated with reckless teenagers, but a symbol of adult responsibility and connectedness. And finally, the wine goblet (or the candelabra—often the gift for girls) has yet another function. It is a kind of trophy, an award for having made it safely through the ordeal, of having passed the test. It is a tangible reminder of the child's triumph. Mazel tov.

The Child's Ambivalence

In families where parents are ambivalent or conflicted about the bar/bat mitzvah, it is very likely that the child will feel confused and conflicted also. But even in families where the parents are united and unambivalent about the importance and necessity of the bar/bat mitzvah, the child may still have doubts, doubts that get expressed in all kinds of ways—verbally or behaviorally, directly or indirectly, actively or passively. It is up to us as parents to help our children make sense of these doubts and to make them manageable. It is up to us first to empathize with what they are feeling, and then to help them put these feelings into context.

Twelve-year-olds, who are just beginning to move out of the stage of thinking concretely and into the ability to think abstractly, have trouble—and rightly so—with the idea that by going through this ceremony they will become men or women, or that they are promising to be *good* Jews (Jews who go to synagogue, stay in Hebrew school, eat kosher food, date only other Jews, etc.). They know they are not adult—not by a long shot—and they *know* (at least most contemporary American Jewish adolescents know) that they (and their families) are not religious; not "practicing" Jews. In fact, the unfortunate truth for most is that they know they can't wait to stop Hebrew school as soon as possible, and have no intention (at least at this point in their lives) of spending the rest of their Saturday mornings in services. Understandably, they recoil from the inherent "lies" they perceive at the heart of the ritual. On top of this, they realize how little Hebrew they really know and they can't imagine getting through all that they'll be required to learn. On the one hand, not only doesn't the bar/bat mitzvah make honest sense, but it scares the hell out of them. On the other hand, they've been hearing about this bar/bat mitzvah all their lives, know that it's expected ("Mom says it's 'keeping Grandpop alive'"), and actually feel more than a little intrigued by the challenge. As for the party and the gifts, they could force themselves.

One child who was especially upset about this idea of proclaiming he was a man when he knew (and he knew that everyone else knew) that he wasn't, was helped by his teacher when he brought this "hypocrisy" up in his Hebrew school class.

Judaism's Developmental Stages

Dr. Cohen explained that in biblical times, twenty was considered the age of adulthood—the age at which one could enter the army or the priesthood. In the early centuries of the common era, however, the Rabbis changed the reckoning and made thirteen not the beginning of adulthood, per se, but the end of childhood. This age fit into a "developmental sequence" that one of the Rabbis had constructed. Pulling out his copy of Pirke Avot (Ethics of the Fathers), Dr. Cohen showed Danny the entire passage in which the age thirteen was embedded. Here it is:

> Judah ben Temah taught: At five a boy is ready to study Torah, at ten he is ready to study Mishnah, at thirteen he is ready to be responsible for the mitzvot, at fifteen he is ready to study Talmud, at eighteen he is ready to get married, at twenty he is ready to provide for a family of his own, at thirty he reaches full strength, at forty he reaches understanding, at fifty he is able to give counsel, at sixty he reaches maturity, at seventy his hair turns white . . . at one hundred he is as one that is dead and has passed from this world.

As Danny could see—and as you can help your own child see—even the early Rabbis knew that the thirteen-year-old boy wasn't a fully matured man. Real maturity isn't expected, as this passage makes clear, until a person is somewhere between thirty and forty. Becoming a Bar/Bat Mitzvah, even for children in fully observant families, means simply that the child is beginning the transition toward adulthood, taking the gradual, evolutionary steps toward full maturity.

While the child's doubts and hesitation make sense from a pragmatic perspective, they make sense from a developmental perspective as well. Almost by definition, adolescents are ambivalent. They are eager to grow up yet afraid to let go. They are drawn to the challenge and frightened by the risk. When you think about it, the colloquial names we call these celebrants—"the bar mitzvah boy," "the bat mitzvah girl"—are precisely accurate. The first part (bar/bat mitzvah) denotes the adult side of who they are, and the second part (boy/girl) reminds us of the other. As parents, we cannot resolve our children's doubts and ambivalence for them. We cannot protect them from the inevitability of healthy adolescent turmoil, but we can help them understand that what they are experiencing is normal, to be expected, and something we will help them with as best we can.

The Sweatbox of Change

One way to help ourselves be helpful is to realize that we are all in this "pressure cooker" of change together. Adolescence, said Nathan Ackerman, one of the founders of family therapy, doesn't happen just to the child. It happens to the whole family. Indeed, the characterization of adolescence as a period of Sturm und Drang may be as appropriate a characterization for us as parents as it is for our children—if not more so. Especially when it is our first child who is entering this betwixt and between stage, we enter also. Just as the child becomes both child and not-child, we become parents of this child and this not-child. Just as they oscillate between pushing away and clinging tightly, we oscillate between holding on and letting go. This pushing and pulling is normal and necessary. You and your child are working to negotiate new rules and new boundaries. You are together in the interregnum, a place where the old ways are dying and the new have not yet been born. It is a place of unbalance. My teacher and colleague, Lynn Hoffman, calls this place the "sweatbox." Old patterns of relating to each other—patterns that used to work quite well—no longer work, yet new patterns, new ways of being in relationship to each other, haven't yet evolved. It is a time of confusion and head-spinning reversals. To the extent that the bar/bat mitzvah is about letting go and holding on simultaneously, it provides timely opportunities for us as parents to talk with each other and with our child about what meanings we each make of the reversals and of this seeming duality—and how we can use it for growth.

One Jewish educator, Treasure Cohen, makes a beautiful commentary on the delicate balancing act that engages us at this juncture. She points out that in Hebrew, the words "hand" (*yad*), "loving" (*yedid*), and "enough" (*dai*) all come from the same root. Knowing when we have held our child enough—at least for the moment and at least in this particular way—is a parental act of love. In this light, the bar/bat mitzvah signals us that it is time to look at the ways in which we are holding and the ways in which we might be ready to begin holding a little differently.

When you look closely, the dilemma is paradoxically perfect. On the one hand, the bar/bat mitzvah is a celebration of the child's coming of age, a celebration of becoming increasingly responsible for one's self, and by implication less responsible to parents. In that it is a celebration of the child's movement *toward* adulthood, it is a celebration of relative movement away from the family (and toward peers).

On the other hand, in that the bar/bat mitzvah is a celebration of the child's coming of age *in the Jewish tradition*, it is a celebration of holding on. It is a celebration of the child's implicit identification with his or her family, its tradition and its future. It is an affirmation of connection and continuity. And it is very much in keeping with some of the current psychological thinking that is beginning to challenge standard notions about teenagers and their parents needing to disconnect from each other. Theorists talk about this new way of thinking as counter-narratives that challenge our either/or ideas about autonomy versus mutuality. What they are suggesting is that as a culture, we need to begin supporting conversations in which the major metaphor of adolescence is not conflict and separation, but relationship and connection. This makes great sense in a contemporary culture that urges teenagers to distance themselves from their parents at exactly the time they are entering an adult world that is so complex and, indeed, dangerous.

The Prayer of Riddance

Set precisely within this context of connection and continuity, the prayer of riddance has great power. This is the prayer traditionally recited by the father immediately after his son's first aliyah. It says, "Thank you God for making me no longer responsible for (the moral/religious misdeeds of) this one." While this prayer has been generally rejected (in all but Orthodox and some Conservative synagogues) as "too harsh," it reflects Judaism's psychological wisdom. It is a statement that makes change explicit and in doing so works to enable the child's growing up and the parents' acceptance of the loss—and gains—inherent in this growth.

Many synagogues have substituted the *shehechiyanu*, the prayer of firsts ("Thank you God for having allowed us to have reached this day"—when our child can say he or she is ready to be responsible.) Although Jewish educators are divided about the appropriateness of this substitution with its altered emphasis, this prayer nonetheless points to some of the same developmental issues inherent in the prayer of riddance.

No matter which (if either) prayer is customary in your synagogue, I encourage you (and/or your Rabbi) to use the occasion as an opportunity to comment from the bimah on the developmental changes this ceremony is marking. It is a perfect opportunity to reflect on the difference between being responsible as a child/for a child and being responsible as a teenager/for a teenager. By talking from the bimah about the developmental changes, we are making explicit what the ritual implicitly celebrates, and acting to help integrate the often conflicting aspects of this family-focused religious ceremony.

What You Can Do to Help Your Child Through the Doubts and Fears

As parents, we can not and should not make preparation for the bar/bat mitzvah painless, but we can help reduce needless suffering. Here are some suggestions:

First of All, Talk

Talk about what's going on and what meaning you make of it. Talk about both certainties and uncertainties. Talk about what you are sure you think and feel *and* about what confuses you. Talk about your mixed feelings about their growing up, about your own growing up, about your own unresolved doubts. Remember, you are all doing exactly what the experts say you're supposed to be doing at this stage in your lives: renegotiating the boundaries between closeness and distance, reworking old habits of holding on and letting go, rethinking old notions about what can and should be voiced. You are doing the "emotional work" that is precisely appropriate. But it *is* work and it is inherently hard.

Talk to your child, but not only to your child. Equally important is that you talk to each other as a couple, with your parents, and maybe also—depending on your family—with your brothers or sisters. To the extent that we use this opportunity to make sense of our own doubts and dilemmas, we enable our children to make sense of things for themselves. Either directly or indirectly, your child will "overhear" your conversations and be informed by them.

When I say talk to your child, I don't necessarily mean *talk* as in "heart-to-heart." When I say *talk*, I mean mostly casual conversations that happen almost incidentally while you and your child are doing something else—driving to the movies, shopping, eating dinner. Heavy, "meaningful relating" (with, God forbid, eye contact) is close to impossible with most children—especially boys—at this age. Unless your child is one of the exceptions, don't even try for "deep dialogue." Listen for their reactions and respond to what they say, but don't wait for answers, much less agreement. Don't expect your twelve-year-old to verbalize what he or she is feeling. Look how hard it is even for you! What's important is for your child to know what you think about this upcoming event (as much as you can articulate it) and *what you expect* from him or her in relation to it.

This is not to say, however, that twelve- and thirteen-year-olds—girls *or* boys—are incapable of serious thought and conversation. In this developmental period where critical thinking is emerging, thoughtful, open-ended conversation is increasingly possible. Be available to it—even when it comes in the form of actions rather than words or in the form of a challenge rather than a question—and respond, as best you can, with your own honesty and openness.

And be ready to *listen* as well as to talk. Remember, thirteen is when Abraham smashed his father's idols. Which of yours is your child questioning? How can you respond with dignity and with respect? And how can you talk about that last blowup when your response (and your child's) wasn't so dignified or so respectful? These will be some of the lessons that last.

Also in the realm of listening, what I would like to encourage is your ability to listen "deeply." While this might at first sound as if I'm suggesting armchair psychologizing, what I mean by *deeply* is that you try to hear what your child is saying at the level of "feeling," not just at the level of words and actions. When Jason won't practice for the bar mitzvah, what might he be saying emotionally about his parents' recent divorce? When nine-year-old Rachel won't turn down the TV so her brother can chant for his parents what he's learned so far of his Haftarah, what is she saying about feeling left out? When Jessica won't practice unless her mother is in the room listening the whole time, what is she saying about her mother's having just been offered a full-time position at the office? In whatever ways you can do it, talk with your children to let them know you hear their sadness, their jealousy, their fears. Share with them what you think might be going on for them and ask what they think about your thinking. This is the kind of listening that encourages them to trust their feelings and to value them. It's the kind of listening that authenticates.

Talk About Religious Ambivalence

In addition to talking to your children about their ambivalence about being part of this evolving family, about growing up and staying young, it is important to talk to them about ambivalence—yours and theirs—regarding Jewish practice and the religious meaning of this event in your lives. This is the time to let them know you appreciate their questions, spoken or not, about how this ritual fits your family if it is not a family that practices many other Jewish rituals (and how it fits if yours *is* such a family!).

Be clear that despite your doubts (whatever you haven't resolved since your own coming of age), you are certain this ritual *is* important—not just to them and to you, but to the generations past and those yet to come. Be clear that you believe in their ability to learn what is required, that you will help them through it in as many ways as you know how, and that only when they are grown up will they truly appreciate the value of having gone through the experience. Indeed, to the extent that you are able, let them know how your own ideas are continuing to evolve, how you are learning about your own values and beliefs through this bar/bat mitzvah process, and how important that learning is to you. Even if they seem uninterested ("Enough already, Dad") or incapable of really taking in what you are saying, by allowing your child to overhear your grappling with the spiritual, religious, and cultural meanings of this passage in your life, you not only allow him or her to know what's meaningful to you, but you provide a model for struggling with life's important questions, a model that will make its mark.

Be clear about where your child has choices and where the decisions have already been made. Find ways to involve him or her in as many of the decisions as are appropriate, and share the thinking behind your other decisions in ways that can be instructive, ways that demonstrate you have taken their needs and preferences seriously.

RON, A FAILED FATHER

Ron, a father whose son's sullenness and reluctance to participate in family discussions about the upcoming bar mitzvah had been a source of great pain and self-doubt, talked about what he had learned at a parents' program on "adolescent identity development" at the junior high school. He talked about his new ways of understanding his son's behavior and how useful this new understanding was. Now, when Jeremy stands listening to the conversation from the doorway rather than participating actively with the family around the table, Ron thinks about this act as an "age-appropriate" expression of ambivalence rather than an expression of outright rejection. Now his son's protests against the "hypocrisy of organized religion" made sense as an expression of his growing "differentiation." They were no longer "proof" that Ron was a failure as a Jewish father.

When Ron was told how some scholars would see the boy's doubts as very much in keeping with the Jewish tradition of critical questioning, he felt even more relieved. And as this relief grew, Ron was able to be more open to his son's challenges and able to engage him in a much less defensive and authoritarian way. Needless to say, the change in Ron began to allow some changes in his son's behavior as well. When Jeremy saw his father being less reactive to his objections, he found that he didn't have to act out his differences quite so dramatically. And, of course, as his behavior changed, his father was able to change even more. Over time, the level of tension and resentment began to subside throughout the family. By the day of the bar mitzvah, what they were proud of most was how they had found ways through the journey both separately and together.

Clarify Expectations and Make Them Appropriate

Children need to know where they have choices and where they do not. They need to know that you understand their doubts and ambivalence, and in fact that you have your own and can empathize. Children love to hear stories about us when we were children. Tell them how you were feeling preparing for your own bar/bat mitzvah. Encourage them to ask others (grandparents, cousins, aunts, uncles) about theirs. Tell them how you're feeling now. Let them know that you know you don't have all the answers, but on this topic of study, you are clear: Preparation for the "ordeal" is an opportunity for them to push themselves to new levels of competency. It is a chance to grow. This is also an opportunity to show them that you have confidence in them and that you support their growth. But at the same time, make sure that your son or daughter knows the limits of what you (and the Rabbi) are expecting. Eddie's story is a good example of unclear expectations.

EDDIE AND EXPECTATIONS

Eddie, a good student and generally happy-go-lucky kid, was becoming increasingly tense and even depressed as the year of his bar mitzvah was getting closer and his parents were beginning to talk with the Rabbi about getting him started on his Haftarah. His behavior was not what his parents would have expected, and they were getting worried. At first they could hardly believe what they were seeing. They couldn't imagine that this was anxiety about the bar mitzvah. After all, he was such a good Hebrew school student. How could he be so intimidated? It was only after they began talking with him directly about their concerns that they understood: The only bar mitzvah Eddie had ever attended was that of the Cantor's son. This child, who'd been studying at the yeshiva since he was five, not only chanted the Haftarah, but read the entire Torah portion, and led the whole service from beginning to end. Eddie thought his parents expected the same of him!

Once they understood this they quickly set the record straight. They arranged a family meeting with the Rabbi and talked together about what Eddie would actually be required to do as a Bar Mitzvah. The expectations were formidable, but they were not impossible. In no way were the parents or Rabbi expecting this child with his Sunday school education to do what was expected of the child with the yeshiva education. Once Eddie heard the difference, his relief was palpable and his entire attitude changed.

While most children have more realistic expectations than Eddie, it is a good idea to make certain that your child knows clearly what is required. A meeting with the Rabbi, the child, and the parents all together in the same room can often help to avoid a great deal of unnecessary confusion and aggravation. It can also be an important symbolic statement about the integration of family and religion. Through preparation for the bar/bat mitzvah, the child's life in the home and the child's life in the Hebrew school become more connected.

In addition to making sure that your child's understanding of expectations is accurate, it is important to make the expectations themselves appropriate. The concept of appropriateness here is relative. What fits one child does not necessarily fit another. What is considered appropriate in one synagogue wouldn't be considered so in another. Within the standard requirements of each synagogue, there is usually a range of what the child might be expected to do. For children like the Cantor's son, leading the entire service is not at all out of the question. On the other end of the spectrum, in that same synagogue, for instance, a child with a severe learning disability might "merely" be required to recite the Torah blessings. For that child, such a recitation would be an enormous accomplishment.

What is appropriate, what will count as a test, what will work to push the child beyond previous limits of learning, what will feel like an achievement, is different for each child in each family and in each synagogue. Most often these variables are computed implicitly by the Rabbi and/or the tutor without much overt discussion. And most often there is a close match between what is possible and what is necessary. Occasionally, however, these decisions require more explicit and expanded discussion. It is important that, as parents, we are part of this negotiation and that our children know we are protecting their best interests. Once they feel that we are assuring their safety, they are more capable of taking the risk, of picking up the challenge.

Our conversations with each other, with the Rabbi, and with other parents can also go a long way in giving *us* the courage to expect more of our children than we had previously thought possible. Our tendency to protect them from "too much" hard work, too much anxiety, and too much pressure can often end up shortchanging them out of opportunities for excelling and feeling proud.

One mother whose son's Haftarah portion had been shortened by half when he complained to the Cantor that he couldn't manage it all, spoke with regret a few months after the bar mitzvah:

"We were sort of misled. I didn't know much about the ritual and didn't know how important the Haftarah was. Kevin and the Cantor kept shortening and shortening it, and we let it happen. I don't know, but I think the Cantor didn't give Kevin enough credit. He could have learned more if she had expected him to. And even though it was a wonderful experience, it could have made him (and us) feel prouder."

Each child's starting point is different. On the other end of the spectrum from Kevin is Avremel, a Hasidic child who had been leading services and reading Torah for years before anyone started thinking bar mitzvah. What would seem impossible for most kids (at least from secular homes), this child simply took for granted. So you'd think that for him, preparing for the bar mitzvah would be a piece of (kosher) cake, right? Not on your life. Not only did Avremel have to chant the Torah and the Haftarah and lead the entire service, but he had to deliver—from memory—two fifteen-minute philosophical treatises—in Yiddish—that were based on the interpretations of his father and his father's father, both of whom were Rabbis. He did it, of course, but only after much worry and last-minute anxiety. When he'd completed the recitation, everyone was thrilled—and relieved. Even for this child, so accomplished in the world of synagogue ritual, the task had to be one that would push him beyond where he had been.

Justin's ordeal was another example of pushing beyond old limits. He was also a child for whom the bar mitzvah was expected to be easy—not because of his religious training, but because of his theatrical experience.

PERFORMANCE WITHOUT PERSONA

Since he was seven, Justin had been singing and dancing in local theater productions, and by thirteen had already played the lead in several large musicals with audiences of many hundreds. It was a surprise, then, to see Justin struggle through the preparations, to see him avoid practicing his Haftarah, to see his public school grades plummet, and to hear from his mother about their escalating conflict. How come Justin couldn't learn these lines as he had learned so many before? How come he couldn't get psyched for this performance as he had for all the rest? Because—it became clear in retrospect—these weren't simply lines and this wasn't simply another performance. In this family, where the father was not Jewish and the mother had given her son the choice of becoming a Bar Mitzvah or not, this decision was big.

Without the protection of a dramatic persona—Oliver in England, or Peter in Never-Never-Land—he would be "on stage" as himself, as one who had chosen to declare his Jewish identity publicly, to use his beautiful voice to sing not show tunes but Torah. Without props, masks, or makeup, he was going to be Justin himself, in his family and in his community. And as himself he was having to find a way to make this identity work for himself not only as his mother's son, but as his father's too.

What became clear by the end of the preparation period when he had begun practicing on his own and had begun showing his excitement about the upcoming event, was that Justin had somehow come to believe in the support for the bar mitzvah that both his mother *and* father were showing. He had come to feel the ritual as an acceptance and not a rejection— and he became open to what it was he was doing. Having pushed the limits of how long he could procrastinate (the tutor had already threatened to "shorten the Haftarah"), Justin somehow became ready to let the process touch him. By the time he had chanted the last prayer on his bar mitzvah morning, it was clear to everyone in that congregation that this was not Justin the actor up there, but Justin the Bar Mitzvah, Justin whose Jewish coming of age they were there to celebrate.

School Grades

One Rabbi I know tells how he encourages parents to be prepared for their children's grades in regular school to drop somewhat while they are spending hours each week preparing for the bar/bat mitzvah. He encourages them to be clear with themselves and with each other about how important the bar/bat mitzvah study is in their minds and what their priorities are. He encourages them to make their thinking known to their children so that they can be relieved of the unreasonable expectation that the usual high level of performance in all subjects and all activities has to be maintained. He also encourages parents to talk to the child's teachers and let them know about the upcoming ceremony and what they, as parents, feel is most important in this period. And finally, he advises parents to talk with their child about which extracurricular activities might need to be put aside temporarily so that sufficient time for practicing is possible.

Clearly, these are difficult suggestions in a secular world where most people think of the bar/bat mitzvah as a "big party" and think of school as "what really counts" (especially now that it's junior high and not just elementary school). Support for the importance of bar/bat mitzvah study is not easily available. This is one of the aspects of the preparation period that forces parents to examine their values. What do we believe is important here? What does our child's other parent believe is important? What do we do with our differences (as well as our agreements)? Is this an area in which we can enhance our capacity as a family for flexibility and compromise? How can we use this opportunity to keep the conversation going about what is important and what we value?

Choose a Tutor Who Can Also Be a Role Model

If yours is a synagogue where parents hire tutors to augment what the children are taught in Hebrew school, look for someone who not only can teach the Haftarah and the prayers, but who can also serve as a role model, a mentor. This can be a person of any age, but often when the tutor is a young adult, he or she becomes a representative of the community with whom the child can relate. Often these young tutors become like older brothers and sisters for the Bar/Bat Mitzvah, and it is the lessons they teach through who they are and how they see the world that stay with the child longest. Because they are older enough, but not—like parents—beyond redemption, our children may be able to talk with them in ways they cannot with us.

On the other hand—there is always another hand in Jewish reasoning—there is much to be said for the tutor as "grandparent," as venerable connector to the past. This, after all, is what the "men at the minyan" were for past generations of B'nai Mitzvah.

THE E-MAILED MINYAN

A friend of mine, who had been sick throughout much of her son's preparation, told me about his tutor—"an older man who made all the difference!" Mr. Samuels was retired and had lots of time to devote to Randy. "He took such an interest and became so much a part of the family. When he went away for two weeks to visit his son and daughter-in-law living in Italy, he E-mailed Randy every day! He had the time and the resources to really help Randy feel safe while I was so incapacitated and his father so busy helping me."

Ask your Rabbi and other parents for tutors they would recommend. No matter what the age, make sure that the tutor is
someone *you* can talk with too. You and the tutor are allies—
working together, not only to teach the material, but to set the
tone, to convey a message of meaning, of substance.

MAKING MISTAKES

One child's parents were worried in an unusual way about his
preparation. Their worry was that Jacob was studying *too*
much, too intensely. It seems that Jacob had taken the sanctity
of the occasion very much to heart and he was petrified of
making any mistakes. "God will be listening to me," he told
his mother tearfully one night. Naturally Jacob's mother tried
to reassure him. Not religiously educated herself, she didn't
know what to say. She tried everything. She assured him that
he would do fine, that mistakes wouldn't matter, that no one
would notice, etc., but nothing she said hit the mark. Nothing
relieved Jacob's anxiety.

It was not until she shared her son's worry with his tutor that
something changed. Simon was a kind, sensitive young man
studying to be a Rabbi. He tutored bar and bat mitzvah children to earn tuition. Jacob liked and respected him a great
deal. The next time they met, Simon initiated a conversation
with Jacob about what he (Simon) understood God wanted
from the Bar and Bat Mitzvah, indeed what He wanted from
all those who pray: "Something called *kavanah*," he said.
"Something that means 'aiming one's heart,' praying with sincerity. As long as you have this sincerity, and you *certainly*
do," Simon told Jacob, "the whole idea of 'mistakes' changes
completely. In sincere prayer, mistakes don't exist."

This, from Simon—a Rabbi-to-be—Jacob could hear. The
drop in his level of anxiety was dramatic. He could study and
he could relax. On the day of his bar mitzvah, his chanting

and his leading of the prayers were not only sincere, but flawless as well.

While some people advise parents who can tutor their own children not to—they contend that children need the space this other adult in their lives can give—I am less dogmatic. I have seen such in-family tutoring work beautifully, and I've seen it go awry. As always, it depends on who you and your child are and what developmental issues are getting expressed through the practicing.

THE IMPERFECT MOTHER

Roz, a Hebrew school teacher, decided *not* to tutor her daughter herself, although she had wanted to dearly. She loved the *idea* of such a mother-daughter experience, but given the reality of their current relationship, it just didn't seem wise. The last thing they needed was one more thing to fight over.

Roz's decision turned out to be a very good one—but in a way she couldn't have anticipated. In the course of preparing for the d'var Torah, Erica and her tutor began talking about heroes in the Bible and about the fact that all of them, in one way or another, were flawed. Not one of our forefathers or foremothers, she discovered, was perfect. This revelation led Erica to some new thinking about herself and about the standards to which she was holding her mother. With the tutor's gentle support and her own stories of mother-daughter conflict, Erica's view of what she and her mother were going through was beginning to change. Not only did the fighting gradually begin to lessen, but by the time of the bat mitzvah, mother and daughter were actually ready to perform a song that they had written together (about their experience as Jewish women!). The moral of this story: When in doubt, opt for some space (and then be welcoming of the closeness it allows).

Find Ways to Concretize the Transformation

How much the child feels changed by the experience and how much others notice changes vary greatly from child to child and family to family. In Orthodox families, the transforming nature of the event is literal. The child is expected to act differently and does. He will put on tefillin [small black leather boxes containing the *shema* strapped on to the forehead and upper left arm close to the heart] each morning. He will be counted in the minyan. He will fast on the days of fasting. And he will eat with the men at the festivals. In families less connected to religious practice, the transformation is more symbolic, usually much more subtle, often not very much noticed, and rarely if ever tangibly marked. This is a loss.

Friedel's story demonstrates one end of the change continuum:

FRIEDEL AND THE FORK

It was two days before the huge bar mitzvah celebration, and there I was in the kitchen of the Hasidic family I was interviewing. The parents were out: Mother was at the airport picking up her parents, and Father was in New York picking up fresh herring. All of the younger children were in school or at the playground with the baby-sitter. I had offered to help with the cooking. My job was the eggplant appetizer—for one hundred and fifty. I'd been left with the task of chopping, and chopping, and chopping. Friedel, the bar mitzvah boy, was in the next room, practicing. Dressed in a white shirt and black jacket with a fedora angled on his head just like his father's, he looked from the back like a little old man deep in study. As I peeked in, I saw him dreamily look up from the page and spy a little toy airplane left on the table by one of his younger brothers. Slowly he picked it up and began etching out flight patterns in the air. Zooming up, zooming down, he was a child again playing with toys. What a snapshot. The textbook's developmental reversals couldn't have been more dramatically portrayed.

A little later, Friedel came into the kitchen looking for something for lunch. He decided to cook some pasta. After watching it boil a few minutes, he asked me to help see if it was done. He handed me a fork and as I was in the process of spearing a noodle he grabbed it out of my hand. "Oh no! It's the wrong fork!" he shouted, looking devastated. It was one from the meat drawer rather than from the dairy drawer. Carefully, Friedel placed the defiled utensil on the window shelf to keep it separate until his mother could rekosher it.

Wanting to make him feel better, I quipped, "It's okay . . . You're not *yet* responsible." "What do you mean, I'm not responsible," he said, glaring incredulously. "I am a Bar Mitzvah! Of course I'm responsible." What I had forgotten was that even though the big celebration with all of the relatives and friends was still ahead, Friedel had, in fact, already had his first aliyah—earlier that week at the Rebbe's minyan in New York City on the day after his thirteenth birthday. I had forgotten that the transforming act had already occurred. Friedel had not. For him, the transition had been complete. He was just as responsible as any other Jewish man.

In this child's observant family, the tangible symbols of his coming of age are clear. Every morning from the day after his first aliyah, Friedel will look and act different. He will be wearing and blessing tefillin. Those straps and black boxes could not be more concrete.

In families not connected to ritual tradition, there are no tangible symbols of the child's having come of age. After the bar/bat mitzvah, the guests go home, the child goes back to school, and life returns slowly to normal. There are no lasting daily reminders that a transition has been marked. To counter this loss, I have taken to suggesting that families *create* such reminders. It is important that the changes we have just celebrated are made visible and anchored. What I suggest is that sometime during the months of preparation, you talk with each other and with your child about *some new privilege and some new responsibility* that you and she or he can agree on that would begin the day immediately following the bar/bat mitzvah, never to be rescinded or rejected. Depending on what fits for your family, these privileges and responsibilities can be in either the religious or the secular realm—or in both.

One family I talked to began—the day after the bar mitzvah—allowing their son to answer the business phone that rang in the house. This was something he had been wanting to be trusted with for years. Another family decided together that after her bat mitzvah, the daughter's allowance would be raised and that she would begin tithing to charity the same percentage of this increased allowance that her parents tithed of *their* income.

Many families mark the child's growing maturity by extending curfews and increasing chores. Some, consistent with the advice of Jewish educator Joel Lurie Grishaver, find ways of changing the family's disciplinary structure entirely. They find ways of replacing punishments such as being "grounded" or "busted" with collaborative problem-solving strategies, such as: Here's what you did wrong. What consequences make sense? What are we going to do about it? Whatever way you do it, the act of discussing, choosing, and following through with something tangible seems to be very useful as a marker of growth and of changing relationships.

In one family, the marker was unexpected: Anna was allowed to eat ice cream in the living room after her bat mitzvah. Although it wasn't the planned privilege I am suggesting, it was a natural and very "sweet" evolution for this daughter of a

Rabbi, a child for whom there was no question about the bat mitzvah's significance.

It was her father who told me the story a few weeks later as Anna listened, grinning.

ICE CREAM AND THE RABBI'S DAUGHTER

"Two days after her bat mitzvah, Anna came into the living room with a dish of ice cream," he began. "We *never* let the kids eat ice cream in the living room," he continued. " 'Either in the kitchen or the dining room,' I reminded her."

"Mommy is eating hers in the living room!" Anna had protested. "Mommy is an adult," reminded her father. "I am too," his daughter said with delight. She'd been waiting for years for this moment.

"But that's not all that's changed," said Anna's mother, adding to the retelling. "She's now capable of baby-sitting and we're helping her get the word out. Six months ago, we didn't feel she was ready. She's really grown up so much through the bat mitzvah preparation. It's hard to believe."

Use the Occasion to Mark Other Changes as Well

As you approach the bar/bat mitzvah, this life-cycle marker, think about changes that are happening *throughout* the family. Here are some questions that might be useful in identifying some of these changes:

- What do you notice about your child's changing?
- What do you notice about *your changes* in relation to his/her changes?
- How do you think your child would describe his/her changes?

- How do you think your child would describe *your* changes?
- How do you think *your* mother or father would describe *your* changes?

Use this occasion to ask.

Think about who you were and how you were when *you* were thirteen. In what ways is your child the same? In what ways different? What characteristics of your child do you want to foster and enhance? What can you share about your growing-up story that might help in this direction?

In what ways can you use this occasion to talk with your son or daughter about what it means to be growing up as a man or a woman in this society? In what ways can you use it to talk about other teenage rituals, like those involving sex, alcohol, drugs?

Two families come to mind here.

One father and son I interviewed talked conspiratorially about "the bar mitzvah secret" that the father had told his son when the two of them were out buying Brandon his bar mitzvah suit.

"Yeah, my dad told me about something embarrassing that happened to him when he was my age," Brandon said, grinning. "And only he and I know about it!" he concluded proudly.

I never did find out what that secret was, but somehow, knowing the father's enlightened sensibilities, I had the sense that it was the beginning of lots more secret sharing—and lots more good communication between these two men.

One mother at a workshop talked about how she made an opportunity to talk about some similar topics she thought were becoming timely.

Among Kenneth's friends, it was becoming customary to have a picture of themselves enlarged to the size of a poster and hung at the entrance to the party hall. There, friends and family could use the attached Magic Marker to inscribe messages of congratulations and good wishes. The poster would then be hung in the child's room along with his or her other poster-sized heroes.

Beatrice used the occasion of hanging the poster to talk with her son about her pride in him, about the tremendous job he had done to prepare for his bar mitzvah and for all of the other ways in which she saw him as "hero." She also talked to him about her hopes for how he would continue to be a hero, how he'd be handling the inevitable pressures of being a teenager in the fast-paced social circle of their neighborhood. "When I saw his image so big and looking so grown-up, I remembered someone saying that not only could the bar mitzvah boy now make a blessing on the Torah, but he could probably now also make a baby. All of a sudden I thought it wasn't still too early to be talking about such grown-up concerns."

It turns out that Beatrice is not alone with these thoughts. Recently I have been hearing of more and more bar/bat mitzvah educational programs that include some discussion of these personal and social issues. Some even include a weekend camping trip, one for the boys and one for the girls, in which the teens can talk with each other, with their teachers, and with some older peers about the pressures and dilemmas of growing up in this culture. This example of connecting "real-life" issues with Judaism's teachings on these matters is clearly the direction in which much of Jewish education is going. If this sounds like something that would make sense for your child and your community, you might bring the idea up with the Rabbi or Hebrew school principal.

What You Can Do to Help Your Child Feel Connected

To the extent that the bar/bat mitzvah is about relationship—the celebrant's relationship to self, to family, to community, to tradition—it is a perfect ritual for this developmental stage in our child's life. In contrast to the emphasis on separation and autonomy that most psychologists had believed were the cornerstones of developmental growth, some theorists are now beginning to understand experiences of connectedness and interdependence as primary necessities for psychological health. In fact, many are beginning to teach that what we call "self" actually exists *only* in the context of relationships—the many relationships that constitute our ongoing interactions. Maybe this is an example of our psychological theories catching up with our folk traditions, but whatever the process, the bar/bat mitzvah's psychological potential is becoming clearer and clearer: *There is no better time than the period of preparation prior to the bar/bat mitzvah for us to help our child strengthen his or her sense of place in the family's evolution—its history and its future.*

In this regard, I would suggest two related strategies for improving and passing on genealogical memory: The family tree and the family album.

The Genogram: A Special Family Tree

The genogram is a shorthand method for mapping intergenerational connections. It is a more graphic and technical version of the family tree. It can be as detailed as you want it to be. But even a simplified version can be complicated (especially with divorces, remarriages, and blended families). Developing the genogram is something you should do with your child, adding information as it is gathered.

Here are some basic instructions:

Women are represented by circles and men by squares (no offense intended). A married couple is indicated by a horizontal line connecting them. (An unmarried couple living together is indicated by a dotted line.) Vertical lines coming down from the horizontal line indicate the couple's children. Here is an example of a typical bar mitzvah family's genogram:

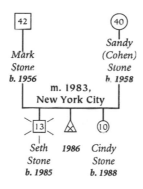

Illustration A

We see that Mark and Sandy Stone were married in 1983, in New York City. Sandy, born in 1958, is forty, and Mark, born in 1956, is forty-two. They have a son, Seth, who is thirteen. He was born in 1985. His ten-year-old sister, Cindy, was born in 1988. There was a miscarriage in 1986.

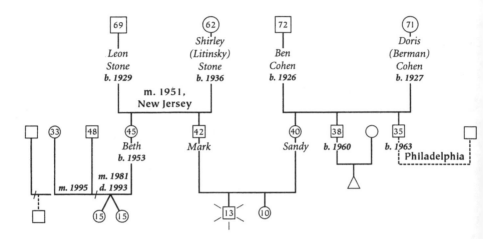

Illustration B

Illustration B enlarges the genogram by including the grand-parents' generation. It reflects the fact that Mark is the younger of two children. His sister, born in 1953, is three years older. Their parents were married in 1951, in New Jersey. Grandfather, Leon Stone, born in 1929, is now sixty-nine. Grandmother, Shirley (Lilinsky) Stone, born in 1936, is now sixty-two. We also see that Mark's sister Beth was married in 1981, and divorced in 1993. She has twin daughters, aged fifteen. Her ex-husband married again in 1995, a divorced woman with an adopted son.

Looking at mother's side of the genogram, we see that Sandy is the eldest of three. Her two younger brothers, born in 1960 and 1963, are thirty-eight and thirty-five respectively. Her middle brother and his wife are expecting a baby (Δ). Her youngest brother is gay. He lives with his longtime partner in Philadelphia.

And now we add the bar mitzvah boy's great-grandparents.

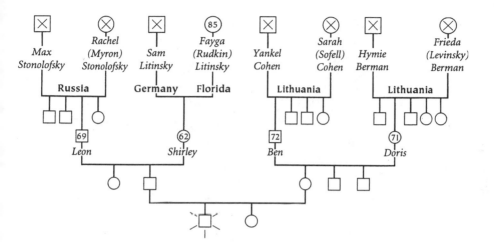

Illustration C

Here we see that they were all born in the Old Country. Three sets from Eastern Europe and one (father's maternal grandparents) from Germany. Of all the great-grandparents, only one is still alive, Bubbie Fayga. She lives in Florida. We also see that the Stone family name in Russia was Stonolofsky. What does Seth know about how the name got changed? What does he know about his father's grandfather, Sam, after whom he was named?

You get the idea.

In order to start, use a big piece of paper and begin with your immediate family near the bottom of the page. Work up the generations from there. The picture will get wider as it gets higher. Extra information that doesn't fit on the page can be collected on a second sheet as "footnotes." Most people find they have to recopy the genogram several times as they collect more and more information and come up with better ways of laying it out on the page. Some families get very creative using different colors for each generation, drawing pictures to depict certain themes, etc.

For those who enjoy computers, there are genogram software packages that lead you through the entire sequence.

Some of the basic information you will want to gather:

- Who is in the family? Where were they born, when, in what order? (Where possible, put them left to right, oldest to youngest.)
- Who was married to whom? When? Where?
- When and where were they divorced? Widowed? Remarried?
- How many births, miscarriages (⚠), etc.?
- Who died? When? Where? From what?
- Who moved from one country to another, one state to another? Why? Was it their choice or did they have to?
- Who was named after whom? What did the names signify?
- What were these people known for? What values were important to them? What made them happy? What made them sad?
- How old are the cousins? Who stayed connected to whom?

For most of us, when we start doing our family genogram what we find very quickly is how much we *don't* know about our families. Given how powerfully they affect us, it is often amazing how little information we actually have. This is a perfect opportunity to begin collecting what we know and investigating what we don't. It makes sense then that many synagogue bar/bat mitzvah programs are now incorporating this kind of family research into the curriculum.

JACK'S DISCOVERY

One interfaith family used this opportunity with amazing results. In an effort to help his daughter fill in some information on the family tree she was putting together for her bat mitzvah class assignment, Tim began calling some old relatives he hadn't talked to for years. In the course of one of these conversations, he started asking about his mother, who had died when he was a teenager. To his amazement, Tim discovered that she had been married and widowed before she married his father. What's more, that first husband had not been Jewish! What a shock. And what relief. All these years Tim had been so sure that his mother would have condemned his marriage to Mary, and would never have been able to understand or accept what he had done. This information was more than a relief; it was transforming.

The bar/bat mitzvah weekend—after the service, during the luncheon, the party, the Sunday brunch—is a perfect time to interview relatives and gather more information. People are fascinated by seeing the family genogram and where they and their immediate relatives fit in the scheme of it.

The process becomes similar to putting together a large jigsaw puzzle. Most people want to help and are eager to fill in missing pieces. Don't be surprised, however, if you come up against pockets of resistance; people who are not eager to answer questions. What you have done, most probably, is come up against some old wound, some story that is still too painful to talk about. What better opportunity to teach our children about sensitivity and respect? Maybe some information is not worth getting if it will cause someone pain. Or maybe it's just not worth getting it from that individual, at that time. Who else in the family might know the story and be more inclined to talk about it? How do we balance our curiosity with our respect for privacy? Again, important moral lessons.

The Family Album: Remembering Is a Mitzvah

Family photographs are like memory windows. They provide openings through which we reenter old worlds. Most children love seeing pictures of their parents as children. There is no better time for looking at such memories than during the months prior to the bar/bat mitzvah. The images we encounter during this period can serve as stimulants to family conversations that are precisely connected to what the bar/bat mitzvah is all about. Gather as many old pictures as you can and make time to look at them with each other, with your children, and with your parents, if possible.

- Who are the people in the pictures?
- Where do they fit on the family tree?
- Who in those pictures are no longer alive? What were they like?
- What might they have thought about the event you are planning?
- What might they have said to the bar/bat mitzvah child if they could have been present?
- Who in the family, with whom we could talk, remembers them?
- What events were being celebrated in those pictures? How? In whose house? With whom? What seemed to be important to the people in those pictures?
- What do you notice now about the relationships represented in those pictures that you hadn't noticed before?
- What do you want your children to notice?
- Who in those pictures is still alive, but no longer in

contact with us? What would it mean if we were to invite them?

- What opportunities could you arrange prior to the bar/bat mitzvah for your parents and your children to look at old pictures together?
- Are there pictures of your bar/bat mitzvah?
- Who has them? What would it mean to ask for them?

FAMILY HEIRLOOMS

One bar mitzvah father who asked his mother for the pictures of his bar mitzvah reported being at first surprised by the amount of resistance he encountered and then very moved by the meaning he began making of it. "I'd thought it was such a simple request," he explained, "but by the time she finally 'found' them (in the top drawer of her bedroom bureau) it was as if she were handing over the family heirlooms. I had to swear to her that I wouldn't lose them, that I would take good care of them, that I would return them. I had no idea how important those faded memories were to her—and no idea of how much *my* bar mitzvah had been *her* event."

Your Album

It's been said that through photography each family constructs a portrait of itself—a kit of images that bears witness to its connectedness.

- What do you want your child's bar/bat mitzvah album to say to future generations?
- What pictures does your child want taken for your future grandchildren to see?
- What do you think your son or daughter would make of such a question?
- What thoughts does it stimulate for you?

If the bar/bat mitzvah is itself a snapshot in time, how can we use the photos we take of it to enhance its substance? One family stumbled onto an answer that worked for them.

FILLING IN THE PICTURE

As part of his preparatory mitzvot, Stephen made a multigenerational collage of family pictures that he attached to the family tree he and his parents had begun putting together. It was a great experience, but also frustrating because they realized how much they didn't know about past generations. What they decided to do was bring the collage and tree to the bar mitzvah party and ask all of the relatives to fill in whatever pieces of information they could. That process, videotaped by Uncle Nate, became the emotional highlight of the party. Some of the adult cousins got so interested that they decided to meet again—as a "cousins club"—to talk more about family and to continue filling in pieces of information for future generations. In this family, the storytelling would continue and the tree would keep growing, long after Stephen's big day.

Chapter 5

Boomers in the Middle: Juggling Your Responsibilities as Parents, Your Needs as Children, and Your Evolving Relationship as Partners

"Here I am planning my child's big day and what's on my mind is more about me than him. What's wrong with me?"

"It's my daughter's coming of age. I should be thinking about helping her develop her self-confidence, her sense of growing maturity. So how come all I can think about are my own needs and fears? How can I be so selfish? My mother was right. I'll never grow up."

With all the emphasis on the bar/bat mitzvah's meaning for our children, we rarely hear anything about its meaning for us as parents. It's no wonder that we feel selfish, self-centered, or just plain wrong to be having so many feelings that are not about our children, but about ourselves.

"If we're old enough to have children this old, we should be old enough to be past whatever it is we seem not to be."

This is one of those primary myths; one of the sources of

unhealthy stress. No, having a child this age does *not* mean that we should be finished growing up ourselves. What it *does* mean is that we should be allowing ourselves to struggle with all of the issues that come up naturally in this period of transition—that come up *especially* as we take on the responsibility of planning a ceremony to celebrate that very transition.

Because the bar/bat mitzvah is a rite of passage not just for the child but for the entire family, it is, in fact, a perfect opportunity for us as parents to foster our own growth as well as our child's. It is not an either/or proposition. Nor is it a zero-sum game—where the energy that goes into working on the parents' needs steals from what's available for the child. Instead, the relationship between our growth and our child's growth is synergistic. At the same time that the process fosters our change, its potential to foster change in our child is enhanced.

Our child's bar/bat mitzvah is a natural opportunity for us to think about our own process of maturing. In some tribal cultures, the boy cannot be initiated into adulthood until his father performs the ceremony called "passing over the fence." In this ceremony the father steps over a stick held by the tribe's elders and recites ritual words of blessing. This act signifies his acceptance of his changing status. He is becoming an "old man."

As contemporary parents of bar/bat mitzvah children, we may not be old men and old women but there's no doubt we are moving toward middle age. How is this process of preparing for our child's coming of age helping us think about our own aging? Our parents' aging? Our evolving relationship with them at this stage in our and their lives? How is it helping us think about our relationships to each other, together or apart? My own family's story is a perfect example, a modern-day passing over the fence.

THE BAR MITZVAH TRIANGLE

It was three months before my first son's bar mitzvah, and the tension was becoming unbearable. "Lucky" Louie had the second longest Haftarah of the year and he'd hardly learned five lines of it yet. To say that I was worried is an understatement. Hysterical is more like it. Every night I'd be in his room "helping him practice," and every night there would be another reason why the practice had to be postponed—a book report due the next day, a favorite TV show, a stomachache. More often than not, the evening would devolve into another tearful heart to-heart in which I would try to convey to my son the importance of this event—not just for him or me or his family, but for the future of the entire Jewish people. Needless to say, this approach wasn't working. The more anxious I got, the more I pushed. The more I pushed, the more Louie resisted. Oh, he wanted the bar mitzvah all right, but he would practice tomorrow. He promised. "And besides, Mom," he'd add, "I don't want to hurt your feelings, but I think religion divides people. Causes wars."

The intensity escalated as Louie's teachers began calling. He was in seventh grade, the first year of junior high. Night after night, for one solid week, it was a different teacher calling to say something was wrong. Louie wasn't concentrating. Louie wasn't doing his homework. Louie wasn't being Louie. My anxiety—and my guilt—were escalating exponentially. What kind of pressure was I putting on my son? Maybe I shouldn't be pushing so hard. Maybe I was doing more harm than good. Maybe if I could just be more relaxed about this bar mitzvah, my child wouldn't be having these problems. But I couldn't possibly relax. Not only were Abraham, Isaac, and Jacob watching, but so were my aunts—Ethel, Edith, and Sarah.

The final straw was the English teacher. That was Louie's favorite subject! Something had to be done. Slamming down the phone, I stormed into the living room where my husband was practicing his bass. "Something bad is happening to Louie and to us," I said. "And if you don't help, there's not going to be a bar mitzvah." (What I had really just said was that if something didn't change, there wasn't going to be a marriage.) Allen put down the bass and to my utter surprise (and enormous relief) said that he'd been thinking a lot about what was happening with Louie and the bar mitzvah and he wanted to help.

A little background here to give you a sense of the significance of this statement: Ever since we'd fallen in love and married fourteen years earlier, there was one major issue around which Allen and I fought. That was Judaism, Jewish tradition, and ritual. Although we were both children of immigrants—people whose hearts and minds, in many ways, were still in the Old Country—on this topic we couldn't have been more different. I had become the devoted Hebrew school teacher holding on to tradition for dear life and he the intellectual, rejecting "irrationality" wherever he thought he saw it.

Every Jewish holiday was a battle. Our fights were so predictable you could set your calendars by them. And the pattern was predictable also. No shouting or door slamming, just lots of intense discussion and quiet tears. Inevitably we'd end up restating our distinct positions as if saying them for the first time and then come to some compromise—about traveling back to Philadelphia for Rosh Hashanah, about the size of the seder, about how much of the Haggadah to read. (Ours was one of the earliest cut-and-paste home editions. Not only was all sexist language changed but every reference to God eliminated.) And then we would joke about the fighting. We would do that regularly too, and so would our guests as they sat with us eating matzoh balls and bitter herbs. The sequence of tension, tears, and humor was almost ritualistic. It was a kind of stalemate that everyone knew about and no one expected us to resolve.

This stalemate included our children. Louie and Eric seemed to take the battleground for granted and managed it rather creatively: Verbally, they took Allen's side, and behaviorally, they took mine. They did what I told them to do, but thought about what they were doing the way their father did. They didn't drink milk with their hamburgers, they lit Shabbos candles and came to services with me, and they went dutifully off to Hebrew school three times a week. But the older they got the more their comments and mocking questions mimicked Allen's.

The polarities were perfectly balanced in another way as well. In our family, everything that had to do with Judaism was in Mommy's territory, and on the other side of the equation, everything that had to do with music was in Dad's. Allen was a musician and filled the house with music as much as I filled it with Judaism. The lines were clear. I couldn't carry a note and Allen wouldn't carry the Torah. So you see, it was no accident that it had been me and not Allen locked in nightly battles with our son, and no accident that I'd been feeling the problem was all mine to handle.

For Allen to say that he'd been thinking about the bar mitzvah and wanted to help was nothing short of a miracle. For the next two hours we sat in the living room talking (and crying) about what we thought was going on with us and with our son caught between us. We talked about what this bar mitzvah meant to our parents—the ones who were alive and the one who was not, the ones who were healthy and the one who was not—and what it meant to us as the first-born children of these particular sets of parents.

What became clear is that we had put Louie in an impossible situation. We had—as my family therapy textbooks would say—"triangled" him into our conflict. For Louie to have embraced bar mitzvah practice would have meant siding with me and, in effect, rejecting his father—the symbol of the very "manhood" he was about to proclaim. What irony! No wonder he couldn't practice, and no wonder he couldn't really say he couldn't practice—and reject his mother.

The next day, Allen volunteered to come with me to the appointment I had made with the Rabbi. The miracle was continuing. It would *never* have occurred to me to have invited him. At the Rabbi's office, we explained what we thought was happening. When we came home, Louie, who knew we'd been at a meeting talking about his bar mitzvah, didn't even ask what we'd discussed. It was enough, it seemed, that we had gone together. That night, Allen told Louie that the bar mitzvah was important "not just to Mommy and her family, but to me and my family also. I know it's a lot to learn, Louie, but I know you can do it, and I will help you." When Allen was a Bar Mitzvah, he had learned the *trope* ["notes"] for chanting the Haftarah and he still remembered them. That night, my husband and my son were in the bedroom together—singing Hebrew!—and I was outside in the hallway crying, this time from happiness.

From that point on, preparing for the bar mitzvah was an entirely different experience. It was now about joy rather than dread. There was still an enormous amount of work to do and plenty of tension and pain, but something was fundamentally different. A couple of times when we were planning the party (a backyard affair under a big yellow tent), Allen and I slipped and referred to it as the "wedding." It really did feel like our celebration. We had each crossed over the fence, and our relationship to each other was now somehow transformed.

How I Understand My Family's Story

Our story is a perfect example of the way in which preparation for the bar mitzvah heats up whatever the family needs to be working on and provides an opportunity for something different to happen. In our case, it was the conflict that Allen and I had so rigidly been maintaining long after we had outgrown the need for it. Although I certainly didn't understand it at the time, this implicit "agreement to disagree" was, I think now, our way of protecting ourselves, our way of holding on to our independent identities (our *ideas* about who we were). Having married in our early twenties, our "adult" identities were still forming and early compromise would probably have been too threatening. Besides, maintaining our distance from each other in this way allowed us to stay loyal to our respective parents. By guarding "tradition," I could continue to be the good daughter to my observant parents, and by rejecting "hollow" ritual, he could continue to be the good son of secularists.

It was not until our conflict became a conflict for our child—not until Louie was becoming "symptomatic"—that we were pushed into moving beyond our rigidly held polarities. *Our old way of handling our conflict over Jewish ritual had worked when we and our children were young. But it was no longer working when—as a family—we were getting ready to move to a new life stage.*

The bar mitzvah was forcing us to break the stalemate. To go through with the ritual would mean that Louie would *publicly* be declaring his identity as a Jew. As long as that meant—in the context of our dynamics—rejecting his father, his resistance to practicing made sense. This behavior, with its negative consequences, was forcing us to relate differently to each other—and ultimately to him. It was our need for the bar mitzvah to happen in combination with our concern for our child's well-being that pushed us beyond the identities that fit for us when we were teenagers but no longer fit when we ourselves were parents of a teenager-to-be. *The pragmatic and emotional pressures that were building in preparation for the bar mitzvah forced us to talk in ways that previously had not been possible.* Through that talk, we were constructing a new story, a new way of understanding ourselves. And as that story emerged, Allen could begin entering the realm of things Jewish and I could begin stepping back a little and give him room to be there. In the space created by the ritual's pressure, Allen found a way to use music as a window instead of a wall, and I found a way to use tradition as an embrace, not a defense.

Our change allowed Louie to change. Because he no longer had to choose between us, he could allow himself to become involved with the practice and take up the challenge of public performance. He still needed to be nudged, but now the nudging could be effective. Louie's bar mitzvah was ultimately a day of triumph for him and for us. And the changes that had begun happening the night the English teacher called are still evolving after all these years.

Coda

There's another piece of our family's story that runs alongside of and intensifies the triangle story. I include it here not only because it is an important part of my experience, but because of the way it illustrates my earlier mention of the myth that other people's families all have such fairy-tale stories. It is a perfect example of how the piece of a family's experience I've extracted to illustrate a point is almost always *only* a piece, not the whole story.

My mother was not at Louie's bar mitzvah. She was in the hospital with yet another descent into the severe depression she'd suffered on and off since I was fifteen. Of course it was predictable: Big holidays, like Pesach or Yom Kippur; important dates, like the anniversary of her father's death; or major family changes, like birthdays, deaths, illness, would almost always send her reeling. Still, it was unthinkable. For the longest time, I couldn't imagine doing this without my mother's presence. How could my child become a Bar Mitzvah without his grandmother as witness? How could I have this joy without her having the joy of seeing it all? She had wanted it so badly. How could I celebrate here with her in the hospital there? The pain was overwhelming, threatening to rob me of my joy as the depression had robbed her.

Three things kept me going. The first was my intuitive (thank God) knowledge that I had to make this good for my son. I had to prevent the sadness from spilling onto yet another generation. I had to protect my child.

The second was the shift in my relationship with Allen. With our having become partners rather than antagonists on this subject of bar mitzvah, I had the strength to resist the despair. Our growth as adults—the growth that the bar mitzvah had pressured us into—allowed me to function as parent to my son (and partner to my husband) rather than simply as daughter to my mother. In this moment, my new role as grown-up mother took precedence over my old role as caretaking daughter.

I am proud of what we did for Louie—and for Eric when he became a Bar Mitzvah and again my mother was in the hospital—but the sadness never goes away.

The third source of strength was my friends. I will never forget the day that Renée and Carol, alarmed by my paralysis, sat me down and forced me to plan the menu—for Friday night, for Saturday afternoon, for Sunday morning. Sitting on each side of me, recipes overflowing, they focused me on the feast we would be preparing together—the kugels, the salads, the desserts; all the little details that, I now see, help make the big steps possible.

Understanding Your Story: Some Suggestions

As parents of a Bar or Bat Mitzvah (especially if it is our first), so much is going on in our lives that it's hard to know where to start thinking about it all. Do we begin with our relationship to our children, to our parents, to ourselves, to each other? On paper it is easy to draw distinctions between people and between generations, but in life, those distinctions necessarily become blurred.

At one moment we are rejoicing about our child's growth and emerging competence and at the next, grieving the loss of our baby—or perhaps crying about the nurturing we didn't get as children ourselves. At one moment we are feeling proud about how far we've come as grown-ups, and at the next, feeling overwhelmed by how far we still need to go—and what that all means as we watch our parents becoming older and weaker. This life-cycle ritual we are planning brings all of these issues into dramatic relief. It's no wonder that we are so full of emotion.

What can we do to manage all of these emotions? Sometimes nothing. Sometimes we just need to allow ourselves to feel what we are feeling and to not even try making sense of it. The feelings are important and simply living through them is all that it takes to get to where we need to be. That's how most of us do it most of the time.

But over the years I have gathered a number of ideas that have been useful in helping bar/bat mitzvah families not only to manage some of the more difficult or conflicting emotions, but actually to make deliberate use of them. I share them here and throughout this book with the hope that something—one idea or another—will have meaning for you in a way that is useful.

Talk

The first thing—as always—is talk. Risking the broken-record syndrome, I am constantly advising people to talk—to themselves (journals, letters, etc.), to each other, to parents, children, siblings, friends. This, I know, is easier said than done. Not only because the topics are often exactly those that have been hardest all along, but because the closer we get to "B" Day the busier we are and the less time there is. But, of course, this is *precisely* when we need to be talking, to be sharing what we feel, and listening to what meaning we are each making of what we feel.

If I were limited to suggesting only one thing, it would be that you put talk on the top of your list of things to do and that you find ways to make it happen.

Schedule Regular Bar/Bat Mitzvah Check-ins

Set aside time each week or every other week for you and your children to talk about decisions that need to be made, feelings that need to be shared, questions that need to be asked, values that need to be explored, stories that need to be told. How is everyone doing—both in terms of tasks and feelings? It doesn't matter that sometimes there won't be a lot to say or that sometimes the meeting might need to be rescheduled. What's important is that everyone knows that that space has been set aside and is there as issues and feelings come up. We don't need to wait for a tearful blowup to begin talking with each other. Putting aside valuable time for this talk vividly conveys to our children the message that this topic is important and worth talking about. The bar/bat mitzvah is not something we are going through mindlessly or routinely, but something we want to make as meaningful as possible—in as many ways as possible for as many people as possible.

Take Time Out for Yourselves

Some parents I know plan a regular time for themselves to have dinner together and talk about bar/bat mitzvah plans, issues, and feelings—that are for adult conversation and not meant for children. How might those first few months of preparation have been different for us and for Louie if Allen and I had been able to talk about what we were feeling instead of having to wait until "symptoms" pushed us into talk? What meaning did our rigidly held ideas for and against Jewish ritual have for us in relation to our parents? What did becoming less rigid about our identities mean—to us and to them? How might things have been different for us as adult children if we could have talked to them?

FEELING ALONE

One mother who heard me talking about this at a workshop came up to me afterward with tears in her eyes. She was married, she explained, to a man who was not Jewish. He was a good husband and good father and was supportive of the bar mitzvah. "But it's all still mine to do," she said. "John just feels so distant. And I just feel so alone." As much as Janice had thought her issues about marrying a non-Jew were resolved, this bar mitzvah was bringing them all up again. It was not that she was doubting her choice, but reexperiencing her pain. And in this unspoken form, the tension between them was growing.

A week later, Janice called. She wanted me to know that "the talking you talked about worked!" Although she couldn't have imagined it earlier, Janice found the courage to tell John some of what she was feeling and it opened up hours of conversation. It turned out that John was feeling equally bad—but from the opposite direction. As a non-Jew, he was feeling increasingly shut out as the bar mitzvah got closer. He had no idea of the meaning Janice had been giving to his silence. Once these interlocking misperceptions were able to be expressed, the dynamics shifted perceptibly. When Janice knew John wanted to be part of the experience, she could let him be there with her. And when John knew she wanted his participation, he no longer felt cut out.

Contrary to what you might imagine, this talking idea is not just for parents who are still together. A number of divorced couples I've spoken with found this "regular" meeting much easier to handle than meetings that depended on one of them calling the other—usually when some decision could no longer be put off or when some crisis had emerged. Other parents I know who are single schedule this kind of meeting with friends—either those who have gone through the bar/bat mitzvahs of their own children or who simply relate to the bar/bat mitzvah child and parent "like family."

Talk to Your Parents

Unlike the regular family conversations I'm suggesting with your children and with each other, this talk with your own parents doesn't need to be regular but it's important that it happens. In some cases such talk can help alleviate anxiety, or even repair some ancient wound. Often we carry around old ideas that no longer fit but which have never been given the opportunity to change. In other cases, talk simply helps strengthen those connections that the bar/bat mitzvah is really all about. It gives us and our children a chance to talk to the elders, and a chance for them to say some things to us. What are your parents' expectations for your child's bar/bat mitzvah? What are they hoping will happen? What are they fearing? What are you worried about them worrying about? What do they remember about your bar/bat mitzvah? What stories can they tell you or their grandchildren about that time? What was your father's bar mitzvah like? What does he remember? What would it be like for your child to hear him talk about that?

Reflect on Differences and Similarities

Photographs can be very useful here. Find some pictures of yourself at twelve or thirteen. Preferably, your bar/bat mitzvah pictures if you have any. Who were you then? Who would that child have imagined you would be today? Look at your mother standing next to you. What do you imagine she was thinking? Who else was standing next to her? Your father? Her parents? His parents? What were those relationships like at that time? What might have been different in the family if things had been different for her? For your father?

Think about what's the same and what's different in terms of the way you and your parents relate to each other now. How do you think your parents would answer that question? What similarities and differences do you notice about your relationship to your parents when you were twelve or thirteen and your bar/bat mitzvah child's relationship to you now? As a child, how did you show your need for independence and for connection? How does your child do it similarly and differently with you? Are there some things about this relationship you would like to change? Are there some ways to use this occasion to talk about those changes, to begin them? Similarly, what do you notice about your relationship that you valued in the past and hope will endure into the future? How can you use this occasion to enhance that possibility?

In one family, where the father's ambivalence about his son's upcoming bar mitzvah was causing friction between him and his wife, a chance discovery of his old bar mitzvah album allowed him to talk about some of what had made him reluctant, even bitter. It also gave him an opportunity to put into words what he wanted to be different for his son. This conversation allowed both him and his wife some new insight into what was happening between them, and some new ideas about how to keep this kind of conversation going.

"It was as if a window into my childhood had been opened and I could see things now that I had no way of understanding then. My feelings make so much sense to me now."

Take Stock of How You Are Changing

Middle-aged (almost) and in the middle, a lot is going on for us. There is no better time than when we are preparing for this ritual of transition to be reflecting on where we are and where we would like to be headed. In what ways are you evolving as a parent, a partner, a sibling, an adult child?

According to psychologists, having an adolescent child helps us with what is called "identity accommodation," the process whereby we reevaluate what we are doing and thinking in response to the new information that we are getting about ourselves—from our child and from the rest of the world interacting with us and our child.

How does thinking about that last fight with your daughter over curfews, or that last painful conversation with your brother about your parents' living arrangements, or that last exchange with your ex-spouse become a source of new information helping you change how you think about yourself and those relationships?

One bar mitzvah mother's reflections illustrate this point perfectly. She was describing a brief moment after the ceremony. It was a very hot day and the party was outdoors:

"I felt torn between myself as hostess and myself as kid wanting to have a good time. Should I stay with my mother and all of the old people under the tent or go out and have fun with the others? My usual way would have been to stay and feel resentful. But this time it was too important. I brought them all cold drinks and appetizers and then let them entertain themselves—which they did quite well, thank you very much! And I went ahead and had a ball."

Mark Your Own Evolution

Find symbolic ways to mark your own growth through this process. One father used the occasion to enroll in an adult education Hebrew class. As a child he had never gone to Hebrew school and had never had a bar mitzvah. What he learned allowed him to read the Torah blessings in Hebrew rather than in transliteration, and when he was called up for the parents' aliyah, there was a sense of this being *his* bar mitzvah too.

One mother used her daughter's coming of age to mark her own by deciding to enroll in law school. It was something she had always fantasized about but never thought she could actually do. In the course of talking with her daughter about the importance of using one's talents and acting on one's dreams, Michelle convinced herself of what she was trying to teach her daughter. By the time her second child, a boy, was ready to become a Bar Mitzvah, Michelle was a lawyer opening her own practice.

Another mother, also inspired by her daughter's accomplishment, decided to become a Bat Mitzvah herself. A month after her youngest child's bat mitzvah, Martha joined an adult bat mitzvah class and began studying in earnest.

But markers don't have to be so ambitious. One set of bat mitzvah parents decided to buy new furniture for their living room. If they were old enough to be parents of a Bat Mitzvah, they reasoned, they were old enough not to have to continue living "like the college students we used to be."

Markers can also take the form of a reward. We all know about bar/bat mitzvah gifts, but what about a gift to ourselves for how far we have come and how hard we have worked? If you think about it, I'm sure you could come up with some gift for yourselves or for each other that you deserve at this stage in your life. What is important here is to acknowledge your accomplishment—as parents, as children, as adults planning this ritual of transition.

Israela Meyerstein, a family therapist and a bar mitzvah mother, made this idea of family evolution an explicit part of her son's formal celebration. This was her third and last child's bar mitzvah. Recalling that Jewish tradition has a ritual celebrating parents at the marriage of their last child, she created a ceremony entitled "The Last Child's Bar Mitzvah: A Ritual Ceremony Marking the Family's Parting with Childhood." It was meant to evoke the "bittersweet feelings of the family" as it was about to make the transition to an important new life stage.

This little ceremony was conducted at the party following

the service. Israela began by introducing the topic and reading several poems about childhood that her father had written when her children were young. She talked about the love her parents and her husband's parents had shown their children and grandchildren and then asked all of the guests to recite with her three blessings—the first looking back with gratitude on the past, the second honoring the present, and the third heralding the future and the world beyond childhood. The ceremony ended as the guests watched a slide show of the Bar Mitzvah's life and sniffed the spice boxes being passed around at each table to "remember the sweetness of childhood as we reach forward toward what comes next."

Although everything I've been talking about applies to all families, no matter what their configuration, I want to first look at the special issues of interfaith families and then of divorced families.

Interfaith Couples: Honoring It All

Recently, I was beginning a parents workshop in my usual way, asking participants to tell who they were, who their child was, when the bar/bat mitzvah was scheduled, and whether or not this was a first.

The initial four people to my left as we went around the circle happened to be men. One after another, they introduced themselves and said they were there alone because their wives were not Jewish. The next person was a woman. Hers, she said, was not only an interfaith family, but an interracial one as well. Her husband was Hispanic and this was all quite foreign to him. The woman next to her also introduced herself as part of an interfaith couple, only it was she who was the non-Jew. "My husband," she said, "knows all about bar mitzvahs and felt he didn't need to come. But in the Protestant church where I grew up, we didn't have anything like this for teenagers and I need to learn. Besides," she added, "my husband seems less sure that the bar mitzvah is a good thing than I do! So without knowing what I'm doing, I'm left feeling most responsible for planning the thing."

The next parent in the circle introduced himself not as part of an interfaith couple, but as part of an "interfaith divorce"! Only the last four people around the circle were Jews married to Jews and the two spouses were there together.

As the membership of this workshop makes clear, the demographics are coming home. According to the 1990 National Jewish Population Survey, half of all Jews who married between 1985–1990 chose non-Jewish spouses. More than half of all Jewish children or potential Jewish children born in the next century will have a parent who is not Jewish. If you are a member of an interfaith family in the United States, you are actually becoming the statistical norm. At this point in our history, only 17 percent of American Jewish families fit what used to be (and in some cases still are) considered "normal"—two born-Jewish parents, in a first marriage, with two children. Today's Jewish families come in shapes and sizes that even one generation ago could not have been imagined. Today, no one blinks an eye when the bat mitzvah girl thanks her parents—all four of them (biological and step), and her grandparents—all eight of them—and then goes on to talk about the lace in the *kippah* (skullcap) she made having come from her step-grandmother's mother in Ireland and the tallit having been bought for her by her uncle and his life partner when they were in Israel.

Whether or not it is comforting to know you are not so unusual, it does not make your situation less complex or less sensitive. As mentioned before, if the bar/bat mitzvah period is a challenge for families where both are Jewish, how much more so for families where one is not? Not only are you dealing with the usual life-cycle issues of this stage in your family's life, but you are also dealing with the additional dynamics of balancing the needs of two very different traditions and the ways those traditions have played themselves out in your history as a couple.

Naturally, interfaith family stories are as varied as the people living them. On one end of the spectrum are Ralph and Jane.

Not only did Ralph's parents practically disown him when he married his Catholic girlfriend, but the young couple could never really come to any religious understanding between themselves either. They dealt with the issues by not dealing with them. The baby didn't get baptized or circumcised. They didn't go to church or to synagogue. There was no tree *and* no menorah. But as the years passed, Ralph was feeling worse and worse about this loss in their lives. By the time their son was eight and his Jewish friends were starting Hebrew school, Ralph insisted that Todd go also. "It's time he learned something about who he is!" Jane didn't interfere with this decision, but neither did she support it. You can imagine what preparation for the bar mitzvah was like in this family.

On the other end of the spectrum are the interfaith couples who have faced the religious differences and have come to enough clarity so that the child does not have to chose between parents.

Joy and Craig decided early in their marriage that although Craig would not convert, he would agree to raise their children as Jews. At first his parents found this a difficult pill to swallow, but they eventually supported their son and daughter-in-law in their decision. By the time of the first child's bar mitzvah, Joy was genuinely able to thank Craig—and his family—for having helped them all come to this day in their lives. It was especially moving, then, when Craig, accompanied by his daughter, sang a Hebrew song they had learned for the occasion. It was about a little bird leaving its parents' nest and both the tune and words were very beautiful. As the congregation joined in (the transliterated words were included in the booklet the family had distributed) the love and support for and from this family could not have been clearer.

But lest you think culture clashes happen only in families where one parent is Jewish and the other is not, there is the example of the observant Jewish family whose daughter's bat mitzvah was being boycotted by the father's ultra-orthodox parents. According to them, a girl reading Torah in the synagogue was a sacrilege.

A Righteous Woman and her Grown-Up Father

"My daughter is so excited and ready to become a Bat Mitzvah," Hannah told me tearfully. "She will be devastated by her grandparents' rejection."

But ultimately, that didn't happen. After many tears and several sessions of couples counseling, Hannah's husband Reuven was finally able to "stand up to his tyrannical father." He told him how they were planning to do the bat mitzvah in accordance with all of the halachic (legal) constraints (a divider between the men and women, on a Thursday instead of a Saturday so no one would have to drive on the Sabbath, and so on) *and* he told him how important his presence was to his granddaughter—and to his son. *He told his father what he had decided as his child's father and he told him what he hoped for as his father's child.* He both stood up to his father *and* stayed in relationship to him. It was a first. And it worked. Bubby and Zayda were there as their granddaughter took "her place among the righteous women of Israel." They still weren't happy about the "transgression," but they did it "for the sake of the family."

Most families are somewhere in-between the various ex-
tremes. The compromises are rarely perfect, but they *are* made.
Wherever you are on this continuum, I encourage you to find
as many ways as possible to help your child not feel torn between loyalties. Help him or her feel pride in their identities as
Jews—and pride as well in the heritage they've received from
their parent who is not Jewish (or from the family who has
objections to the ritual). Find ways as a family for the non-
Jewish parent and extended family to participate and to contribute. Depending on the norms of your synagogue, might
Judd, the non-Jewish father, stand with Yael, the mother, as
she blesses the Torah? Might his sister, Aunt Kathleen, read a
poem, or a prayer? Might Grampa Anderson sing a song?

During the party, where religious guidelines are usually set
by the family rather than the Rabbi, the ways for non-Jewish
family members to contribute, and to be honored, are myriad.
At Rachael's bat mitzvah, her non-Jewish grandfather—a pot-
ter—presented her with a beautifully crafted Sabbath set: wine
cup, challah platter, and candleholders. His wife, a weaver,
completed the presentation with a specially woven challah
cover, with the Hebrew letters spelling "Shabbat." At Terry's
bar mitzvah, it was his non-Jewish Aunt Carrie who made all
of the desserts. She loved to bake and this was her way of
expressing her love for her brother and pride in her nephew.

In addition to finding ways for non-Jewish relatives to contribute, I encourage you to find ways of publicly (and privately)
appreciating their support. Some Rabbis make a special point
of publicly acknowledging the non-Jewish parent's (and his or
her family's) contribution to the raising of this child as a Jew.
"Statistically, only fifteen percent of children of interfaith families become B'nai Mitzvah," said one Rabbi talking from the
bimah to the non-Jewish father and his parents. "You should
be applauded."

A more common opportunity for expressing appreciation,

of course, is at the party and in particular at the candle-lighting ceremony. As the O'Reillys marched up proudly to light a candle at their grandson's bar mitzvah party, the band broke into a rousing rendition of "When Irish Eyes Are Smiling." When the Galowowski grandparents came up at their granddaughter's party, it was a polka that they skipped to.

Whatever the tune, the meaning is clear. All of the heritages are being honored. Even as we celebrate this child's coming of age as a Jew, his or her whole family comes with them. Everyone—as much as it is possible—needs to be incorporated and appreciated.

Interfaith Witnesses

I can't end this section on interfaith families without some stories about the interfaith audience-congregation. As interfaith families as well as interfaith neighborhoods and friendship groups grow, the makeup of bar/bat mitzvah "congregations" becomes ever more diverse. It is not unusual now to see people of all colors and all religions attending a bar/bat mitzvah. This diversity makes my penchant for people-watching even more compelling. At one bar mitzvah I attended, the faces of a Protestant family stuck out for me vividly. The father's cousins and their two children had traveled east from Colorado. I didn't know who they were until after the service, but something about them made me know they were strangers. Maybe it was their wide-eyed, freckled faces and perfect decorum (mother wore a pillbox hat and white gloves, father sported a bow tie, and the children sat between them upright and silent throughout the long service), but somehow they looked as if they were sitting in the pew of a church. Only this was a synagogue and the sights and sounds were very different from anything they were used to. This was the family's first time in a synagogue and, not knowing what was expected of them, they were clearly on guard wanting to be proper guests. It was fascinating to watch them watching. At first their faces were unreadable, but as the service progressed you could see how engrossed they were—especially during the Torah service with the elaborate rituals and increasing intensity. You could also see how impressed they were as the Bar Mitzvah began chanting his Haftarah and how amazed they were at how long it was and how much he seemed to have mastered. And finally, you could see the surprise when it was over and the congregation started shouting "mazel tov" and broke into song. By the end, they were clapping with the best of them—and crying too, as the parents spoke of their pride in the child and their hopes for his future.

When I spoke with these cousins at the kiddush (blessing of wine and refreshments after ceremony), they couldn't stop marveling at how wonderful it all was. "We knew from Cousin Paul that this bar mitzvah thing was supposed to be something special, but we had no idea! We are so glad we made the trip!"

During another service, one little Catholic boy—a friend of the bar mitzvah child—was there alone, without his parents. They had dropped him off at the synagogue door with a reminder to be on his best behavior. William also had never been in a synagogue and was fascinated by all of the activity—and drama—surrounding the Torah. He had heard in Catholic school about the holiness of the "Scroll of Moses," and he stood with his mouth open as the majestic Ark was opened and the Torah removed. He was practically transfixed as he listened to the cantor wail the Shema, and visibly excited as he watched the Rabbi and cantor making their way slowly through the congregants crowding around to kiss the Torah. It was more than he could resist. By the time the procession had reached his section of the room and all of the arms around him were stretched out to kiss the Torah, William's arm was stretched out too. Without thinking, he did as the others, touching the Torah with his prayer book and then touching it to his lips. And as soon as he did, the shock of his action hit him. Looking around furtively to see if anyone had witnessed his religious transgression, William quickly crossed himself and sat down. From where I was standing—several rows ahead of him—I could practically see his heart beating in his little chest. His friend's bar mitzvah was more than he'd expected.

Divorced Couples: Partners No Longer, Parents Forever

Stories about, and advice for, divorced couples permeate this book. Still, a few specific words:

There are few events in our lives that highlight the pain and the complexity of divorce more than our child's bar/bat mitzvah. Just as you are celebrating the coming of age of this child you conceived together, you are most dramatically reminded of the fact that you are now not together. It is a complex and very difficult moment. But it is also one filled with potential for good. From all the conversations I've had with divorced parents for whom the bar/bat mitzvah was ultimately a healing experience, the one constant refrain—despite all the variations in their respective situations—was the desire to make this a good experience for the child, one in which he or she was not torn between parents. It was like a mantra: "This has to be a *simcha* for Stevie"; "We have to find ways to hold our pain and not let it spill out onto Stephanie"; "We have to swallow the anger and focus on what we want Robert to be able to look back on"; "We have to find ways to talk to each other so that Sandy can talk to us"; "We have to keep in mind what this event is for and what values we want Michael to come away with."

THIS AMAZING KID

One mother, a few months after her daughter's bat mitzvah, described how hard she had worked during the planning period to make the event positive and how difficult she felt her ex-husband had been at every turn. Needless to say, when I talked with Richard, he had the same story, only the roles were reversed. It was he who had been trying and she who had been so difficult. But both, it turned out, described the same experience on the bimah. It was after their daughter had led the service, blessed the Torah, chanted the Haftarah, and delivered a d'var Torah that was wise beyond her years, that they each found themselves so filled with pride that "there was no room for anger." Standing on either side of their daughter as the Rabbi made the traditional blessing, they looked at each other over her head and knew, they said, that "despite all that we couldn't do together, we had, in fact, created this amazing kid." They could not help themselves, they said, but kiss each other as they stood there kissing their daughter. And for their daughter, the moment was complete.

Not all bar/bat mitzvahs have such storybook endings, of course. In fact, there are families where the bar/bat mitzvah simply can't happen at the appointed time (if at all) because the parents are in too much pain to do what it takes to keep the ceremonial space sacred for simcha. Perhaps they are in the throes of the divorce and actively battling over custody with every decision becoming, literally, a court case. Or perhaps there has just been a devastating death or a catastrophic medical diagnosis. And even when the trauma is not this obviously all-encompassing, there is no end to the possible variations on the theme of suffering. Betrayals in the preparations, battles on the bimah, tragedies on the dance floor—we've heard it all.

But these are not the stories I want to focus on. Families in these extreme situations need more than a book like this. They need all of the love and all of the professional wisdom they can gather to help them reclaim their lives. And they need to be free—at least for the time being—of the impossible expectation that they can orchestrate a celebration in the midst of their loss. For most other families, those for whom this book *is* intended, what I have found is that when parents are able to keep the focus on the child's happiness and on what meaning they want the experience to have for their child, the outcome is usually more positive than anyone would have anticipated. This fits perfectly with what theorists are telling us about the new realities of family relationships: Our child's well-being, they say, depends not on the structure of the family, but on the quality of the relationships in them. When parents are able to focus on creating positive relationships, there are no limits to the miracles. (See "Talking to Our Ex-Partners," in Chapter 8, for more specifics on this situation.)

Repeatedly I am told that the idea of thinking ahead about what stories they hope their child will be able to tell *their* children about this bar/bat mitzvah keeps parents focused on what they have to do in order to "make it a *simcha* for Stevie." I hope this idea helps you and your family as well.

Chapter 6

Gender and the Ritual

So far I have made little or no reference to issues of gender. Most of what goes on for us as parents of B'nai Mitzvah and for our children as the celebrants has more to do with our generation than with our sex. Yet to varying extents the gendered histories, ideas, and expectations informing the ritual very much influence what we do and the meanings we make of it. In this chapter I want to explore what is unique about the bat mitzvah in reference to a daughter's development and what is unique about the mother's role, regardless of whose ceremony it is, her daughter's or her son's. At the end of the chapter, I'll focus on the father's more commonly understood role.

Our Daughters and Triumph: The Bat Mitzvah's Voice

Throughout this book I have been referring to bar and bat mitzvahs as if they were interchangeable, as if there were no distinctions between the two events or between the boys and girls who are central to them. But of course there are differences. Not only do boys and girls develop differently in our culture, but the two ceremonies have very different histories and some very different emotional resonances.

It is not an accident that most bat mitzvah girls need less coaxing in order to study, want more involvement in planning details, come up with creative additions to the traditional ceremony, and tend to approach the event with more enthusiasm than their brothers. Not only are girls generally more emotionally and physically developed than boys at this age, but they are approaching a religious event that is in a very different stage of historical and cultural development than the bar mitzvah. Because of its newness, a bat mitzvah has not *yet* become as routine, or as fixed or obligatory as its male counterpart. There is more sense of choice and more permission for innovation.

BETTER THAN A WEDDING

One girl, whose parents had been completely uninvolved with synagogue life, decided on her own that she wanted to go to Hebrew school and become a Bat Mitzvah.

Her parents watched with amazement as she followed through with her studies (all four years of it), led them through the preparation, and ultimately triumphed through a performance that sparkled with her brightness and passion. A few weeks later, her mother, still clearly moved by how meaningful the process had become for them all, recounted her daughter's assessment: "You know, Mom, when I started this, I knew it would be hard and that I would learn a lot, but I didn't know how much and how good it would be. Really, Mom, I think it's even better than a wedding!"

Bar mitzvahs go back to the fourteenth or fifteenth century. Most bar mitzvah fathers were themselves bar mitzvah boys. Until recently, when a Jewish boy was born, it was a given that (God willing) there would be a bar mitzvah thirteen years later. The bat mitzvah dates back only to 1922, the day when the daughter of Mordechai Kaplan, founder of Reconstructionism (the most recent branch of Judaism), was the first Bat Mitzvah. Judith's ceremony was a groundbreaking event. But the idea took time to spread. Even today, most bat mitzvah mothers have not themselves been bat mitzvah girls. And it is unlikely that many of today's bat mitzvah parents had thought about their infant daughters twelve years ago as future B'not Mitzvah.

It is only very recently that the bat mitzvah has become—in all but the most orthodox communities—almost as expected as the bar mitzvah, and that the bat mitzvah girl is permitted—in fact, required—to perform the same ritual acts as the bar mitzvah boy. For many years, the bat mitzvah ceremony reflected Judaism's ambivalence about women and public ritual. It was held on Friday night when the Torah is not read, rather than on Saturday morning when it is. The bat mitzvah girl did not bless the Torah, or, in fact, even touch it. In most early ceremonies, she simply gave a d'var Torah and led some of the prayers.

Despite these cultural, historical, and familial differences, however, *the potential effectiveness of today's bat mitzvah is the same as that of the bar mitzvah.* It is not the child's gender, but his or her position in the family that is important. There is much recent research on women's psychological development that leads us to understanding the bat mitzvah not only as equally useful, but as *especially timely* for our adolescent daughters.

According to Carol Gilligan, the researcher most associated with this work, middle-class girls, beginning around age eleven or twelve, seem to move away from the confident, morally articulate preadolescents they had been and toward the stereotype of the confused, hesitant teenager with which we are all familiar. Gilligan says that between the ages of eleven and sixteen, the young woman's "moment of resistance," her "clarity of vision," goes underground. She becomes disconnected from herself in a misguided attempt to stay connected to others; she loses her "voice," her right to take care of herself, if she perceives that caring for herself is in opposition to caring for others. What then could be more timely than a bat mitzvah? At precisely the point in her development when her self-confidence is in danger, the young woman is given this opportunity to take center stage, to push herself through the ordeal, to demonstrate her competence, and to speak—indeed to sing—out loud. It is a perfect counterweight, an implicit message that she deserves to be the focus of attention, to be listened to, respected, admired, and honored, and that she deserves to be held accountable to the same degree as her brother. What a gift.

A colleague of mine, a feminist psychologist well-versed in Gilligan's theories, found herself overwhelmed by what she was feeling in relation to her daughter's bat mitzvah, the ritual that would—as she herself put it—give voice to her daughter's growing maturity:

"Despite all I knew academically, I could never have predicted the emotional power of the event for my daughter or for me as her mother. I could see her blossoming before my eyes, growing up and speaking out . . . and getting ready to need me less (okay, *differently*). I was so filled with pride *and* with pain that I could hardly contain myself. I had always loved the fact that we were so close to each other and I know that I will come to love seeing her more independent and self-assured, but in that moment, I was just blown away. Now I *really* understand what it means when we say that for mothers and daughters the bat mitzvah is not about separation and loss, but about intense 'renegotiation of connections.' "

SOPHIE'S DAUGHTER

Sophie is another mother who took ideas about voice very seriously.

Having grown up in a home (and at a time) where she'd learned that nice girls don't express—or even feel—anger and don't take up much space, Sophie flirted dangerously with anorexia as a teenager. She spent much of her young adulthood in therapy and recovery programs. By the time she'd met and married Ed, she'd come a long way, and their relationship was surprisingly balanced and healthy.

Sophie had been determined to raise her children differently from the way she had been raised, and both she and Ed felt proud of themselves as parents. By the time of her first child's bat mitzvah, the fruits of their efforts were supremely visible. Shira (whose name means *song*) was a lovely young woman, known not only for her kindness and her intelligence, but for the strength of her convictions and her ability to articulate them.

When she began preparing for her bat mitzvah, she wanted it to demonstrate her coming of age not only as a Jew but as a woman. With her mother's help, Shira researched ways to enhance the traditional ceremony and incorporated several of them into her performance. One of the things she did was to pick, from among the possible dates for the bat mitzvah that the Rabbi had offered, the Sabbath in which the Torah reading featured a woman. The portion read on Shira's bat mitzvah was about the midwives who defied Pharaoh's instruction to kill Jewish baby boys, and about Miriam, who protected her brother Moses. In her d'var Torah, Shira spoke about what these women symbolized for her as a young woman entering the twenty-first century. Shira also involved her girlfriends in the ceremony. Not only did those who had already become B'not Mitzvah share an aliyah, but they and the others who were still preparing for theirs read in unison a poem and a prayer about strong women. One of her friends with whom she had been talking about women in Judaism even suggested to Shira that they put up a *mechitza* (the divider behind which traditionally observant women sit), and have the men in the congregation behind it this time. Shira and her mother both thought better of this idea!

In my experience with bat mitzvah families, I have learned of many creative ways of using the occasion to nurture and celebrate the young woman's unique identity. Some girls and their mothers, in the months preceding the ceremony, attend Rosh Chodesh (the beginning of the month) ceremonies, monthly gatherings of women in the synagogue to celebrate the new moon and the female cycles with which it is associated. One bat mitzvah mother I talked with said she was planning a private ceremony with a small group of female friends when her daughter would begin menstruating. That ceremony would incorporate some of the Rosh Chodesh symbols and would make linkages between the girl's physical, emotional, and spiritual development.

Some girls use traditional women's folk art to enhance the passage. They weave or embroider their own tallitim or kippot. Others dance a piece they choreograph based on their Torah or Haftarah portions, sing a related song they composed, or read a poem they wrote. Others perform a play about Jewish women in history whom they've researched.

The details are not important here. You can find wonderful ideas and fascinating background information in a book on bat mitzvah written by Barbara Diamond Goldin entitled *Bat Mitzvah: A Jewish Girl's Coming of Age* (Viking, 1995). What *is* important is that our daughters use this opportunity to express themselves as emerging Jewish women. Whether they choose to express their (feminist) identities by doing it "exactly like the boys" or by doing it decidedly differently from the boys is entirely up to them. Some girls, like some feminist scholars, choose to emphasize the similarities between men and women, while other girls, and other feminist scholars, choose to emphasize the differences. What matters is not their approach, but that they make the most of this opportunity to express both their individuality and their connectedness as women, *and* their connectedness and their individuality as Jews.

A caveat: Whenever I seem to be speaking about *all* boys or *all* girls, I am uneasy. Such generalizations are never *all* true. Without a doubt, there are girls for whom the danger of losing one's voice could not be more remote and there are boys for whom the bar mitzvah is an opportunity they approach with great enthusiasm and creativity. My generalizations are simply that—generalizations. We all know exceptions.

A footnote: What I find so interesting from a sociohistorical perspective is the way in which the bat mitzvah's ability to incorporate creative approaches is now influencing the bar mitzvah's ability to do the same. It is not an accident that as the bat mitzvah ceremony—with all of its innovations—becomes more accepted, the bar mitzvah is also becoming more innovative. Without a doubt, as women (both our daughters and ourselves) enter the sphere of public ritual, public ritual is changing—not only for us, but for the men with whom we share the space. And like the paradox at the heart of the bar/bat mitzvah ritual, it is to the extent that Judaism can evolve that its continuity is assured.

We move now from a focus on our bat mitzvah daughters to a focus on ourselves as bar/bat mitzvah mothers.

The Bar/Bat Mitzvah *Balabustah:* Mother's Role in the Family's Rite of Passage

It was three months after her only child's bar mitzvah, and Stacy was talking about the part she'd played in making it the success it had been. She was giving herself the credit that most bar/bat mitzvah mothers don't know they deserve:

"It just underlines how important family is to me. I felt real good about myself in terms of all that warmth flowing from family and friends. *I felt responsible for having created the space in which that warmth could have happened.* I'm happy it happened for Seth. I don't know what he may feel but I think it was important that all of those people showed up for him and if I should die tomorrow, I think it will now be important to him to keep up with the family."

In almost all of the bar/bat mitzvah families I have ever talked with, there has been the implicit assumption that Mother is the one in charge of the details. She is the manager of the event, the keeper of lists. Of course there are exceptions, but they *are* the exceptions. In most cases, Mother is in charge of the overall gestalt. She is responsible for making the event gracious, harmonious, beautiful, and tasty. No matter how much a feminist, no matter how much she is helped, no matter how egalitarian the relationship with her partner or spouse, in most cases we think of Mother as the one responsible for the domestic (as opposed to the religious) details. She is the preparer of food, provider of comfort, protector of harmony.

And when I say *we*, I mean all of us—women and men alike. We have all absorbed this expectation about who is in charge of what regarding bar/bat mitzvah preparations. Just listen to the jokes and the stories, and you'll know how the genders are locked in and caricatured: Father is the proud elder welcoming his son into the world of men (and lamenting how much the whole thing is costing). Mother is the hysterical hostess running all over for the perfect tablecloth colors. Of course, this is an exaggeration, and of course, the dynamics are changing—especially as it is now our daughters as often as our sons whom we are welcoming into adulthood, and especially as women are increasingly taking on roles of religious leadership in synagogues. But my point is that the work mothers do in organizing their child's coming of age ceremony deserves recognition, not ridicule.

I believe that for first-time bar/bat mitzvah mothers, our child's rite of passage is as much a milestone for us as it is for our child. Our "ritual ordeal" comes not in the form of a public performance but in the form of a private one—one that begins months before the first guest arrives. What we are being tested on, by ourselves as well as by others, is our capacity as *balabustah*—competent homemaker in the best, most sacred sense of the word. We are not only managing the logistics of the largest, most complicated, most costly, and most emotion-laden event in our family's experience so far, but we are bringing together everyone who is important in our lives and in our child's life in order to celebrate *harmoniously* our child's (and our family's) coming of age in the Jewish tradition. This is no small challenge.

One woman I heard about became so distraught that—as her adult son described it years later—she "took to her bed" for two weeks afterward. "It was the biggest performance of her life," he said, "and *she* was a concert violinist!" I hesitantly share this story as a dramatic extreme. It is not, I repeat, *not* the norm. In fact, most of us get through the challenge amazingly well. And as we do, we succeed not only in organizing a successful event, but in creating a safe experience through which our entire family deals with the intense and complicated emotions inherent in being a contemporary Jewish family evolving (read *aging*) through the life cycle.

Our success also demonstrates our own growing maturity, in at least two ways. One way has to do with our skills, and the second with our capacity for making emotional connections. In orchestrating this complicated and complex event, we demonstrate what has been described by anthropologists as women's "capacity for sustained attention to multiple and competing needs." On any given day we could be practicing with our child, pacifying a younger sibling, ministering to an ailing mother, consulting with the caterer, and preparing the list of aliyot—not to mention maintaining our full-time professional schedules. This is a skill that needs to be acknowledged and celebrated rather than taken for granted or ignored.

We also demonstrate our growing maturity through the ways in which our orchestrating helps us and those close to us feel connected. Many experts in the field of women's psychology are beginning to think that women's emotional development occurs not through a progressive series of separations—as was earlier thought—but through the experience of feeling empathically connected. Indeed, our sense of continuity with the past is what allows us to move forward; our sense of connectedness is what allows us (and ultimately our children) to grow up.

If developmental growth is about connecting and differentiating, the bar/bat mitzvah is a perfect metaphor. The celebrants are symbolically declaring their separation from parents—but through a ceremony that binds them to us fundamentally. For our children, it is an episode of individuation in the context of connection. For us, as mothers, it is an inverse drama, an episode about connection but in the context of differentiating. Everything we do, from deciding on the guest list to getting our child to write thank-you notes, is about relationships and connections. In addition, everything we are doing, we are doing as an *adult*, in charge of the event. For most of us, the last major life-cycle ceremony of this magnitude and importance was our own wedding, and there we probably shared management of the event with our mothers. This time our mother is our guest and we are fully in charge. The event we organize will reflect *our* values, *our* standards, *our* accomplishments, *our* growth. *In the process of creating the vehicle through which our child's voice is heard, we as mothers are, in fact, finding our own.*

To illustrate, here are some women reflecting on their own experiences:

Shelly has three children, now all grown. At the time of her first child's bar mitzvah, she was a single mother, her husband having left her a year or two earlier. Shelly was determined—as she had always been—to show everyone, especially her mother, how self-reliant she was. "What a nightmare!" she laughs, looking back. "Everything that could go wrong did. Here I was, 'Little Miss Competence,' and the roof was falling in on my head. The day my mother arrived to help with the cooking—I was having a luncheon in the house—the phone was disconnected (I'd forgotten the bill), the washing machine broke, and maggots infested my kitchen cabinets (the larva in the whole grains I'd bought three weeks earlier chose this day to hatch). If I could live through that, I could live through anything. One way or another we cleaned it all up, got the phone reconnected, the clothes washed and the food cooked. Oh, yeah, and my son was great too. But no doubt about it. *I* was the one being tested."

Another mother, whose story wasn't as dramatic, talked about the meaning of the preparation decisions in terms of her relationship to her parents. "With every little detail, I had to go through this 'values clarification' thing. How much was I going to do it for them (their way) and how much was I going to do it for myself? It was resurrecting old issues from our wedding. Like about food. Ari and I are vegetarians, but my parents wanted us to serve meat at the wedding dinner, so we capitulated. But that was then. This time we didn't have to give in to anybody. It was all us!"

In another vein, one recent bat mitzvah mother was talking about the importance of her extended family having come and what she noticed about herself in relation to them.

"I had this feeling of giving back to my family. All of these cousins I hadn't seen for years. They *all* made the effort to come. I have memories of our playing together as children in my aunt's backyard—'cause that's how I knew them. I didn't know them as adults, but suddenly, there they were—grownups. I feel like somehow this was *my* coming out as an adult. 'Here is my family,' I was saying. 'Here is my daughter. And isn't she great!' It was like introducing myself as a mother to all of my family."

Paula, reflecting on her son's bar mitzvah a month earlier, talked about changes in perceptions about herself. "I tend to see myself as shy," she said. "Being a Gemini, I have a shy side. But I also really like people. I like talking and kibitzing. So I always wonder what side of me will come to the fore. The last couple of years, it's been much more the sociable side, but with all these people coming, I was afraid that my shy side would come out. But it didn't. I really got into the people. I just couldn't talk with everyone enough. Circulating, laughing it up. It was a really pleasant surprise. The old myth about myself, 'You are shy and you don't know what to say in social situations' is gone. It just blew away. And maybe it's gone for good. Maybe I don't need to hold on to that piece anymore."

Jan, a single woman whose daughter's bat mitzvah was still a year in the future, was another parent who was struck by what was happening prior to the event. Jan was short, bubbly, and good-natured. She was glowing with happiness as she talked about the plans she and her daughter were making. "We're thinking about Anita making her own tallit and about maybe using some of my grandmother's lace and some other pieces my mother brought back from Israel. You know I'm a quilter, and the fact that she wants to do it this way really touches me. I'm just filled with emotion. Oh . . ." she said, searching to find a way to express her excitement, "I don't know, but I just feel . . . taller."

Pamela, a lesbian, talked about her experience with astonishment and tears. Although she had been living for eight years with Janet and Janet's daughter, who was five when they met, it was not until Mandy's bat mitzvah that Pamela found herself coming out publicly—as Janet's partner and, more significantly, as Mandy's second mother. "I had no choice but to voice my love and my pride as the coparent I had been all of those years. Somehow my happiness overtook my fear and I could publicly own my relationship to Janet and *our* daughter. In retrospect, I see that no one but me was surprised. What a liberation."

Here is one more story to illustrate what these mothers and I have been talking about:

GLITZ AND GRANOLA

Barbara and Bill were both born and raised in New York City. They met in college and moved to New England as soon as they married. They were drawn to the little country town because of the lifestyle it allowed them to enjoy: low-keyed, low budget, low stress.

When they returned to the city for visits home, they bought their sons sports jackets so they wouldn't embarrass their grandparents in shul and Barbara always packed her dressiest blouse for the same reason. She tried as much as possible to appease her mother and avoid the old fights. She wore her long hair up, put on lipstick, and wore "real" shoes (instead of "those schleppy sandals" her mother hated). For his part, Bill also tried to keep the peace, to keep the conflict about lifestyles and values to a minimum. He even submitted to wearing a tie for Aunt Lil and Uncle Al's fiftieth anniversary.

But now the event they were anticipating was their first son's bar mitzvah. Now New York was coming to New England. After the glitzy dinner dance that Cousin Sheldon made for his daughter's bat mitzvah in New Jersey last month (that everyone was still raving about and—if truth be told—even Barbara and Bill enjoyed), what would the family think about the potluck party they were planning for their son's big moment?

For a long time, they put off telling their parents about their plans. They would never understand. New York and New England were different planets. And this bar mitzvah was risking a collision. Of the two, Barbara was most upset. Somehow Bill seemed to care less about what the families would think, but for Barbara this was becoming a larger and larger worry. By the time she and I talked, the anxiety was becoming paralyzing. For all these years, she had been able to negotiate the two worlds. She accommodated her parents when she was with them, but lived in her own home according to the values she and Bill believed in and wanted to instill in their children. Her son's bar mitzvah was forcing Barbara to deal with the difference between herself and her mother and to deal with the consequences of that difference. Robby's ritual of individuation was becoming hers also.

As we talked, Barbara was beginning to understand her anxiety and was beginning to see the need to take some control over it. What she decided to do was write a letter to her mother—telling her about her plans and what it meant to her to have all of her friends helping to prepare the meal. Barbara and Bill were members of a *havurah*—a friendship group that celebrated holidays and simchas together—and this shared cooking was their tradition. She also told her mother how sad she was knowing that her mother would probably not approve. She told her mother how important it was to her that her child's bar mitzvah give his grandmother joy. She wasn't asking for advice, she said, but she just wanted her mother to know what she was feeling.

To her surprise, Barbara's mother wrote back to her (she'd been expecting, at most, a phone call). In her letter, her mother talked about how moved she was that Barbara cared so much to share these feelings with her, how important her grandson's bar mitzvah was, how proud she was of the way Barbara and Bill had raised him, *and* how lucky she thought they were to have such good friends.

Clearly, something important had shifted and the relief was felt throughout the family.

Moving on, some thoughts about fathers:

Changing the Generational Guards: Father's Role

Father's role in the contemporary bar/bat mitzvah is not much better understood than Mother's. But *traditionally*, it is much clearer, certainly more public, and dramatically less ridiculed. Until a relatively short time ago—and even now in more traditional congregations—the mother is more or less consigned to the role of spectator during the actual service. She has no public presence. The father, on the other hand, is publicly central. Within Judaism's patriarchal tradition, the father is implicitly the representative elder whose ranks his son is joining. Although many of our stereotypical expectations are, in general, beginning to change, especially in reference to our daughter's bat mitzvah, the father's role is still more specifically defined. Traditionally it is the father who implicitly passes on the secrets of the tribe. It is he who publicly recites the "prayer of riddance," declaring that this child is now responsible for his own moral actions. Since it is still the fact that in most cases the father has gone through this rite of passage himself, while the mother has not, it is the father who embodies the family's sense of loss, the sense of the changing of generational guards. "Just yesterday" it was he standing in the place where his son now stands, and "overnight" he has become his father. In bar mitzvah after bar mitzvah, grandfather's shadow (living or dead) is palpable as father and son stand together on the bimah. Stan's story is a dramatic example:

GENERATIONAL TREASURES

Stan's father was always sickly. He died when his son was twenty-one. Although Stan didn't tell me about it (his wife did), his only child's upcoming bar mitzvah was bringing up a lot of sadness that Stan hadn't allowed himself to feel in years. During a visit to his ailing mother's apartment in New York, Stan rediscovered an old strongbox his father had used for storing valuables. Whatever money had been in it was long gone, but the ritual objects that had been important to his father were still there—his old tallit, his tefillin, and a dog-eared prayer book. Without giving it too much thought, Stan brought the safe home with him. When Kenny, the bar mitzvah boy-to-be, saw the "cool" old box, he wanted to know where it had come from and what was in it. Stan was surprised by the intensity of his son's interest in its contents *and* in the stories he found himself telling about them. All kinds of memories were flooding back, and Kenny wanted to hear more and more about what it was like when his father was a boy living in Coney Island and going with *his* father, not only to shul, but to delis, ball fields, and all-night poker games.

On the day of the bar mitzvah, Kenny did a great job and everyone was thrilled, but the emotional highlight of the service came *after* the shouts of mazel tov. It was then that Stan joined his son on the bimah to say a few words of pride and appreciation. Barely choking back the tears, Stan presented to Kenny—one by one—his father's treasures. As he put each one in his son's hands, he talked to the boy about what his father used to tell him as a child—about the world being good and about his responsibility to make it even better. And he talked about what he thought his father might have said to his grandson had he lived to this day. There was no mistaking Stan's grief. He was mourning not only the loss of his son's childhood but mourning his own loss as well. And in that mourning he was connecting his son to his past and simultaneously making way for the future. It was a quintessential bar mitzvah moment—an intensely moving comingling of family and tradition.

From the perspective of psychological growth, it is the symbolic enactment of the father's transformation that child development theorists say is necessary for the adolescent's transformation. With the passing on of his father's legacy, Stan was crossing the ancient fence. At his son's rite of passage, he was redefining himself both as son and as father. His growth would clear the way for his son's growth, which would in turn further his own.

In this ceremony, Stan was doing something else as well: He was dramatizing—and enhancing—his connection with his son. And according to some, like family therapist Terry Real, who are now doing research on identity development in adolescent boys, this relationship is crucial. It is *the* critical variable, they say, for the boy's development of a stable sense of identity and a positive attitude toward himself as male. Contrary to previous thinking, these researchers believe, it is not the degree of masculinity measured in the father but the warmth of the father-son relationship that is the determining factor. Warmth, attachment, empathy: precisely the relational characteristics the contemporary bar mitzvah celebrates. How different this male-bonding ritual is than those we usually see on the courts and fields and rings. How different and how powerful.

Gender Politics

This exploration of the differences between the mother's and father's traditional roles is *not* about whether or not such differences are appropriate. That is another book. The point I want to make here is the importance of acknowledging and examining what is happening for us as men and women, mothers and fathers, daughters and sons. Given the increasingly egalitarian ideas taking hold in many congregations, and the fact that bat mitzvahs are becoming as much the norm as bar mitzvahs, traditional gender distinctions are beginning to soften. But they won't melt overnight. These distinctions go way back and have lots of resonance—not only in traditional Judaism, but in our secular culture as well.

Family therapist Olga Silverstein puts it most succinctly in her book *The Courage to Raise Good Men* (Viking, 1994) when she says that in our current cultural context, each sex is required to "halve" itself. By this she means that girls and women are required to inhibit the development and expression of their public, assertive sense of self, and boys and men are required to inhibit the development and expression of their capacity for emotional connectedness. Clearly the bar/bat mitzvah is about connecting the halves.

One father, half joking about his pride in having resisted tears, talked about deliberately *not* looking at his parents when he was on the bimah talking to his son.

"I knew if I looked at them, I would lose it." But then, he went on, he happened to see his two college roommates who had "come all the way from Texas" to be there with him. "I couldn't believe it," he said, shaking his head, "the two of them were bawling like babies. And one of them isn't even Jewish!"

Ourselves as Children Growing Up

Male or female, mother or father—we are all touched deeply by the emotional power of our child's bar/bat mitzvah. And to the extent that it does touch us, it has the potential to be useful. In what ways can you imagine its usefulness for you—not only as your child's parent, but as your parents' child? As you plan your child's rite of passage, what tests are you yourself passing through? Which still make sense to you as an adult with a child who is getting ready to be an adult? Which tests no longer make sense? Which messages about how to be a good mother, a loyal son, a responsible sibling, do you value and want to preserve, and which are you now getting ready to leave behind?

Given what we have seen of the contemporary bar mitzvah's capacity for enhancing both emotional expression and public voice, I think the point has been made: This family rite of passage makes good developmental sense—for our children and for us.

Part III

The Spirit

Chapter 7

Mocking the Mock Lobster: We're Not Religious, So How Come This Actually Feels Sacred?

The put-downs are legion and you've heard them all:

"Who are they kidding? The family isn't religious and having ten bar/bat mitzvahs isn't going to change a thing. They won't be back in the synagogue again until next Rosh Hashanah . . . maybe."

"It's a hollow performance, an empty sham; an excuse to get the kitchen remodeled like the Goldsteins."

"It's a rite of passage all right—for the parent: 'Look, we are old enough to have a kid who is thirteen, and rich enough to invite everyone to celebrate that with us.' "

It is easy to dismiss today's bar/bat mitzvah as hollow and meaningless. It is easy to focus on the family's lack of religious practice, the child's mindless memorization, and the party's tasteless glitz. It is easy, that is, if you don't bother looking more deeply.

Brimstone and the Bar Mitzvah Lady

Some years ago I did a presentation for bar/bat mitzvah parents in a wealthy suburban temple. It was designed as a Sunday morning brunch and I was the guest speaker, invited by the school principal. I deliberately arrived early in order to be able to chat informally with some of the parents before the talk. The principal arrived a few minutes after I did, but then was called away to deal with one of the students. He pointed me in the direction of the social hall and I was on my own. As the parents came in, they helped themselves to the lox and bagel buffet and took seats at several round tables set up in front of a podium. It was clear that people were sitting with friends and had a lot to talk about with each other. It was also clear that they were ignoring me. They knew who I was, not only because I was the one none of them had ever seen before, not only because I had already put on my name tag, but because I was actually going up to people and introducing myself and handing out blank tags and Magic Markers for them to use. In the past it had been my experience that there would always be at least two or three people who would eagerly come over, introduce themselves, offer me coffee, tell me about the synagogue, and generally try to be hospitable. And even in those places where people were shy, I could always initiate enough small talk to put us both at ease.

This time it was different. It was as if this crowd was angry at me. It was as if they hadn't wanted to be there, as if I was responsible for them being there and they really didn't want to hear what I was going to say. In any other circumstance I would have taken their behavior personally. What had I done to offend them? Why were they (literally) turning their backs to me? But, of course, I knew that whatever was going on wasn't about me. They didn't know me from Eve and didn't have a clue about what I would be saying. All they knew was that this was a program for parents of the sixth grade Hebrew class, that the guest speaker was going to talk about "bar/bat mitzvah and the family," and that they were required to attend.

Thankfully, this "social" period didn't last too long. The principal returned and formally introduced me and my talk. Almost reluctantly, it seemed to me, people stopped talking with each other and turned their chairs—most of them, anyway—toward the podium.

As I began talking, I was struck by how stiffly everyone seemed to be sitting, how—almost defensively—they seemed to be listening. But as my talk went on, I could see people beginning to relax, actually softening in response to what they were hearing. Occasionally something I said hit a nerve and a husband and wife would look at each other knowingly, or chuckle softly in recognition. By the end of the talk, I could see that most of the audience had become engaged with the ideas I was sharing and some were actually asking questions and volunteering comments.

Clearly, I had touched many of them, but I was still in the dark about their initial response to me. It was not until the formal presentation was over and people were gathering around and telling me their personal stories that I understood what they had been afraid of.

These were almost all secular or minimally affiliated Jews. They were planning huge (read expensive) bar/bat mitzvah extravaganzas and they had been expecting that I—"the bar/bat mitzvah lady"—had been brought in to admonish them for it. Their earlier rudeness was their way of steeling themselves against the fire and brimstone they'd been expecting. All of the things they were worried about or ashamed of—their lack of religiosity, their child's eagerness to quit Hebrew school, the amount they were spending on the black-tie-optional dinner dance—all of this they were expecting me to "throw in their

faces." They could hardly believe that I was not only not condemning them, but that I was actually finding meaning in even
their children's bar/bat mitzvahs. It was such a relief. What they
were saying was that, despite how hollow it might look to others, and even—at times—how confused they were about it
themselves, something about this event really did feel important. They couldn't actually say what that was, but they certainly *felt* it. Finally, here was some confirming "authority."

One couple's story brought this home to me most dramatically.

As her husband nodded in agreement, Mrs. Clark defiantly
informed me that no matter what anyone had to say about it,
she was planning a party for her second daughter's bat mitzvah
that was going to be "as big and as special" as the party for
her first daughter had been. "She's going to have all the balloons and glamour that her older sister had!" As I listened,
Mrs. Clark went on to reveal the emotional meaning behind
the intensity. "What my father said to me after that first bat
mitzvah, I will never forget!" she explained. "He said that if I
never did another thing for him in his whole life, I had done
enough. For *his* daughter"—who had married a man who was
not Jewish—"to have raised her children as Jews and to have
given his granddaughter 'such a big bat mitzvah,' this he could
hardly believe. He was thrilled."

By now Mrs. Clark was too choked-up to continue, and Mr.
Clark took over. "My father-in-law died last year, so now this
second bat mitzvah is even more important. Even if we have
to take out a second mortgage, it's worth it."

For better or worse, what looked to the world like hollow
excess had a different meaning for this family. For them, it was
a statement about forgiveness, about healing, about holding on
to the past even as the present was so radically different. And

maybe it was also a statement about the future and how the generations will continue to be connected—in ways that we cannot, in the present, predict.

Clearly, the Clarks' way of indicating the ritual's importance is not the way the Rabbis and Jewish educators would prefer, and in fact the Clarks *could* have done more to enhance the event's spiritual and cultural significance (without having to give up the balloons and glamour). Still, the emotional meaning for them was very real and very powerful.

Spirituality and the Secular Norm

In today's secular world, the Clarks are statistically more the norm than the exception. The intermarriage rate is now over 50 percent and only 20–25 percent of American Jews regularly participate in Jewish religious or cultural activities. They are the norm also in that as bar/bat mitzvah parents, they feel self-conscious about their lack of Jewish practice, their lack of "religiousness," as they would put it. Although many of the families I talk with are less defensive, perhaps, than the Clarks, they are no less worried. Yes, they are sure their bar/bat mitzvah is Jewish, but they are also sure that it's not sufficiently spiritual. Over and over I am asked for ideas about how to make the event more spiritually meaningful for families who have been—in general—nonobservant, confused, conflicted, or even hostile to religious ritual.

I have a number of thoughts in response to this request. And my thinking has evolved over time. Almost twenty years ago when I began my research on bar mitzvah and family development, no one took this ceremony very seriously or expected much from it. It was a family gathering that happened to occur in the synagogue and in the banquet hall, with little "real" religious significance. No one expected the kid to be any different (except that he would be "done with Hebrew school"), and no one expected the family to become more observant. More often than I care to remember, the mere mention of this topic would be followed by someone telling another horror story—either why he hadn't stepped foot in a synagogue since his own bar mitzvah thirty years ago, or how some family feud had started at a cousin's bar mitzvah and continues to this day. Always, there was some can-you-top-this example of materialistic excess like, for instance, the "shop-till-you-drop" bat mitzvah party theme with each table sporting the name and logo of another famous department store. The fact that the bar mitzvah wasn't really about religion seemed to be a foregone conclusion.

Trying not to be defensive or dejected (at that time, I shared much of the pessimism), I consoled myself with the thought that my research wasn't about the religious aspects of the event, but about its developmental possibilities. I wasn't looking at how the bar mitzvah made the child or the family better Jews, but how it made them better able to launch an adolescent. Without explicitly understanding it, however, let alone being able to articulate it, I was not without bias. It was my unspoken expectation that the bar mitzvah *would* be more developmentally/psychologically useful for families more connected to Jewish practice and less useful for families less connected to it.

Lots has changed since those days in the early eighties. To some extent, my thinking has moved with the zeitgeist. Our culture's overall attitude toward ritual has evolved quite dramatically. As a secular society, middle-class Americans have become much more respectful of the power of ritual and much more interested in that which we characterize as spiritual. Disillusioned with the capacity of science and technology to make the world a better place, we are casting about for other answers. Hence, our current return to roots and religion.

As for the change in my hypothesis about the relationship between religiosity and ritual efficacy, what I'd expected turned out not to be true. No connection was shown in my research between the family's level of religious observance and the ritual's developmental usefulness. The Hasidic family aside (there, the shared expectation about transformation is absolute and literal), it could *not* be said that the bar mitzvah had developmental consequence only for families who were involved in Jewish practice. Instead, what I found in my study was that the bar mitzvah had tremendous developmental potential for all of the families and a great deal of emotional (and at times spiritual) power even for families who seemed very cut off from the tradition. For example, in the family for whom this was the first bar mitzvah in three generations, there was no doubt that something spiritual was happening.

I have since talked to hundreds of families and attended hundreds of ceremonies, and what I see—even in those that seem on the surface to be *all* surface—confirms what I earlier sensed: Something sacred seems to be happening on that bimah and in that chapel, and even if it's only for a few seconds, it is profound.

What accounts for this phenomenon? Is it that as a society we have more respect for the power of ritual and thus fulfill our expectation that it will be powerful? Is it that as secular, nonpracticing Jews we have fewer and fewer opportunities to enact our Judaism publicly so that the few remaining occasions—the bar/bat mitzvah being one of them—take on greater significance than they ever used to? Clearly there are no simple answers. But in my search for ways to understand what is happening for us, our children, and our parents at this juncture in our lives, I've come across a number of ideas that I believe to be relevant.

The first idea has to do with the sense I mentioned above of something sacred happening on the bimah—"if only for a few seconds." In an article about research on contemporary Jewish life, Arnold Eisen, a professor of religious studies, says that we cannot measure the quality of a family's Jewishness by the quantity of time it spends in Jewish activities. Spirituality doesn't happen when we accumulate a sufficient number of Jewish chips. Although we're used to thinking, he says, that the more daily Jewish activities people have in their lives, the more Jewish they are, this might *not* always be the case. "The most meaningful times we have in our lives are often brief moments or even fractions of moments." In general, he goes on, we know where the substance, as opposed to the routine, is, "so why not let it be the same in [the realm of] Jewishness?" How helpful this is in understanding Mrs. Clark and her passionate defense of her experience, how helpful in understanding the intensity we observe on the bimah whenever there is a bar or bat mitzvah family standing up there in tears.

The writings of Rabbi Lawrence Kushner also help me understand what it is that feels so meaningful. In one of his many articles on Jewish life, he writes that life-cycle rituals are occasions during which one generation *hands itself over* to the next. It is a chance to "realize our place in the ancient fabric [of which we are a part], and [to] stand reverent. . . . This reverence before the generations past and future may be the root experience of the holy. We meet God in the faces of our parents and our children . . . for in them we behold our own birth and our own death."

"What is so powerful," he asks, "about the great life passages that they evoke such emotional and religious intensity?" And this is how he answers: "After two decades of trying to help Jews find meaning in the great events of their lives and build institutions where that can happen gracefully, I am convinced that the answer lies in the dynamics of the family. First comes family, then comes religion."

So much for my attempt to keep separate the secular and the sacred, the dynamics of family and the dynamics of religion. *In our Jewish cosmology, the everyday is holy. Our relationships to our parents and to our children are sacred. And it is this Jewish emphasis on the sacredness of relationships that creates for us the link to increased meaningfulness and, indeed, spirituality.* To quote Rabbi Kushner once more, "These emotionally powerful events are religious precisely because they touch us at our core—whether or not we ourselves are religious."

Putting These Ideas into Practice: Enhancing the Bar/Bat Mitzvah's Spiritual Meaning

God and the Greens

The Greens were a decidedly secular, urban couple. Eric was born Jewish. Jen had been raised Protestant but converted before the wedding to please Richard's mother. Neither thought much about religion one way or the other. If anything, Eric was mostly put off by what he felt were his parents' parochial views. The younger Greens' passion was reserved for local politics. They'd been most active in organizing neighborhood efforts to help the homeless. When their son, Peter, was eight, his best friend was being enrolled in Hebrew school, and Peter wanted to go also. Eric was surprised by his son's interest and surprised also by the pleasure he found himself taking in it. For whatever reasons, Peter seemed to like going to Hebrew school, and Eric seemed to like that he liked it.

It was not until Peter was eleven and a half and came home talking about the fact that in a few weeks the Rabbi would be meeting with parents to discuss bar mitzvah dates that Eric began to question what this all meant. It was one thing for his son to go to Hebrew school, but an entirely different thing for the family actually to have a bar mitzvah! That was a public commitment to Judaism that he didn't know if he or they were ready to make. Wouldn't it be a sham, a farce? After all, they never went to the synagogue, they didn't celebrate the holidays at home—and they didn't believe in God. What kind of Jews were they and what kind of bar mitzvah could it be? The more he thought about it, the more troubled he became.

Talking to Jen wasn't much help either. She liked the fact that Peter was interested in Judaism, thought a bar mitzvah would be fun, and told Eric the decision was up to him and Peter. This was *his* tradition, not hers. She would go along with whatever they decided.

Eric was left no choice but to make an appointment with the Rabbi. With much hesitation and with what was, for him, an unusual inarticulateness, Eric talked about his reservations and doubts. To his surprise, the Rabbi was not surprised. It seemed that lots of bar/bat mitzvah parents had been expressing similar worries. They were perhaps not as clear about their dilemmas as Eric, but they were nonetheless concerned about not being religious enough or spiritual enough to make their child's bar/bat mitzvah feel "honest." In response, the Rabbi said, he was planning an adult education class for bar/bat mitzvah parents and the focus would be precisely these concerns.

What Eric learned in that class began to open up new ways of thinking about Judaism and his relationship to it. What struck him most was Judaism's emphasis on human relationship. According to the Rabbi, Eric told me later, Judaism is as much about our relationship to people as it is about our relationship to God. Whatever enhances our connections to others (our family, our community, the world) enhances our Jewish spirit(uality). In this context, Eric's long-standing and deep commitment to people and to issues of social justice had much deeper roots in his tradition than he'd known. Impressed, he repeated the Rabbi's quotation from the Book of Hosea: "It is kindness that I desire, not sacrifice." "In other words," Eric concluded, "God is more concerned about how we treat each other than about how we pray."

In the class on God and our ways of believing, Eric went on, the Rabbi said that "in Judaism we talk less about God's essence and more about the way God is 'encountered.' 'Ask,'" said the Rabbi, " '*not where is God, but when is God?*' If God is in our actions, our deeds, then Jewishness resides in all sorts of unexpected places." Again Eric was struck by this thought. And when the Rabbi asked the parents to think about talking to their children about these ideas in relation to bar/bat mitzvah preparation, lots of connections began to emerge.

That night Eric talked to Peter about what he had been learning and thinking about and how that fit with what Peter was hoping his bar mitzvah would mean to him. Together the two of them began to think about how the family's work with the homeless and Peter's attraction to learning about his Jewish heritage meshed. Together they developed a "mitzvah plan," something the Rabbi had suggested. It was a list of thirteen mitzvot or good deeds—some for Peter to do alone, others for his parents to do, and yet others for the whole family to do together as part of the bar mitzvah preparation.

Some were actions that involved more political work on behalf of the needy, some were about reading books on Jewish history and practice, and a couple focused on learning more about family members lost in Europe. The final item the Greens came up with was a decision to do something as a family to celebrate one new Jewish holiday each year. The holiday they chose to begin with was Sukkot, the harvest celebration. It was the one closest to Peter's bar mitzvah date. It was, not accidentally, a perfect choice. In preparation for building the sukkah, they began reading about its meaning in terms of Jewish history and symbol. The connections they made between their wandering forebearers and their contemporary ideas about shelter and communal responsibility were profound.

On the day of his bar mitzvah, Peter talked about the mitzvot he had done in preparation for "becoming a man," and his father talked about his own preparations for this "becoming." On the day of his son's bar mitzvah, Eric formally thanked his parents for having passed on to him his Jewish heritage and acknowledged its link to his social consciousness. For him, the bar mitzvah was now spiritually "honest." For all who knew the family history, it was amazing.

The Greens' story is clearly exceptional. Although it often happens that our child's upcoming bar/bat mitzvah restimulates our spiritual doubts and uncertainties, it is not often that it leads to such dramatic resolution. More commonly, we are aware of discomfort but don't feel we can do anything about it. It's too late to change, we tell ourselves; even if we wanted to, we're not going to become different people—with different family backgrounds, living different lives. So what can we do but try to ignore the doubts—sweep them, so to speak, under the consciousness rug. That's what most bar/bat mitzvah parents, disconnected from the tradition, do. But not all. In fact, more and more of the parents I talk with are looking for other responses. They simply can't tolerate the idea of just "going through the motions." They want what they and their child are going through to have some kind of spiritual/religious significance. They are becoming increasingly intent on using the opportunity to make new meanings for themselves and their families. As one mother put it, "I want it to be a ritual, but I don't want it to be ritualistic!"

"Spirituality" Suggestions

Here are some of the suggestions I've gathered from talking with parents along the whole continuum of "spirituality." Maybe one or two will be helpful as they are or as catalysts for your own ideas.

Once Again, Talk

Talk to each other and to your child about what can make this experience most meaningful. What moves you emotionally, what moves them? *The task is less about finding meaning in the bar/bat mitzvah and more about putting meaning into it.* Even if your child doesn't engage in this conversation actively or articulately (and most can't), it is crucial that he or she knows this is important to you and that you are talking about it and thinking about ways of embracing and enhancing its significance. Acknowledge the disparaging images often associated with contemporary bar/bat mitzvahs—and acknowledge (if this is the case) your own ambivalence, not only about the ceremony, but about Jewish ritual in general. Be clear about what's important to you in all of this—*despite* the ambivalences. Talk about the bar/bat mitzvah's significance (if this is your situation) in terms of your family's past *and* its future. Talk about the significance for the parent who is not Jewish as well as for the one who is. And talk about how this all *fits* in the family's evolution.

Talk about what it would be like if you *weren't* having this bar/bat mitzvah. What would be lost? Who would be most disappointed? What would grandfather have said about this? What would a future great-grandchild say?

Together, figure out ways of counteracting the negative images or feelings that the bar/bat mitzvah is a farce; an empty performance. Invest time and energy, not just money, in what you are doing. Once you begin to do this, the Rabbi's words may evoke in you a different response. As one mother told me after she began using her daughter's bat mitzvah practice as an opportunity to begin studying again herself, "Now when the

Rabbi talks about the significance of the bar/bat mitzvah, I feel like he's talking about us, not just about some other family."

Another set of parents I spoke with used this idea to talk together about the "rat race" they'd been in and hating for years. Their desire to make their son's bar mitzvah more meaningful became the incentive they'd needed to begin reordering their priorities. They decided to end their workweek early on Fridays and actually have dinner together. Once they saw that this was possible, they decided to incorporate some challah and some wine. By the time I saw them again a few months later, they were lighting candles and singing along with a tape of Sabbath songs. They were delighted with themselves and felt that this previously unimagined Sabbath time together was making preparation for the bar mitzvah an entirely different experience. Indeed, they felt it was changing them as a family.

Encourage Connections with the Extended Family

Use this as an opportunity to foster your child's sense of connection with and concern about family. Encourage your child's curiosity about his or her ancestors and where they all connect on the family tree. (Use the genogram described in Chapter 4.) In what ways can you help your child understand him-or herself as a link between the past and the future? In what ways do you understand *yourself* as such a link? Might this be a time for your son or daughter to begin calling grandparents themselves—to ask how they are, to tell them about the bar/bat mitzvah plans, to ask questions about family? Might it make sense to plan a trip to distant grandparents or to some segment of the family who haven't been seen in a long time or in which, for instance, a new baby has been born? This is a wonderful opportunity to reinforce your child's larger sense of family.

And speaking of larger family, quite a number of families are using the period of bar/bat mitzvah preparation as a time to schedule a trip to the Holocaust Museum in Washington, D.C. Many of these families make it a point to take only the bar/bat mitzvah child on this visit. They tell the younger siblings that they will take them when they are in the process of preparing for *their* "coming of age."

Link Joyous Occasions with Charity

Talk about ways of linking the money being spent on frivolities to money being given to charity. In Jewish tradition, simchas and *tzadakah* (righteous giving) always go together. At every Jewish wedding in Eastern Europe, there was a beggar's table—a tangible way of sharing the family's wealth and happiness with the poor.

Mazon, which means food, is a contemporary version of this linkage. This Jewish organization responding to hunger suggests that families donate 3 percent of what they pay for the bar/bat mitzvah to feeding the poor. What this means is that for every thousand dollars you spend on the event, you pledge thirty dollars to Mazon. (You can write to them for information at 12401 Wilshire Blvd., Suite 303, Los Angeles, CA 90025, or ask your Rabbi for details.)

Also, in addition to any monetary contributions you decide to make yourselves, what portion of his or her gift money does your child want to pledge to charity? Which charity? Discussion of this kind is Jewish spiritual practice.

You might also talk to the caterer about donating leftover food to a local shelter, and to each other about how it would be for you and the children to bring the floral centerpieces to a local nursing home after the party. Some families are now creating centerpieces from art, music, or sport supplies (depending on the child's interest) and then donating them to local schools.

Whatever you choose to do, don't just do it, but be sure to talk about it with your child. What *are* your values about sharing your good fortune? This is an opportunity to strengthen them and to pass them on.

Make the Idea of Mitzvah Come Alive

The bar/bat mitzvah process is a golden opportunity to foster your child's sense of Jewish values. If, as Eric Green's Rabbi told him, "God is in our deeds," what activities can we encourage *in ourselves and in our children* that reinforce our idea of being spiritually connected to our Jewish history and values?

The word *mitzvah* in the term bar/bat *mitzvah* is translated not only as "commandment," but as "righteous deed" as well. How can we make the most of this natural link between religious practice ("commandments") and good deeds (acts of human kindness and decency), between the spiritual and the ethical, between being "religious" and being connected to Judaism's emphasis on mercy, compassion, and social justice?

In rabbinic tradition, we are told that being "responsible" as an adult means being involved in the "three pillars on which the world stands": study, religious practice, and righteous deeds (community service). In some Israeli kibbutzim, and increasingly in the United States, children arrange to carry out thirteen mitzvot of their choice in any combination of these three categories.

When Rabbis talk about "core Jewish values," they are talking not just about keeping the Sabbath or keeping kosher; they are talking also about the concept of *derekh eretz*, the idea of basic decency and courtesy. And they are talking also about the ideas of *g'milut hasadim*, about deeds of loving-kindness. The idea of such deeds is broader than the concept of charity de-signed to help the poor. These deeds emphasize the need to do more than one's minimum interpersonal duty. Traditional ex-amples include feeding the hungry, providing clothes for those without them, comforting mourners, and treating others with dignity and respect.

In what areas does your child want to do righteous deeds? (Not *does* he or she want to do them, but *which* ones?) In what ways can he or she demonstrate decency and courtesy? Like the Orthodox boy who puts on tefillin before his bar mitzvah only as practice, and then begins doing it afterward for real, and for the rest of his life, what good deeds can your child come up with that he or she can do as "practice" before the bar/bat mitz-vah and then can do "for real"—and for always—afterward?

In Jewish thought, *action is the antecedent to belief.* Children learn the meaning of mitzvot by *doing* them. Just as we don't wait for our children to be ready to study, we don't wait for them to be ready to think about helping others. We structure ways for them to help and *then* it becomes part of their con-sciousness, part of what they expect of themselves.

Talk with your child about which mitzvot make sense in terms of interest, time commitment, and practicality: Volun-teering in a hospital? Nursing home? Soup kitchen? Blessing the challah and the wine? Lighting candles? Studying some piece of text? Watching a movie, or attending a concert with Jewish content? *The process of preparing to become a Bar/Bat Mitzvah is a natural gold mine of opportunity for moral devel-opment. Whether your child chooses an ethical mitzvah like vis-iting the elderly, or a ritual mitzvah like regularly reciting a certain prayer, he or she is enacting the spiritual development that the ceremony is meant to celebrate.*

After visiting a homeless shelter—one of her thirteen mitzvot of preparation—Amanda decided to include on the invitation a request that guests bring to the bat mitzvah old winter coats they no longer wore. She arranged with the Rabbi to use one of the classrooms as the drop-off site. By the time the ceremony was over, the room looked like a rummage sale. That Monday, Amanda and her parents picked up all of the coats and brought them to the shelter. The coordinator was thrilled. And so was Amanda. She has been organizing school collections—food, baby clothes, kitchen supplies, you name it—ever since.

Amanda's story, an example of how preparation for the bar/bat mitzvah can work to raise the child's consciousness about the needs of others, always reminds me of one of the ironies imbedded in the process: *At the very moment in their lives when all eyes are on the child, the child's eyes are becoming capable of looking beyond him/herself. The natural process of maturing psychologically combined with the ethical teachings of the mitzvot work to raise the child's capacity for empathy and compassion to a level previously not possible.*

One Jewish educator, Joel Lurie Grishaver, refers to the bar/bat mitzvah process not as a coming of age, but as a "coming of mitzvah." He says that what the child does is less important than how he or she does it. What is important is the spirit, the values, the attitude with which they approach the process. In this respect, Grishaver's book, *40 Things You Can Do to Save The Jewish People* (Alef Design Group, 1993), is a must read. His chapter on bar/bat mitzvah is right-on.

Do as We Preach

Talk together about ways the adults in the family can also become more committed to righteous deeds. This is a way of demonstrating to our children *and to ourselves* the seriousness of what we are doing and the importance of what we value. In what ways do *we* want to do more in the areas of study, prayer, community service? Here are some possibilities:

- What would it be like for you to do what the "rat race" family did?—to establish Friday night as the one night you all eat together, to make the meal into a festive celebration of the Sabbath? What would that feel like in your family? Is it at all possible? How might you ease into it? What would you have to do/learn to be able to arrange it? Could you manage it even once a month? Could it be done with friends or with another bar/bat mitzvah family or two?

- What adult education class in the synagogue might you join as part of the bar/bat mitzvah preparation? What would you like to learn about on your own? Ask your Rabbi to recommend some books.

- Learn the meaning of your child's Torah portion and Haftarah with him or her. Demonstrate that the meaning is important; these are not just nonsense syllables to recite by rote. Indeed, these texts contain our people's sources of hope. What a great conversation to have with your child, especially in a world so full of cynicism. Ask your Rabbi for books that interpret each section. There are fascinating stories that make the text come alive.

- Or start to study Hebrew if you've never learned to read it. Might this be something your child could teach you from the *aleph*-class (first level) textbook stashed away in the back of the closet? What would it mean to your child to see you doing "homework" yourself each night? Whatever you choose to do in this area, begin doing it early in the process. Not only is there more time at this end of the preparation period, but this kind of learning will enhance the context of everything else that is being done and learned.

- According to the Rabbis, we should have a fixed time each day for Jewish study. Might this be the year to start this tradition in your family?
- Plan to attend services together—not simply because it is "required" as part of the synagogue's preparation program, but because of the opportunity it provides: to spend a few hours together as a family, to become more acquainted with the liturgy and with the customs of the service, to allow yourselves to feel (if this is your situation) less like a stranger in the congregation your child is "entering." If you can't get everyone in the family to go, take those who will. And maybe go out to lunch afterward. Make the time together pleasant, something to look forward to.
- If, as author and poet Catherine Madson has put it, "holiness is not a kind of essence, but a kind of activity," talk together as a family about what other things you can do to infuse holiness or meaning into the everyday "rituals" of life—our hellos and good-byes, our morning greetings, bedtime routines, mealtime habits, etc.
- Purchase trees or donate books in honor of guests. Have certificates at each place setting.
- Make a donation to the synagogue in honor of the Bar/Bat Mitzvah or in honor of those receiving aliyot.
- Invite guests to bring donations of food or clothing to the synagogue's tzadakah collection site.
- Read *Putting God on Your Guest List: How to Reclaim the Spiritual Meaning of Your Child's Bar or Bat Mitzvah* by Rabbi Jeffrey Salkin (Jewish Lights Publishing, 1992). It is a wonderful guide to enhancing the bar/bat mitzvah's spirituality. Another excellent book to help you become more knowledgeable about the bar/bat mitzvah is called *Bar/Bat Mitzvah Basics*, edited by Cantor Helen Leneman (Jewish Lights Publishing, 1996).

- Tell your Rabbi what you are thinking about and doing and ask for further suggestions.

Remember the Rabbi who suggested that parents talk with their child about curtailing some extracurricular activities during the months of preparation? Well, what would it mean in your family if you announced that during these months of preparation *you* also were curtailing some of your "extracurricular" activities (like the tennis tutorial or the poker pack, or something else that was fun for you) in order to study along with your child, or to take some class at the synagogue, or to volunteer at the local nursing home, or . . .

While most advice books tell you not to let the preparations for the bar/bat mitzvah take over your life, what I am suggesting is that you find some ways to make it actually change something in your life. Finding some regular way to enact even some small piece of what the bar/bat mitzvah symbolizes emotionally or spiritually could make a surprising difference. You never know.

Chapter Eight

The Period of Preparation: It's Part of the Ritual

"No matter what happens tomorrow, it's already been worth it."

It was the day before his child's bar mitzvah and Dave was musing about the months of hard work and intensity he, his son Noah, his wife, and his ex-wife (Noah's mother) had just been through. Before they'd started planning it, he had worried terribly about how they were all going to manage—especially as his new wife was not Jewish and (on top of that) had become pregnant just when he and Janine had begun talking about invitations. Looking back now, he was amazed at how far they had all come. Six months ago, the amount of work and potential for conflict had felt overwhelming. He could hardly believe how much they'd been through and how much they'd all grown. He was feeling so good about what they'd accomplished, he said, that he almost didn't need the ceremony in order to feel proud. "Sure, there was plenty of tension and we each had to swallow a lot, but somehow we all seem to be closer to each other now, more accepting of where we are in life, more clear, at least, about what we all want for Noah. I don't know, but all I can say is that something's different and we're all really excited."

With all of the attention focused on THE BIG DAY, most of us miss the importance of what's happening prior to that day. Most of us don't notice that it is really A BIG YEAR: The changes the ceremony is meant to mark have already begun happening. In fact, *preparation for the ceremony actually fosters those very changes we are looking forward to celebrating.*

In this chapter I want not only to draw your attention to the value of the preparation period, but also to suggest ways of making the most use of this period.

Preparation for a Sacred Event Is Sacred

For most of us, the process of bar/bat mitzvah is implicitly divided into two spheres: That which is sacred and that which is profane (secular, ordinary). Most of us automatically put the ritual on the bimah into the category of the sacred and everything else into the other. To my mind, the dichotomy is less sharp. While what happens in the synagogue is clearly the most "religious" part of the process, in some very real ways the period leading up to the sacred ceremony is also sacred—or at least very special. Important things are happening for us in this part of the experience, and to the extent that we notice their value, we increase that value.

People actively preparing for any sacred life-cycle ritual have already entered into a state of sacredness. The closer to the ritual date, the more intense this state becomes. Anthropologists talk about this as a liminal (in-between) period, a time enveloped by an atmosphere of impending holiness, specialness, excitement, danger, and transformation. Edwin Freidman, a Rabbi and family therapist, calls it the "hinges of time," the period when relationships "unlock" and the family is most open to change.

Just think about the label *bar/bat mitzvah family.* What was going on for you the first time you heard yourself referred to by that title or began thinking of yourself in that way? Once we take on the identity as "a family preparing for a child's coming of age in the Jewish community," something changes. We know ourselves and are known by others as something special, something we were not before we took on that title, before we began talking about and planning for the event.

When does preparation begin? Obviously it begins at different times for different families. Some families start thinking about the bar/bat mitzvah at the bris or at the naming ceremony. Others wait until they are enrolling the child in Hebrew school. Yet others begin imagining their own child's event only after bar/bat mitzvah invitations from cousins, friends, and neighbors start pouring in.

The Browns' son was ten when this preparation period began. They had just returned from a wonderful trip to a cousin's bar mitzvah in California.

What was most meaningful, Mrs. Brown said, was the time they spent in their cousin's backyard with the extended family they hadn't seen for years. In particular, she got to talk at length with some very lovely relatives on her father's side whom she'd almost forgotten. What was even better was the way their children and hers hit it off. It was as if they'd made friends for life. So how was Mrs. Brown beginning her family's preparation? She was getting estimates from landscapers. What trees and bushes could she plant now that would provide shade and beauty for her relatives in three years? Not your usual idea of preparation, but preparation nonetheless.

In general, however, when we talk about the preparation period, we are usually talking about the three- to six-month period in which we are most actively engaged in the details of planning, studying, arranging, etc. Thinking about these months of preparation as sacred gives them new meaning and importance. Not only does it take some of the pressure off of the big day (no longer does everything that is important about this process have to happen on that one day or one weekend), but it gives new meaning to all of the hard work we are doing and all of the anxiety and emotionality we are experiencing during the big year surrounding the day. If changes are already happening and if the specialness has already begun, it's no wonder that we're feeling so emotional; no wonder that we seem to be investing these mundane details with such intensity.

If this is actually a sacred time in our family's life, then we don't have to feel embarrassed or guilty for all of the time we are spending planning for the event and thinking about its meaning. If this is sacred time, then we can decide to protect it from polluting distractions—like longstanding fights about custody, money, or our brother-in-law's jealousy—that take the family's attention away from what is important. If this is sacred time, it makes sense that we do all that we can to keep the family focused both on the event and on what's going on in our lives that the event is meant to celebrate.

Therefore, what I would suggest is that you:

1. Acknowledge the significance of this preparation period.
2. Give yourselves permission to devote as much time and energy to it as you need.
3. Decide to make the most use of this experience for your child and yourselves as you possibly can.
4. Decide to use the ritual to do what it was always intended to do: Encourage changes and deepen connections.

Think of this period of preparation as a sacred few months devoted to new questions, new ways of thinking, and new ways of acting. In the service of this sacredness, the rest of this chapter is devoted to ideas about talking, ideas about making meaning and about connecting with those who are important to us. A brief coda at the end presents a few additional ideas that aren't directly about talk.

How to Make the Most of the Preparation Period

Once Again, Put Talk on Top of the List

Without exception, every bar/bat mitzvah family I've ever spoken with had a "things-to-do list." Some were scribbled on scraps of paper, others were computerized and color coded, but few had on them what I would consider the most important item: TALK—talking to each other about what we are thinking and feeling, dreading and hoping. Talking to each other about what all this means to us and how to make it even more meaningful.

There are obvious reasons why talk is not on our list. The first is time. With a thousand and one things to do, the idea of taking time out to talk with each other is often the last thing we would think of. The second is that talk is hard—especially during a time in our lives when so much is going on, and when so much of what is going on is difficult or confusing. It is, understandably, tempting to avoid talk by immersing ourselves in tasks.

As Jewish educators are beginning to recognize the importance *and* the difficulty of talking, some synagogues are now offering workshops focused *specifically* on family communication.

In one such innovative workshop, entitled "Celebration and Negotiation" and described by authors Ann Hartman, Sally Weber, and Rabbi Stewart Vogel, children and parents are asked to write responses to such statements as: "What Bar/Bat Mitzvah means to me," "What I am looking forward to," and "What concerns me the most." The anonymous answers are read aloud by the workshop leader and participants are asked, "How many of you think your parents/child wrote this response?" Imagine the discussion as family members asked each other, "Why didn't you know that was mine?" or "How could you think I'd write that?"

The third reason that talk is not on our lists is because it is something we take for granted, not something we think about as a separate item. And it is not something we've been taught is important in terms of bar/bat mitzvah. If anything, we worry that we're talking about nothing else *but* the bar/bat mitzvah. But the talk I am suggesting is different. It is talk, not simply about content (who, what, where, when), but talk that reflects on that content: Why? How come? What if? How is it that it feels so important to me that Uncle Jake has the first aliyah, or that Aunt Molly approves of the party? In other words: What is the history of our ideas about this content? How is it we've come to think in this way and what implications does this have for the future?

It is worth doing whatever you can to overcome the resistance to this kind of talk because it is this kind of talk that helps us make meaning. It helps us open up spaces for new ideas and it helps us deepen connections. So talk to everyone, early, and often. Keep communication open. Discuss everything from the most mundane details to the most profound feelings. Explore ideas about preventing what's feared and ideas about ways of turning what's hoped for into reality. Talk about how hard it is to talk. Give yourselves permission to stumble, to become upset, to need time to think about what you are feeling.

Saying the Unsaid

Use the bar/bat mitzvah as an opportunity—like birthdays, anniversaries, Mother's Day—to make explicit things we usually leave unsaid. Do not assume that others know what you are thinking, feeling, needing. Putting our thoughts and feelings into words not only gives others important information, but often gives *us* new information. It gives us a new perspective on our ideas that we have been taking for granted and it gives us a new way of thinking about these ideas. This perspective is vital because *what we think and feel about what we are doing ultimately determines the meaning we make of what we are experiencing.* And this exchange of meanings is mutually influencing. By sharing what we are feeling and thinking about the bar/bat mitzvah with others in the family, we help them make their own meanings, which they then share with us and thus inform the way our own meanings evolve. This may seem convoluted, but it is actually the way we make sense of everything in our lives.

Talk cannot bring back the parent who will not be there, but it can change how we feel about that loss and what we do with the feelings. This difference can be profound.

Looking back at it, Sally had only one regret about her daughter's bat mitzvah. She was sorry that her speech to her daughter on the bimah hadn't included something about how proud her mother would have been had she lived. "I was afraid that if I mentioned my mother I would lose it. But so what if I'd cried? I wish I had thought this through differently."

What might have been different for Sally had she talked with her husband, daughter, or her father about her fear of breaking down on the bimah? What might they have said that might have given her the permission she hadn't been able to give herself?

Think of the preparation period as a sacred few months devoted to new ways of talking to each other, a kind of experiment. And to the extent that some part of the experiment is successful, you might actually be developing new *patterns* of communication that will fit better for you as a family with a teenager than the old patterns that fit when your child was younger. This shift would be another expression of the "passage" you are celebrating.

Talking to Our Children

Talk to your child about bar/bat mitzvah hopes, fears, meanings. This is the perfect time to talk about ambivalences—theirs *and* yours. Help your child raise questions. Show them that the bar/bat mitzvah is *not* all about answers. Not only is this honest, but it's Jewish! It is part of our tradition to critique and to challenge what is handed down and also part of our tradition to answer questions with more questions. As adults, we do not have to have all of the answers, we just have to be honest with the struggle and clear about whatever it is we *are* sure about (like the importance of making this bar/bat mitzvah as meaningful as possible).

One great way to get into this kind of discussion is to look with your child at pictures of previous bar/bat mitzvahs—especially your own. After all the jokes about nerdy haircuts and weirdo clothes, talk about the best and the worst memories of the event that those pictures bring back to you. What was it about *your* bar or bat mitzvah that you would want to capture for your child's rite of passage? What was it about that event that you would do anything to make sure *doesn't* get repeated in this generation? Use talk about these pictures to help your child know what you're thinking about and hoping for. Use them to help you listen in to what's going on for your child as well. If yours is an interfaith family, what life-cycle events in the non-Jewish parent's history bring up a similar range of feelings: baptisms, confirmations, weddings? Bring those pictures out too. Talk about what was going on in those pictures and which aspects of it relate to the bar/bat mitzvah.

Talk to your child about growing-up hopes and fears. Use this occasion as the marker that it is. Talk about what kind of teenager you and they hope they are becoming. Talk about the implicit and explicit messages they are receiving about being a man or a woman in this culture. What is the meaning of their maturity in terms of sex and sexuality, alcohol and drugs? What new responsibilities and privileges do you and they feel they are ready to take on? Talk about ideas—yours and theirs—about boundaries, about growing independence and growing responsibilities. Talk about the ways in which your relationship to each other is changing. What do you each make of the friction that seems to be escalating between you? In what ways might your fighting with each other ultimately be helping both of you let go and stay close at the same time? Talk about how to make this talk emotionally and literally "safe." Don't expect agreements, affirmations, feedback, or even eye contact, in some cases. The only ground rule is that the talk be civil and respectful.

Some families I've spoken with decided to set up *conversational listening zones*: Agreed-upon times—every Sunday night before *The Simpsons*, or every other Wednesday after Hebrew school—at an agreed-upon location—a certain corner in the family room, or a particular couch in the living room—where the family would gather and everyone would take a turn expressing anything they needed to *without being questioned and without expecting that the others would respond.* It was a way of allowing the parent or child to simply "overhear" what the other was thinking or feeling about something that seemed too loaded to talk about in a more usual manner. In this zone, no one is supposed to respond, but to just listen. The freedom not to answer and not to defend allows all kinds of new thoughts to emerge and eventually to be put into words.

If the listening-zone idea seems too contrived, try something like the good old-fashioned family meeting: A regular "check-in" time to catch up or to say things that feel important or difficult. Whatever format you choose, what's crucial is that you don't wait for tensions to build so that talk becomes even harder. The *regularness* of these talks is what's most useful about them.

A Surprise in the Zone

The Roberts were one family that tried the listening-zone idea. Bruce was a psychologist and liked the notion of structuring a space that was explicitly labeled as safe. He was especially concerned about his son Graham at this time since he knew the upcoming bar mitzvah would be a poignant reminder of Graham's mother's death from cancer five years earlier. He didn't know exactly what he was imagining would come of it, but he was hoping that somehow this zone would allow some space to talk about this loss and might—in addition—allow some insight into the escalating tension between the bar mitzvah boy and his fifteen-year-old stepbrother, the son of Bruce's second wife of two years.

When the appointed time came, Bruce began the round by talking about how they could incorporate Graham's mother's memory into the service and about his concern that his two sons were fighting with each other so much. What emerged as each family member had a chance to speak was the stepson's feelings of jealousy and of shame. Never having had a bar mitzvah himself—despite the fact that he was Jewish—Russ was feeling jealous of all of the attention being focused on Graham and was feeling ashamed of his feelings. Not only did he not want to make his mother feel bad (after all, he knew it was enough of a struggle for her just to have raised him by herself, let alone to think about Hebrew school and bar mitzvahs), but he felt doubly bad to be jealous of Graham, who didn't even *have* his mother.

What a surprise for Bruce. Here he was so concerned about Graham and his loss that he hadn't realized what was happening for his other son and *his* loss. This insight opened the way for much conversation and many new plans. Having learned in Hebrew school that it was never too late to become a Bar Mitzvah, it was Graham who suggested that Russ begin studying with a tutor. "There are still months left and he can learn to read the Hebrew and learn the blessings so he could have his first aliyah at my bar mitzvah also!" Everyone thought this was a great idea. Russ not only learned the blessings but eventually began taking Hebrew as a language in high school and joined the local Jewish youth group. In the process, Bruce was able to talk to Graham about what his ideas and generosity of spirit meant to him—how much that way of being in the world reminded him of Graham's mother and what a great legacy he was enacting. This thought became part of what Bruce spoke about to Graham from the bimah on the day of the bar mitzvah. Everyone who had known Graham's mother knew this to be the best tribute she could possibly have been paid.

Talking to Our Partners

Use this occasion to talk about things you used to talk about, things you've never talked about, things you feel are too hard or too sensitive to talk about. In the service of your child's successful transition, what do you need to discuss, resolve, get through, compromise on? How might the two of you use something like the "listening zone"—for this and all kinds of other topics?

One interfaith couple, each in their second marriage, took this idea to heart and compiled a joint list of all of the topics and issues that they found were starting to come up for them as they began planning the wife's daughter's bat mitzvah. Having each gone through the pain of dissolving marriages, they were both determined not to repeat old patterns. Where both had avoided talking about difficult issues in their former marriages, they were eager to use the bat mitzvah to make things different this time. They decided to meet for an hour and a half each week—in a restaurant—to make whatever bat mitzvah decisions were necessary at the time *and* to talk about the list, one item each meeting. They chose a restaurant because it was both private and public enough. It was a space where they wouldn't be interrupted, but also where they wouldn't let their emotions get out of hand. In addition, they chose a restaurant because it was—like the therapist's office—a place they could leave after the time was up.

Talking to Our Ex-Partners

If preparation for the event is complicated for parents who are together, how much more complicated for those who are not!

Communication between former spouses can be a minefield. Planning for the bar/bat mitzvah, a happy transition, inevitably brings up memories of the family's most painful transition: its dissolution. And no one has to tell you how easy it is to contaminate the new with the old. In divorced families, the need for creating safe spaces for talk is all the more crucial, and it demands all the more commitment and creativity.

Like little else, the bar/bat mitzvah highlights the fact that despite the divorce, you are still parents. No matter that you are no longer married to each other, you are still this child's mother and this child's father. *Despite the pain and disappointment between you, the love for your children and your hopes for their future are as profound as ever. Preparation for the bar/bat mitzvah is an occasion to act on that love and those hopes.* With more or less modification, all of the suggestions about talking are applicable in situations where parents are no longer partners.

Whatever the specifics, the most important message divorced bar/bat mitzvah parents can convey to their children is that they do not need to choose between their mother and their father. "No, this does not mean we are thinking of getting back together again, but it does mean that we both love you, that we both want this event to be joyful, and that we are both going to do everything we can to make it so." This is a lot to ask when the pain and disappointment are still raw. Even in families where there has been lots of healing, this event tends to reactivate old wounds. But our child's happiness is the goal nonetheless. Use whatever talking and listening formats you can establish for expressing your sadnesses as well as your hopes. To the extent that they can be discussed, the pain, resentment, and disappointment sometimes become less powerful and less necessary to act out. Make as many opportunities as possible to let your child know about the pride and hopes you still share.

One divorced couple for whom face-to-face conversations

were still too painful decided to write letters to each other instead. This correspondence allowed them to work out some of the more contested decisions about their daughter's bat mitzvah and ultimately allowed them to arrange to have dinner together with her a month before the ceremony. There, they emphasized their mutual happiness about Gail's growing maturity and about her upcoming ceremony of passage.

Another divorced couple who also couldn't meet together alone arranged through their respective new spouses to meet as the four adults in the bar mitzvah boy's life—to plan the event and to work out the details. Since the new spouses were not as emotionally reactive as the former couple, they were able to keep the conversation focused and civil. As these meetings became more routine, the tensions seemed to dissipate over time and the bar mitzvah turned out to be an amazingly happy time for the child and for all of the parents. As one of the grandmothers in this large family put it, "for a divorced couple, they did wonderful!"

Talking to Our Parents

Talk to your parents about the hopes, needs, sadnesses, and appreciations that are alive for you as you prepare for their grandchild's bar/bat mitzvah. Talk about your feelings, and about the importance of this event for *you*. Just that. Not what you want them to think or feel about it, but how *you* are thinking and feeling about it. Remember Barbara (Chapter 6), who was worried that her mother would be disappointed in the potluck party? She told her mother why she felt it was important that she do it her own way. And she was prepared for her mother to argue the way she had when Barbara was a teenager. She was shocked that her mother now saw the value of her daughter's way. That understanding would not have happened if Barbara had not used the pressure of what she was feeling as a catalyst for communicating.

Talking to Extended Family

Tell your aunts, uncles, and cousins what it means to you that they are coming from so far and with such effort to be with you. Tell them what you are wishing for and what you are worried about. Tell them about your hopes that your children and theirs will enjoy playing with each other, about your fear that your aunts, who have been feuding with each other, will use this occasion for another eruption. Talk ahead of time to people you know might be difficult.

One mother, lamenting a detail she hadn't considered, talked about what she might have done differently: "I should have thought more about my family's dynamics. My brother always got his way with everything. He was the one who was going to drive my mother and uncle to the bar mitzvah. I should have realized that he would want to leave early (in order to get back in time to watch the football game). I should have talked to him ahead of time and insisted that he plan to stay and let my mother and uncle visit longer. I really feel sad that they weren't there for the whole party."

Use this opportunity to reconnect with people who, for whatever reasons, have become distanced. Preparation for the bar/bat mitzvah is both incentive and "excuse" for making the connections you've been meaning to make for years.

"We've been planning Gabriel's bar mitzvah and I can't get you out of my mind."

"We are planning Mara's bat mitzvah and I can't bear the

thought of your not being here with us. You used to be such an important part of our family. We really want you to come."

Talking to Friends

Talk to friends about ways they can help: assisting a family member who is likely to need support, staying close to Uncle Abe who gets disoriented, putting up one of the guests, hosting the Friday night dinner, and so on. It is a mitzvah to give others a way to do a mitzvah (like contributing to another's simcha).

Talking to friends is critical, especially if you are single.

Jean's support group became her family as she planned her daughter's bat mitzvah. Rejected by her parents after having come out to them as a lesbian, Jean developed a strong and loving family of friends. Both she and her daughter felt held and encouraged by this close circle of support, and when Jean began to feel overwhelmed by all that the bat mitzvah entailed, they were there for her.

Talking to Other Bar/Bat Mitzvah Families

Gather advice and suggestions from experienced parents. Ask your Rabbi to start a parents' support group or start one yourself. Ask others about their experience, what they would recommend and what warnings they could offer. Talk to your Rabbi, your child's teacher or tutor. Talk about meanings, ambivalences, hopes, and expectations.

One congregation I've heard about has developed a buddy system where experienced families are paired up with first-time families. Not only does this format help with the sharing of practical information—like who has the keys to get into the synagogue so the flowers can be delivered, or what caterer has the best reputation for which kinds of specialties—but it helps with emotional support and understanding as well.

When I was going through the experience for the first time, there was no such thing as a buddy system in the synagogue I had recently joined, but one woman—a veritable stranger— came forward to befriend me as much like an angel as a buddy.

FRANNY AND THE BAR MITZVAH SUIT

At the one informational meeting my synagogue held for parents of children who would become B'nai Mitzvah that year, I made some comment about how expensive everything was— even for the backyard event we were planning. After the meeting, Franny, a mother of four boys and one girl (this was her baby's bat mitzvah), came up to me and, without a moment's hesitation, offered to give me one of her sons' bar mitzvah suits for my son to wear. "Jeff's built like Louie," she said, "I'm sure it will fit—and it's practically new. He only wore it once." I ultimately didn't take Franny up on her offer—my father was going to have the *nachas* (pleasure) of buying his grandson "the" bar mitzvah suit—but I will never forget her kindness. Whenever I think of Franny—even so many years later—I remember that little suit and I still feel warmed.

Franny's gesture had a profound impact. Although I certainly didn't understand it at the time, I think the power of her outreach had as much to do with the timing as with its substance. In retrospect, I see that as a first-time bar mitzvah mother two months before the event, I was already in the altered state of one preparing for something sacred, if not something dangerous. I was feeling vulnerable and this unexpected generosity from a stranger shot right to my heart.

Appreciating Appreciation

Throughout the months of "preparation talk," take time to notice, appreciate, and comment on each other's positive characteristics, new competencies, efforts to help make the event a success (little brother allowing big sister to practice undisturbed; Aunt Doris's offer to write a poem; your neighbor's offer of her freezer). According to the Rabbis, the act of praising someone is considered a "minor mitzvah." They say that such praise leads people to additional mitzvot.

Talking About Talk

Now that we've talked (a lot) about putting talk on the list, here's one final suggestion: Talk about the talking. Talk about what these conversations have been like for you. Should they be more frequent? Less frequent? Who else needs to be included?

Tell Stories: They Are a Special Kind of Talk

Stories have a special place in Jewish life. It is said that Jewish theology is a narrative theology. It tells us a story. In fact, the theologian was originally "the one who told the tale," the tale of creation, of exodus, of Abraham and Isaac.

Here are two favorite pieces about stories:

> *My father, an enlightened spirit, believed in man.*
> *My grandfather, a fervent Hasid, believed in God.*
> *The one taught me to speak, the other to sing.*
> *Both loved stories.*

*When I tell mine, I hear their voices whispering from
  beyond the silent storm.
They are what links the survivor to their memory.*

—Elie Wiesel

There is a well-known tale about the eighteenth-century
founder of Hasidism, the Baal Shem Tov, who was known as
a miracle worker. Whenever misfortune threatened the Jews,
he would retreat to a particular place in the forest, light a fire,
say a prayer, and the evil would be averted. The next generation, faced with disaster, also went into the forest to the holy
place. They had forgotten how to light a fire, but they could
still say the prayer, and they too avoided misfortune. When the
third generation got into trouble they did not know how to
light a fire or say the prayer, but they knew the place. And they
were saved also. Then came a generation that knew neither fire,
prayer, nor place. All they could do was tell the story. And they
too got their miracle. Remembering was enough.

During the months prior to the bar/bat mitzvah, family stories are especially important. Jewish ethnographer Jack Kugel-
mass calls them "the most enduring architechture of memory."
They are what connects us and helps us make meanings.

Tell stories about past bar/bat mitzvahs. Tell stories about
what your bar/bat mitzvah was like (or a sibling's or a cousin's
that stands out in your memory). Tell these stories to each
other, to your child, to your parents. Ask your father (or uncle)
to tell his bar mitzvah story. What memories can your father
or mother share about their son's bar mitzvah?

Again, think about the ways in which your parents' stories
about your bar/bat mitzvah are similar to or different from
your own stories about that event.

What stood out for them? For you?

What do you think the differences and similarities will be

between *your* child's stories about this upcoming bar/bat mitzvah and your own, fifteen years from now?

Preparation Principles

As we come to the end of this chapter on preparation, and look
ahead toward the next section that deals with the actual weekend, I want to offer a few summary suggestions for making the
most of this period of preparation. The seven pieces of "advice"
that follow can be considered overall principles. They have to
do with the entire event.

Be Kind to Yourself

This is a big moment in your lives. You've worked very hard
to get to this place. Make sure you have enough help and have
built in enough support so that you can actually enjoy the
weekend along with your guests. Think creatively about what
you all need and how you can ensure it will happen.

This advice is especially important for interfaith families,
divorced families, gay and lesbian families—all families where
additional issues intensify the inherent complexity and where
the supports that are usually taken for granted may not necessarily be in place.

Share the Simcha

Involve as many people as possible in helping you with the
hundreds of discrete tasks involved in making the weekend go
smoothly. Don't hoard them all for yourself. Besides the fact
that learning how to delegate is another mark of maturity (no
longer needing to be like your mother—a do-it-all-myself

martyr), letting friends and family know you count on their support helps them feel connected to you and more secure about themselves. Involving them early in the preparation increases the pleasure and satisfaction they will derive from the actual ceremony. Also, in the process of involving others in the preparation, we give them an example of how to ask for help. This is a hard thing for many of us to learn, and so the demonstration is a gift.

Claire said it perfectly after her daughter's bat mitzvah:

"It's not easy for me to ask for things from people. So I really had to think about who I could ask favors of and what I could ask. Asking for even the smallest favor made me assess my relationship and see where I could take risks and extend them."

Again, it is a mitzvah to give others a role in your simcha. By actively contributing to your happiness, it becomes their happiness also. And to the extent that we share our happiness, our happiness grows. Ask people to help with the cooking, cleaning, schlepping, transporting, etc. From friends who host some out-of-towners to friends we ask to help by passing out little cups of wine for kiddush at the end of the service, they are doing mitzvot that you had the mitzvah of asking them to do.

Marcie's friends still talk about how much they enjoyed the evenings they spent cooking with her for her son's bar mitzvah ten years ago. "It really gave us a way of showing her how much we loved her and how happy we were for her," said one of them. "Yeah, and it showed me that it was good to be able to ask for help," said another. "Yes," said the third, a single mother, "and when I started planning for my daughter's bat mitzvah the next year, I knew I was not alone, that I could count on my friends."

Attend Other Bar/Bat Mitzvahs: Your Presence Is a Gift

Attend other bar/bat mitzvah ceremonies in your synagogue or in other synagogues. *Your presence adds meaning.* You do not need to be an invited guest in order to participate in the regular Sabbath service. You are not simply an outsider in an audience of strangers. By virtue of the moment, you are symbolically a representative of the Jewish community into which this Bar or Bat Mitzvah is being welcomed. Your presence is an embrace. Your witnessing this family's simcha contributes to their simcha. It is enough just to be there, but if you are so moved, you can enhance the gift of your witnessing by phoning or writing the parents later in the week and letting them know what meaning *their* event had for you. Learning about such an unexpected effect amplifies their more private happiness.

In addition, attending other bar/bat mitzvahs will help you become more comfortable in the synagogue (if this is a problem for you). In any case, it will give you a taste of the many possible variations and will help you develop a better sense of what you want or don't want "your" service to feel like.

Take Time: Give Yourself This Gift

If possible, take time off from work the week before the bar/bat mitzvah to attend to last-minute details in a more leisurely way. One father took the week off even though his wife was at home handling most of what had to be done. "I wanted to be as involved (in the preparations) as possible," he said. "And I'm glad I was. It's amazing the pleasure I got in helping my daughter dip the strawberries into the chocolate coating for the special treat she wanted to make for the luncheon. We had such a good time laughing together and licking the extra drops of chocolate."

Lest you jump to conclusions and condemn this father for strawberry dipping as his way of being involved, this man was a Hebrew school teacher who had actually tutored his daughter through her Torah and Haftarah studies himself. Becoming involved with the strawberries and the excitement of last-minute preparations was a gift he gave himself—and his wife as well. Knowing she could count on him to help with whatever details needed attention was a relief she appreciated. But even more, she loved seeing the love between her husband and his little girl. These moments were treasures.

Take Time to Talk

Maybe it's "enough already," but I can't make a list without this item.

Talk to each other and to your children about the meaning you want this celebration weekend to have. Talk about what it would be like not to feel pressured into doing it like the Cohens down the street or the cousins in Chicago. What would it be like not to feel pressured into spending more than we can or want to spend? What would we be giving up? What would we be gaining? For whom would it be hardest not to do the party the way everyone else does? The pressure from our peers can be intense and the pressure from our child's peers can even be cruel. Maybe it is too hard to do it differently, or maybe as a family you don't want to do it differently. *What you decide is less important than* how *you decide—and what meaning you make of what you decide.*

Talk about what it means that Judaism values joy and celebration. We are all so used to hearing about the sadness and tears in our tradition. How can we take this joyful aspect of our heritage to heart also?

Think Ahead About the Weekend's Timing— Its Beginning, Its End, and the Spaces in Between

Looking ahead at the event—from the first trip to the airport to picking up early guests, to the last trip to drop off the last departing ones—it seems like such a huge amount of time to fill and be responsible for that we wonder how we'll get through it all. But in retrospect, the weekend will probably be over before you fully realize it's happening. After planning for so long and thinking about it in such detail, most people talk about the experience as having flown by. They describe a sense of having gone through the weekend in something that is "like being in a trance." "It was if I had been on another planet," said one mother. "I felt like I was floating in another time zone and when I woke up it was all over." "I didn't get to pee all day," said one mother in amazement.

In and Out of Time
One bar mitzvah boy, commenting on his sense of time, talked about how simultaneously normal *and* abnormal he felt.

"I thought I would be slow and dragged out and, you know, real tense, but it was pretty casual. I felt really casual when I woke up. First I took a shower like a normal shower, put on a suit like I was going to somebody else's bar mitzvah. I just sat up there and before I knew it even, boom, boom, boom, just like that everybody had their aliyahs and all of a sudden, I'm in my Haftarah. It just happened. And then it was over. It was like a surprise."

What all of these people are describing is what anthropologists call "liminal time," time that is altered, special, transformative. They talk about the experience of being in this space as being *both in and out of time*. It is the period during which participants are caught-up in the uniquely pleasurable connectedness of "communitas" and get carried along by the event's momentum. Although the intensity of this experience varies for each person and from one moment to the next, the weekend's overall feeling of specialness is usually hard to miss. And it's usually hard to see it end also.

Acknowledging the Pain, Prolonging the Pleasure

One of the disappointments I hear about repeatedly is how abruptly the whole thing ends. "Before I knew it, it was over and everyone was leaving."

Part of this sadness, of course, is inevitable and built into the meaning of the experience. For most of us the experience *is* ending. Extended family and old friends are generally not part of our daily lives. They are *not* always gathered around and wishing us well. This loss is real. Real also is the recognition that this exact same gathering will never happen again. Even if no one gets sick or dies between now and the next family gathering, we and those we love will never again be this young and in this place in our lives. The clock *is* ticking. And the poignancy of the moment is reflected in that sense of letdown, that sense of time having flown by. This *particular* bar/bat mitzvah (or wedding, or bris, or anniversary) really is possible only once in a lifetime.

Although nothing can change these realities, many families have found ways of extending the pleasure and also protecting themselves from this sudden collapse at the end of the weekend. Arranging ahead of time for some special relative or some old friend to stay on for a few days after the party allows us to benefit from a more gradual tapering off of the intensity. It allows us some space to luxuriate in the success of the experience and to share the pleasure with others. It also allows us some space and assistance in thinking about whatever was painful or disappointing during the weekend.

Time Out

Having now talked about the before and the after, a few words about the "during." Anticipating how hectic the weekend will be allows us to build in some respite, some moments of quiet and connection. Some parents find it useful to arrange ahead of time some private spaces to "check in" with each other and with their children. With all of the guests and all of the activities, it's easy to lose touch. Some families agree ahead of time to some special signal they can give each other to indicate that some time alone is needed—for a talk, a tear, a hug.

One woman describing a particularly painful exchange with her sister right before the party Saturday night, talked later about how valuable the "time-out" signal had been for her.

"What she said hurt me so badly, I didn't think I could face the party. But luckily Bob and I had talked about the possibility of this kind of thing happening and what we would do if it did. I gave Bob 'the signal' and the two of us went to the private alcove we'd designated earlier. All I needed was a chance to say out loud what my sister had said, how it made me feel, and what I had come—over the years—to understand about that feeling, and then I was able to go back to the party. Those few minutes alone with Bob saved the day."

Carved-Out Spaces

Another kind of "carved-out" space is that which we plan with some special friend or relative who's come from far or whom we haven't seen in years and with whom we want to make sure we have time to talk. Let that person know early how important it is for you that the two of you have some time together and arrange a mini date during the weekend. I can't tell you how many stories of regret I hear about important people having come and gone without our having even five minutes of private time together. Think ahead about who these people are and make sure those moments happen for you. Be reasonable in your expectations. You can't possibly have "meaningful conversations" with everyone who comes.

Make Money Matter

There is no way to talk about bar/bat mitzvahs without talking about money. If you've read this far, you know by now that I don't subscribe to the automatic perspective that big is bad and small is good. What kind of celebration and how much we will spend on it depends entirely on who we are, what we do, where we live, what we've known in the past and what we want for the future. Although there are some affairs that we would probably all agree go overboard in terms of extravagance and taste-lessness, most of us would probably draw the line at very different places.

Wherever that place is for you, what is crucial is that you think about the meaning of that line, about the meaning you make of how much you are spending, and that you discuss that meaning with each other and with your child. What are we saying to ourselves, our families, our children, and our friends and community by how we decide to celebrate? How do we express the notion that this is *both* a birthday party for a thir-teen-year-old *and* a much wider celebration of the family and its tradition? How do we do that without overshadowing the accomplishments of the child, and without—as they say— turning it into a wedding?

How can we use this preparation for the event as an opportunity to talk to our child about the meaning of money and how we choose to spend it? In what ways does the party express our joy? In what ways can we—at the same time—share our joy with others? Increasingly, families are now deciding ahead of time to tithe a percentage of what they spend on the celebration to charity. (See discussion of Mazon, p. 169). Families are also now talking ahead of time about how they understand the monetary gifts the child will be receiving. How much is your child free to spend as she or he chooses? How much must be saved, and for what? How much might be given to a charity that the child selects? How might he or she personally deliver that donation? Or would it make sense that it be donated anonymously? Again, there is no one right way—except what is right for you and your child.

GRANDFATHER'S MEMORY

One family in a wealthy suburb was increasingly uncomfortable with the prospect of making their son's bar mitzvah party like all of the black-tie affairs they'd been attending in the neighborhood. Spending money wasn't the problem. They had plenty. But what *was* the problem was Father's memory. Ted had grown up in a working-class family whose values he felt were being lost to his son's generation. Despite his best intentions, he found himself surrounding his children with all of the luxuries and expensive toys that their friends' parents bought.

But the prospect of capitulating to these pressures with the bar mitzvah was more than he could tolerate. In long and intense conversations, he convinced his wife about the appropriateness of a simpler affair, a luncheon—in the synagogue, no less—with a relaxed backyard party at night.

He then had to convince his son. To his surprise, Josh was more open to making it "like Grandpop would have wanted" than Ted had expected. In fact, their conversation about Grandpop and what he was like when Daddy was little was one of the highlights of the preparation period. Josh had so many questions and the talk reminded Ted of all kinds of important memories. What was even more surprising, however, was the reaction of the guests. Although Ted was prepared to defend his decision, he found he didn't have to. The neighbors, it turned out, were impressed with Ted's "down-to-earth" values, and found the whole experience a meaningful change of pace. Some, in fact, followed suit with similar celebrations for their children.

Bar/Bat Mitzvah as Wedding

Since I mentioned the word *wedding* a few paragraphs ago, let me digress. Everyone knows that the worst "put-down" of the party's extravagance is to say it was like a wedding: "If that's what they do for the bar/bat mitzvah, what will they do [read: *spend*] for the wedding?!" "Next thing you know they'll be having the kid smash a glass!" While most of us are uncomfortable with this comparison, there are some other interesting interpretations.

Sociologist Stuart Schoenfeld, looking at this trend toward lavish parties that rival weddings, sees meaning where others see only loss of meaning. He talks about the fact that contemporary bar/bat mitzvah parents are generally older than their counterparts in previous generations. By definition, they have collected more friends, colleagues, and neighbors than the younger parents of the past, and have also amassed more resources to pay for a bigger party that can include all of these people. So on that basis alone, he says, it makes sense that today's celebrations are bigger. But he explains the growth in another way as well. Just as contemporary bar/bat mitzvah parents are older, so too are their parents older. For many, the traditional hope that Bubbie and Zayda will live to dance at their grandchild's wedding is becoming less and less likely to be realized. In this context, "a big affair—like a wedding" takes on new meaning. In addition, as this generation of children becomes statistically more likely to marry someone who is not Jewish, this might be the family's last chance for a "Jewish affair."

Part IV

The Details

Chapter 9

Details and Hidden Treasures: Imbuing the Mundane with Meaning

You've heard about devils in details? When it comes to bar/bat mitzvah details, we should look, instead, for angels.

Most popular wisdom advises us to "relax!" and not make such a big deal about the planning details. Who cares if Aunt Gloria sits next to Uncle Morton or next to Cousin Dave? What difference does it really make how the invitations are worded—as long as we get them out? What difference does it make if Scott puts the tallit on by himself or if we drape it around him?

My advice is the opposite. I say that the details *are* important and worth lots of thought. They have rich symbolic potential for enhancing the ritual's power to mark transitions and open the way for connections. (And if you don't believe they are potent, just look at what happens when they go awry. Who doesn't have some horror story about a family rift that began at someone's wedding, or funeral, or bar mitzvah? Invariably it began with some detail, some perceived offense.)

In Chapter 8 we talked about the preparation period as sacred time. In this and the next three chapters, I look at the individual tasks or details you are working on during that period as sacred also. And I include here not only those details associated with the ceremony in the synagogue—who gets which aliyahs, who makes speeches, which prayers are read and by whom—but the details associated with the secular, prosaic aspects of the weekend: the invitations and the transportation, the food and the flowers, the lodgings and the logistics.

For most of us, thinking about caterers and seating arrangements as sacred is a conceptual stretch. It certainly was for me. But as I've come to experience it through my research, and as I hope I have been demonstrating so far, the distinction between the secular and the sacred—especially in Jewish tradition and especially as it pertains to a Jewish life-cycle ritual—is very blurry. The bar/bat mitzvah preparation details, no matter how seemingly mundane, contain within them the possibility of becoming something more than they appear to be on the surface. They are imbued with the *possibility* of the sacred.

This is so for two reasons. One, because they are meant specifically to enhance the effectiveness of the sacred ritual, and two, because they are all about relationships. *Because the bar/bat mitzvah ceremony is about our relationship to God, to Jewish tradition, to our children, our parents, our community, our selves, all of the details that enhance the process of connection are therefore infused with this possibility of "holiness."* For instance, the decision to include or exclude someone from the invitation list is not simply a statement about how many people we can afford to feed, but a statement about the people we count as family, the people we want to share in our happiness, the people with whom we want to stay connected.

Food details are another good example: The decisions we make about food are not simply about the latest fashion in caterers (be they kosher or otherwise), or about who can prepare the most variations on the theme of kugel, but about the meaning of feeding our family and friends, about what folk-lorist Maury Sachs calls the "embedded love message" in our hours and hours in the kitchen, and about the way those hours bind us together with those who eat what we offer. The symbolism surrounding food abounds: Whether we focus on Rhonda's freezer that got fuller and fuller as her heart filled with joy (and also with terror that there wouldn't be enough to eat); or on Marcia's sadness as she came home after the party to empty shelves that had been so full with anticipation in the morning—"They're like the nest that will soon be empty," she lamented, only partly in jest—or on the "famous" chopped liver that grandmother came "special from Israel" to prepare for her only grandson, we see that food has as much to do with the heart as the stomach.

In this light, preparation details—those long lists of things to do and decisions to make—become something more than chores. They become symbols with larger meanings. And as with all symbols, they are "multivocal": They express multiple meanings simultaneously. It is up to us to determine which meanings we want to notice and give voice to.

In this chapter we look at three details that come early in the process: decisions about whom to invite, decisions about where they will stay, and decisions about how to word the invitations.

The Guest List: From Minefield to Gold Mine

"I'm so excited. I want to invite everyone we've ever known. But maybe I'm going overboard. Maybe I'll end up making 'strangers' feel uncomfortable, or obligating people who can't come, or making the whole thing too big and impersonal, or maybe . . .

"I'm so overwhelmed, I can't even bring myself to begin making the guest list. The thought of dealing with all those people at once is terrifying."

Whether yours is closer to the first or second of these voices, the guest list is no small detail. It is usually one of the first tasks we tackle, and it has the potential of hitting us with many of the hardest questions all at once—before we've had a chance to begin thinking about what we're really doing and what it all means. Questions like: Who is in our family? Who is no longer in our family? Who might not be here by then, and if they are, in what health? Who in the family has needs that conflict with the needs of others in the family? Whose conflicting needs are we going to meet? Whose can't we meet? How do we make choices among friends, colleagues, neighbors? How do we invite some and not others? Whose feelings are we going to hurt? And besides, how do we pay for any of it? Can you believe what the invitations themselves cost!

There is no way to make making the guest list a simple task. It is an inherently complex compilation of human connections, past, present and future, and by definition fraught with potential land mines. But by the same human token, it is also a *gold mine.* When you think about it, how many opportunities do we have in a lifetime to name those who count as kin and community, and to call them together in celebration? How many opportunities are there for such a conscious assessment of who is important to us and to our children? *How many opportunities do we have for deliberately enhancing our network of connections and for teaching our children about the importance of those connections? Embedded in the act of creating the guest list is a potential bonanza.*

One pragmatic solution to the desire to invite more than we can accommodate (because of space and/or cost) is to create a second, backup list. The first list contains the names of those we are definitely inviting, no matter what, and the second, names of those we would invite if we could. As "regrets" arrive in the mail, people from the second list can be invited in their place.

Bar/Bat Mitzvah as Ritual of Reunion

All over the country people are organizing family reunions, events to gather scattered family for the purpose of meeting and spending time together. Such gatherings are antidotes to what sociologists call "kinship fragmentation," the breakdown of our sense of familial connectedness. In contemporary Judaism, the bar/bat mitzvah weekend implicitly serves this function. The guest list names those we identify as family—and those we want our children to know as family, now and in the future.

Some of you may balk at this idea. Many parents I've spoken with say they want the event to be "intimate." They want to invite only those people their child knows—"So when she or he looks out, it won't be at a sea of strangers." Whatever way you do it will be right for you. But in most cases when I am asked for my opinion, I find myself on the side of inclusion.

All things being equal, I encourage you to use the invitation as an opportunity to make contact with as many family members as possible. Use it for anything from ending old feuds that go back generations, to meeting new babies of cousins twice removed. These far-flung relatives are part of your child's inheritance. This network of kin you are invoking is one of the most precious gifts you can give. What we are saying to our child is, "Look at how many people you are connected to and who are connected to you." As one bat mitzvah child put it, "It was weird having all those relatives thrown at you all at once. I didn't know a lot of them but it was kind of nice knowing they were there—all together—even if I really didn't get to say anything to half of them."

Even if many on the list don't come, and even if those who come aren't seen again for years, the sense of being related to so much family in so many places helps children feel anchored, attached in time and space. Who knows which little cousin and your child will someday befriend each other in some distant place?

LIZA, LAURIE, JESSIE, AND KATE

Liza wanted to invite her aunt, whom she hadn't seen or heard from in many years, to her daughter's bat mitzvah. She remembered being very close to Aunt Laurie as a child. In fact, she still had the doll Laurie had brought her from a trip to Spain. It would be wonderful, she thought, not only to see this aunt again, but to have Jessie meet this special woman in her family. The only problem was that Liza's mother had had a falling-out with this sister fifteen years ago. The two hadn't talked to each other since. What would her mother think if Liza told her about this wish? Would she feel betrayed? Would she refuse to come? The fight had been very bitter and Liza knew she didn't know half of what was involved. What should she do, she asked me, at a presentation I was making at her synagogue. "Talk," I said as usual. "Talk to your mother about what it would mean for you and for your daughter. Ask her what it would mean for her if you talked to her sister."

When Liza called me a week later, she was full of news. She'd taken my advice, and to her surprise discovered that her mother had actually been longing to see her baby sister again and had been secretly hoping that it might happen at her granddaughter's bat mitzvah. She would never have volunteered such information, of course, "but since Liza brought it up, and since Liza thought it would be good for Jessie . . . "

The reunion of the sisters was heartfelt and important. And the added bonus was Laurie's granddaughter, Kate, who also came. She was visiting from Canada. No one could believe how much Jessie and Kate, second cousins once removed, looked like sisters. It was uncanny. As of this writing, they are regular pen pals and Jessie will be spending part of her next summer vacation with Kate and her whole family in Ontario.

Cousins Are the Best

Although the details vary, Liza's story is not unique—especially in regard to the cousins. Over and over again I hear from both parents and children how important the connections at this generational level feel. Whether it's about how far mother's cousins had to travel to be there, or how wonderful it felt to have father's brother's son read from the Torah at his cousin's bar mitzvah, or simply how much fun it was to see all the little ones playing together, this is a relationship that seems to hold particular significance at this life-cycle event. It also has significance in terms of the future: When we are gone, this is the generation of kin our children will have as family.

So I encourage you to do what you can to make it possible for cousins, big and little, to come. I've heard about all kinds of creative ways to arrange for baby-sitters, alone or in pairs, from the hotel or from the neighborhood, to stay with groups of cousins who are too young for the party. These gatherings often become little parties themselves where the kids have a ball with each other before the sitters (try to) put them to bed. By arranging these accommodations ahead of time, the big cousins—the children's parents—feel really welcomed. They don't have to choose between being with you and being with their children for the weekend. And on top of that, they get the pleasure of having their children know and be known by the rest of the family.

216 Whose Bar/Bat Mitzvah Is This, Anyway?

Whom Else to Invite?

It is a blessing to bring people together for a simcha. In sharing our happiness we not only give others a gift, but our own joy is enhanced. So invite as many people as you can. Make priorities. More people, one less costly gimmick. I've almost never heard someone say, "I wish we hadn't invited so-and-so." Instead what I hear repeatedly are regrets about who hadn't been invited. "If only I'd known it would turn out this wonderful, I would have invited his teacher my coworker our doctor our neighbor." "So-and-so would have enjoyed it so much. If only I'd thought to invite them." The only names on the list I would think twice about are the business acquaintances and distant neighbors. This is not a time to repay social obligations.

Distant Relatives

Even when you know distant relatives or old friends can't come, send them an invitation anyway. Tell them in an accompanying note that you're not really expecting them (and definitely not a gift), but want them to know that you are thinking of them, that they are counted as part of your family, and that you want them to be part of your child's life. You have no idea how honored people can feel by such acknowledgement, and how touched. Those who live far away from most of the family often feel more cut off than we realize. By including them on your guest list and letting them know how important they are to you, you often allow them to feel connected in ways they didn't think they were anymore.

One of the Waldman cousins surprised everyone by coming from Arizona to Jonah's bar mitzvah in New Hampshire. It turned out he was using the occasion for a number of purposes. Not only was it a neutral place where he and his estranged brother (who was coming from New York) could meet, but it was a chance for him to think more about whether or not to plan a bar mitzvah for his own son. Micah was still only nine, but he would need to start Hebrew school if it was going to happen. This was a big concern for Tom since he'd married a woman who wasn't Jewish. So far they hadn't really dealt with the issue of religion and tradition, but his son's development and his cousin's son's bar mitzvah were making him think more seriously about what he wanted for his own family.

The Congregation

Bar/bat mitzvahs are celebrations of community, not only of family. Every bar and bat mitzvah is a symbolic statement that the Jewish community is continuing, that it has a future. Members of the synagogue, of the "regular congregation," are representatives of that larger community. They represent the elders who take in the initiate. They are important as witnesses and as celebrants. Whether we know them well or not, whether they know us well or not, our experiences are connected. Our child's coming of age in the Jewish community is a gift to the community. The community's presence is their gift to us.

The current trend toward separating the bar/bat mitzvah ceremony from the larger congregation is consistent with our secular culture's move toward privatization. To me, it feels like a mistake. To not share this event with the community is a missed opportunity to enact the fundamental linkage between the child and the community's "elders." They are the "village" our children need.

Increasingly, congregations are searching for ways of dealing with the problem of regular synagogue-goers staying away on the days when there is a bar/bat mitzvah being celebrated. Somehow they've begun feeling like intruders at a private social function, like audience rather than congregants. Is this happening in your synagogue? Talk to your Rabbi, to other parents. What can you do to resist this trend? An open letter of sincere invitation in the synagogue's bulletin? A certain number of aliyahs set aside for congregants? A festive kiddish/light lunch for family, guests, and congregants to share together? Find out what's possible. Make your own suggestions.

Non-Jewish Friends

And what would it mean for our children to invite some of their non-Jewish friends? Depending on where you live, this is either the regular custom or something quite unusual. There is the well-known story of one child named Aaron who decided, with his father's encouragement, to invite one of his non-Jewish friends, but was surprised by the response. His friend thanked him for the invitation, but asked if he came, would he have to watch? "What do you mean?" asked the Jewish boy. "You know," said his friend. "Would I have to watch you be 'hacked'?" The gentile child who had had little contact with Jews and no experience with this celebration, had confused the bar mitzvah with the bris. No wonder he was hesitant!

What an opportunity this turned out to be for Aaron. Although at first he was taken aback by how little his friend knew about Jews, he soon found himself describing a lot more about Jewish customs than he would have imagined he knew. Maybe he had learned something in Hebrew school after all. But this demonstration of knowledge was not all that surprised him. What got to him most, he said later, was the feeling of pride he had in talking about the bar mitzvah and the other customs. "It was really cool!"

On the other end of the spectrum is the Jewish child who doesn't feel the coolness. Increasingly (and sadly) I am hearing stories about bar and bat mitzvah children being reluctant to invite non-Jews. Especially those in communities where there are relatively few Jews, some children talk about feeling "weird." They are afraid of what their Christian friends will think of "all those guttural *ch* sounds" and embarrassed by what they expect will look strange to strangers.

What is there to say to this but, again, "Talk!" Beyond lamenting the anti-Semitism that these children are internalizing, we have to use these situations as opportunities for teaching and for learning. If this is part of your family's story, talk to your children about the ideas and experiences behind their concerns, about what those concerns mean to them—and to you, and talk about how things could be different. Maybe you're shocked by your child's ideas and, then again, maybe you're not. What can you and they do to make things at least feel different? What can you do to cope with the reality of anti-Semitism, while resisting its poison? Talk to your child, to each other, to the Rabbi, to teachers, and to other parents about the way anti-Semitism gets expressed in your community and what can be done about it. To the extent this is possible for you, make it a public conversation. If you and your child are feeling it, so are others in the community. You will have a mitzvah to help such a dialogue happen.

And even if you think your child's reluctance to invite non-Jewish friends is less about anti-Semitism and more about their fear of being different from their peers in *any* way, talking is still crucial. The injunction to conform to peer norms is frighteningly powerful. Mary Pipher, author of the best-selling *Reviving Ophelia: Saving the Selves of Adolescent Girls*, calls this the child's "social anxiety." She says that the message teenagers are responding to is that "not pleasing others is social suicide." It is critical that young teenagers have places where it is safe to talk about the effect of the culture on their lives and the decisions they make about their lives. Planning for the bar/bat mitzvah offers countless opportunities for talking about messages. Make use of as many as you can.

Guest List as Teaching Tool

The guest list is a perfect opportunity for demonstrating the values we want our children to learn. Even if they aren't usually part of our conversation about which family, friends, and neighbors to invite, what values are they absorbing as they *overhear* our adult conversation about these decisions? What are they learning about inclusion, generosity, kindness? And what are we helping them learn as they create the guest list of their friends and schoolmates? What would it mean for them to include the child who seldom gets invited to parties? A lesson in empathy and compassion here is not simply a lesson in social etiquette. It is a lesson in Jewish values.

And speaking of lessons, think about inviting your child's teachers. The Rabbis tell us that those who teach our children Torah deserve a special place in our hearts. They are like surrogate parents. Inviting the Sunday school teachers acknowledges and honors their role. Also think about inviting those public school teachers who have been special. This is another gesture toward integrating the secular and the sacred in our lives and in our children's identities.

Guest List as Gift and as Guide

The process of completing the guest list with all of the names, addresses, and phone numbers is in itself an experience in connections. Who in the extended families keeps the information, the family's memories? How easy is it to get it from them? Which aunt knows the names of grandfather's cousin's kids? How about their ages? Which of those extended relatives know the names of your children? Do you know where all the names go on the family tree? Some families I've talked with make copies of the family names, addresses, and phone numbers they've collected and share them with siblings and cousins. Who would appreciate such a gift in your family?

Another way of thinking about the guest list is as a kind of map with which you can help your child navigate the extended family territory. What distinguishing story can you tell your child about each of the names on the list to fill out the terrain? How many of the people you are inviting has your child never met before? Who of this list do you think would be most pleased to know your child? Who on the list do you think your child would most enjoy getting to know? How might you tell that person you think that?

Fern, one bat mitzvah mother who heard this idea, decided to invite her own freshman English teacher and tell her how important she had been. This was someone who had taken a particular interest in Fern and had mentored her through some very rough times. She hadn't thought of Professor Sloan in years, but suddenly she wanted her and her daughter Melissa to meet. When the invitation arrived, Dr. Sloan was sick with cancer and couldn't attend. A year later, in remission, the teacher called her former student to tell her how much it meant to have been remembered on such an occasion, and then invited her and Melissa out to visit. The reunion and the introductions were more wonderful than Fern could have imagined. Her teacher, it turned out, was a Holocaust survivor and not too many years earlier had become a Bat Mitzvah herself. She'd dedicated her studies to her lost family, and this meeting with Fern and Melissa became another opportunity to remember.

The Out-of-Towners and Lodgings: It's Not Just About Logistics

With families so scattered geographically and the number of out-of-town guests growing, the issue of lodgings has become more central. What are the messages embedded in our decisions about where our guests will sleep?

She'll Be So Hurt When She Finds Out

Lodging was one detail Ruth worried about a lot. How was she going to break the news to her mother and father that she wanted them to spend the bar mitzvah weekend in the hotel with all of the other out-of-town guests—and not in their "own daughter's" home? Her mother would be so offended. But on the other hand, there wasn't room in the house for her parents *and* Barry's parents. How could she have one set of parents with them and not the other? And besides, even if she had room for all of them, she really didn't want *any* of them staying with the family during these nights. Given the commotion and level of activity she was anticipating, she felt strongly that their home should be a place of respite and calm—especially for the bar mitzvah boy who was already hyper enough.

What surprise and relief when Ruth finally visited her parents and told them her plans. Not only was her mother not insulted, she seemed to like the idea of being put up in a "fancy" hotel. Besides, she had already thought about it and didn't want her daughter to have to worry about taking care of her when she had so many other things to attend to. When had her mother become so understanding? And how many sleepless nights could Ruth have avoided if she'd talked to her earlier?

Another family's hotel story has an altogether different set of meanings.

Harmony and the Hospitality Suite

Joan and Dan had painfully divorced some years ago but were sharing custody of their only daughter. Joan had remarried.

Her new husband was not Jewish. Money was tight for every-one in this family, and all of the bat mitzvah decisions had been made with cost in mind. The only exception was the question of which hotel should house the out-of-town guests. According to Joan, it had to be one with the best hospitality suite, the one that would be most comfortable for guests from all three of the extended families to be together in—for the Friday night deli dinner, Saturday afternoon relaxing, and Sunday morning brunch—so that the bat mitzvah girl "would not be pulled apart." If all of the sides of her family were together, Joan reasoned, her daughter would not have to choose between the two sets of parents. The plan worked beautifully. Not only did it take the pressure off of Karen, but it allowed a kind of camaraderie among previously distant ex-relatives that no one had thought possible.

"To see my ex-mother-in-law helping my stepson fix a plat-ter for dinner Friday night was unbelievable," Joan exclaimed later. "It really set a tone of harmony that carried through the whole weekend."

Whatever your decisions about housing, the point—as al-ways—is not what you decide, but how you decide. In what ways can you use this detail in the service of what you want this bar/bat mitzvah to be all about?

On Reading (into) the Invitation

The wording of the invitations is another ostensibly secular example of these what-difference-does-it-make details. Of course, what's most important is that they are sent and that people come. But the decisions that surround these invita-tions—wording, color, style, size—have symbolic potential that we can use consciously if we choose. More literally than most symbols, the invitations are "texts" that get "read," that is, interpreted by the reader. It is not just the factual information that conveys meanings, but the paper the facts are printed on, the graphics surrounding the facts, the number of envelopes holding the facts. These are all symbols that we use to make meaning.

In a sense, the invitation is the family's first public statement about what they are experiencing, what is important to them, and what they want their guests to share. It is a kind of preview of what is to come. It is a statement about joy and about welcome. Whether the invitation includes the names of both of the divorced parents or only one parent speaks volumes about what is happening in the family. Whether or not the invitation contains Hebrew words or symbols speaks volumes about what aspects of the ritual the family is emphasizing.

Whenever I think of invitations, one family's story always comes to mind:

Since the divorce five years ago, Roberta and Greg had shared custody of their only child. Zach had alternated each week between his parents' homes. When I first met them—three months before the bar mitzvah—tension was mounting. The invitations had not yet been written, much less printed and mailed. What was the problem? The wording: Who was extending this invitation? Greg had remarried last year and Roberta felt strongly that the name of her ex-husband's new wife not be included in the invitation. "After all," she said, "Zach is my child, not hers. She didn't diaper him when he was a baby, or take care of him when he was sick." Stepmother Marianne, as one might imagine, was equally adamant; she was "paying for part of this shindig" and given the custody arrangements, she was "definitely helping to raise this bar mitzvah boy." Poor father (not to mention son) was caught smack in the middle of these two very strong women and their equally legitimate claims.

It was Roberta, in charge of the invitations, who came up with the compromise. And it was fascinating: Zach's middle name was her maiden name, which she had never relinquished, and his last name was his father's surname. By using Zach's full name and saying "the family of Zach Lerner Feinberg fondly invites you to . . ." both the mother's name and the father's name were included and the stepmother's name was neither included nor excluded. The father and mother were united so that their child did not have to choose between them. Through this logistical detail, the mother was protecting emotional connections and the family was developing and practicing ways of negotiating change. Also, through this invitation, they were instructing their guests about their commitment to compromise and harmony.

In the Gordovsky family's invitation, the huge ornate Star of David superimposed on Anton's Hebrew name symbolized not only that this event was Jewish, but that it was *publicly* Jewish. This ceremony, it was saying, would be a far cry from his secret bris in Russia. This would be a celebration not only of Anton's coming of age, but of the family's triumph and of their religious freedom. They had not lost their connection to Judaism despite years of repression, and the invitation made that abundantly clear.

A Hasidic family's invitation in Yiddish announced yet something else. Signed by the father and his "very good friend" (his wife), it was stating not only that the bar mitzvah was happening, but that it was being celebrated as much as possible as it had been in generations past. The mother's agreeing to her husband's wording the signature in this traditional way (rather than including her name) was her statement about the importance of tradition.

In a strangely similar way, the Reform family's shiny invitation (with its clearly etched maroon letters) encased in three shiny envelopes and separated by three sheets of tissue, spoke dramatically of their emphasis on their peer group's conventions. Indeed, the invitation lived up to the formal attire used for such occasions among their circle of friends. While some would condemn this kind of dress and invitation as "too ostentatious," in the context of this family's history and its way of making meaning it was a sign of their coming closer to what they identified as "Jewish." After three generations of having abandoned the ritual of bar mitzvah altogether, this event (and this way of doing it) was an expression for them of having returned to the fold.

Again, the point I am making, of course, is not about a right or wrong way to do any of this, but about the opportunities embedded in even the most mundane details (the guest list, the hotel, and the invitation) for expressing ethical and spiritual values that are important to us as Jews—no matter where we are on the spectrum of traditional observance.

Chapter 10

The Ceremony: The Dramatic Center

How much we can do to shape what happens during the service on the bimah depends mostly on the customs and traditions of the synagogue in which the bar/bat mitzvah is taking place. In some synagogues the service is highly prescribed and the opportunities for variations are relatively few. In others—usually the more informal congregations—the opportunities for individual variations are much greater. Whatever the parameters of your setting, here are some thoughts you might consider as you think about details of the ceremony.

It's a Drama: So Make It Dramatic!

For observant Jews who go to shul regularly, the meaning of what is happening on the bimah is clear. Among these participants is a shared understanding of what the prayers and practices mean and a shared appreciation of the drama inherent in every word, in every act, and in every service (whether or not there is a bar/bat mitzvah). For those in the synagogue less connected to the tradition—and for all kinds of reasons, this number is growing astronomically—the meanings are much less clear (if discernible at all), and the powerful unfolding of the drama can be missed entirely. It is for this second group that we need to think about ways of strengthening the clarity and the impact of the experience. We do this through words and through actions: what we write, what we say, and what we demonstrate. Here are some examples of what I mean.

Handing Down the Torah

One popular response to this need for explicit enactment involves calling all of the generations of the family up to the bimah and literally passing the Torah from the arms of the grandparents, to the arms of the parents, to the arms of the bar/bat mitzvah child. When I first saw this rite performed, ten, twelve years ago, I thought it was unnecessary if not downright hokey. After all, I thought, doesn't everyone know that this passing of the Torah (and all that Torah stands for) "from generation to generation" is what the entire experience is all about? How could the meaning be any clearer? Doesn't this literal enactment trivialize the larger meaning? I've now come to see its value. Given who is currently attending bar and bat mitzvahs (in some cases as many non-Jews as Jews, and often more secular than observant Jews at that), we do need ways of making the ceremony's implicit meanings more explicit and therefore more accessible to everyone.

Putting on the Tallit

Another example of dramatizing what happens naturally is when the Bar Mitzvah (and in a growing number of synagogues, the Bat Mitzvah) is asked to stand and publicly bless and put on the tallit "for the first time." Until recently, this is something the child would have done privately at the beginning of the service. Focusing public attention on this act, and often involving the parents and grandparents in it, reinforces the idea of "firsts" and provides an opportunity for the Rabbi to explain what the tallit and its fringes implicitly symbolize. This allows more of those witnessing the event the possibility of feeling those meanings as well.

It is also another one of those details that allows us to enact meanings that are important to us. In terms of traditional symbolism, wrapping ourselves in the tallit is a statement about wrapping ourselves in the commandments that the tallit fringes are meant to remind us of. It is also a statement about being wrapped in God's love and taking on the responsibilities of our tradition. But how we choose to enact the child's first wrapping is an opportunity to add to and enhance the traditional symbolism.

The child who stands up and puts the tallit on him- or herself while saying the prayer that sanctifies the act is symbolically making a statement that emphasizes growing maturity and independence. The child who stands up with parents or grandparents who dramatically place the tallit around the child's shoulders as the prayer is recited is symbolically emphasizing generational connections. It is specifically the parents and grandparents who have wrapped this child in his or her connection to Judaism. In each case it is a statement about the child's coming of age and taking on both the protection and the responsibilities of the tradition, but which of the dual aspects gets highlighted—change or continuity (transformation or preservation)—is up to the family to decide.

In the Bergen family, this little detail became a saga. Jason's grandparents had been to Israel the year before his bar mitzvah and had bought him a tallit that they were excitedly looking forward to presenting at his bar mitzvah. As Jason and his parents were thinking about the meaning of donning the tallit, Jason most liked the idea that he was making a statement about growing up and assuming adult responsibilities. He wanted to do it himself. But he also didn't want to deny his grandparents any pleasure. His compromise was thoughtful and creative. It was also something his parents commented on when they spoke to him publicly about their pride in him. At the point in the service where the Rabbi would ask him to stand and put on his tallit and say the blessing for the first time, she would first ask the grandparents to stand and present the tallit to him. She would tell the congregation where it had come from and even say a few words about the grandparents, about their long-standing involvement in Jewish practice, and about the generational connections this rite was meant to symbolize. Jason would then take the tallit, recite the prayer, and wrap it around himself.

Constructing a Bar/Bat Mitzvah Booklet

Since the Rabbi can't be explaining everything all of the time for each bar/bat mitzvah, many families have begun putting together supplemental booklets of welcome and information that guests can read throughout the service. I think this is a very useful idea and provides additional opportunities for enhancing meaning. Whether you do a booklet or not, I do recommend at least a handout that includes the names of those who are being called up for aliyahs (and any other honors) and how they are related to the bar/bat mitzvah family. Knowing who the players are enhances our appreciation of the drama and its meaning.

Each family does the pamphlet differently. It can be two sides of one page or a many-paged opus. But most often it is written from the parents' perspective and contains explanation, information, and appreciation. At its most basic it includes:

1. A brief description of the service and how the bar/bat mitzvah ceremony fits into it. (Don't hesitate to ask your Rabbi for help here. Such descriptions and explanations are easily available.)
2. The names of those being called up for the aliyahs and all other honors—and their relationship to the Bar/Bat Mitzvah.
3. A statement of thanks to the relatives and friends who have come to share the family's milestone.

More elaborate efforts include special prayers, special readings, pictures, poems, family history, and so on.

One highly intellectual family wanted the traditional service, the traditional prayers, and traditional melodies, but was uncomfortable with the traditional translations that contained what they considered "archaic and sexist language." So they put together a Xeroxed pamphlet to be used instead of the regular prayer book. It included all of the prayers (plus the Torah and Haftarah portions), but instead of the traditional translations, they inserted alternate selections: poetry, readings, new prayers that fit with the idea of the Hebrew text but were more consistent with this family's values.

Another family used the brochure as a memorial to members of the family who had been killed in the Holocaust and included photographs that the one surviving great-aunt had saved. Yet another included a description of the charity the family was tithing the celebration to, including information for others who might want to contribute. In a similar vein, some brochures explain the theme the child chose to explore and weave into the event—for example, universal peace efforts, ecology and Jewish holidays, or rabbinic teachings on what it means to mature. Some brochures are written completely, or in part, by the Bar/Bat Mitzvah. These are often supplemented by siblings' illustrations or additions. In one, a cousin's wood-cut graced the cover.

It goes without saying that if you choose to do these pamphlets, the more they become family projects, the better. Again, it is the process, rather than the product, that is important.

Punctuate the Passage

Another opportunity to intensify the drama and enhance its impact is at the end of the Haftarah when the final prayer is completed. At that point the child usually begins breathing differently and might even break into a smile. For the celebrant, this is usually the emotional climax of the entire experience. They've "passed the test," "lived through the ordeal," "done what they'd thought they'd never be able to do."

Mark this moment. Punctuate it with shouts of mazel tov, with singing, clapping, laughter, and tears. Make sure everyone attending knows that the dangerous part of the journey has been completed safely. The initiate has come through, and the transformation has occurred.

In some congregations people in the first few rows throw candy symbolizing "the sweetness of Torah" (and then the little children scamper up, collect the bounty, and provide a measure of comic relief). At one bar mitzvah recently, members of the family's havurah got up after the final blessings and danced around the congregation. In whatever way feels appropriate to you personally, and is acceptable in your congregation, it is important to make this point in the ceremony dramatic and joyful.

How much drama is necessary varies. In an orthodox shul where everyone understands the significance of what just happened, proud smiles and whispers of mazel tov are all that may be required. But in other situations that wouldn't be sufficient at all. In the B'nai Mitzvah ceremonies I've attended where this moment wasn't marked dramatically enough for an extended family unfamiliar with synagogue tradition, there was a clear sense of confusion, if not letdown. "Is it over?" "Did he do it?" Neither the child nor the witnesses had the sense of closure that is required in all such rites of passage. No matter what comes next and whatever else the child might do in the service, this particular moment needs to be dramatically proclaimed.

What comes next, in most cases, is "the speech," another detail that gets worked on during the planning period.

"Today I Am a Man; Today I Am a Woman": The Speech Is Important

Originally, the speech was the d'var Torah, the Bar/Bat Mitzvah child's teaching on the Torah and Haftarah. In immigrant America, the speech became a perfunctory statement of thanks the bar mitzvah boy would make sometime before the service was over. Mainly he would thank God, his parents, the Rabbi, his teachers, and all of the relatives who came there to be with him. The classic story associated with the bar mitzvah speech is about the reluctant child whose parents bribed him into practicing by reminding him of all of the presents he would be getting. When it was time for Yankele to make his thank-you speech, he was so focused on the prospect of presents that instead of beginning with the "Today I am a man" line, he slipped and said, "Today I am a fountain pen" (the most popular of bar mitzvah gifts; the immigrants' symbol of the "professional" future they wished for their son).

Today the gifts are different, and so is the speech. In most cases it is usually expected that the talk will include some words of thanks but that the central focus will be the child's interpretation of the Torah or Haftarah portion. It is more like the d'var Torah of old. In some congregations, this is a requirement and in others, an option. In my experience, whatever it takes for the child to do this speech, the extra effort is worth it. It is a part of the test that serves several functions. First of all, it forces the child to make some meaning out of the often mean-ingless (to him or her) nonsense syllables he or she is learning to chant. This effort to interpret the text stretches the child in ways different from the workout provided by the chanting and the prayers. Over and over again I hear stories about how sur-prised parents are by the connections their child made between the ancient text and the contemporary world, surprised by their insight, and their sensitivity. The only disappointment I ever hear related to the speech is that it was read "too fast," or "too softly."

Writing and delivering a speech is a task that everyone can understand and appreciate. It is not only something that all the witnesses can relate to, but something that the child also sees as a valuable skill for the future. Unfortunately, this is usually not thought to be the case when it comes to chanting Torah and Haftarah—though some Jewish educators are beginning to report some progress in this area. More and more bar/bat mitzvah programs are encouraging children to learn the trope, the "symbols" for the traditional chanting of the Torah and Haftarah, rather than learn "their piece" by rote. By learning the "notes," they come away from the experience with a tan-gible skill: They will be able to chant *any* Torah and Haftarah they can read. And even if they don't make use of this skill for a long time, if ever, it is a fundamentally different learning experience.

The speech or d'var Torah has another function that I al-luded to earlier. In the context of classic ritual performance, it stands for the "rite of reversal" often embedded in ceremonies of transition. To the extent that the child becomes the teacher, explaining the text to the adults, it is an important component of the ritual passage. During those few minutes of teaching, the boy "becomes" a man, and the girl a woman.

In Praise of Praise: The Parents' Speech Is Also Important

There is another speech increasingly associated with the contemporary bar/bat mitzvah. It is the speech the parents make to the child that acknowledges their pride and happiness—not only in what the child has just done, but in what they have learned about that child watching him or her prepare for doing it. What they are describing is their pride in, and hopes for, the young adult the child is becoming.

For many parents, this is the scariest part of all. The idea of standing on a stage and talking to our children can be overwhelming. Not only is public speaking not our thing, but how do we get through it without breaking down? A friend of mine says she starts to cry every time she even thinks about talking to her son at his bar mitzvah. And his is still two years away.

Despite these fears, I encourage you to think about making such a speech. Whether you do it as part of the service or at the party afterward (many Rabbis decidedly do *not* encourage parents to speak from the bimah), it is an important opportunity on many levels. You could even do it as a prayer that you've written to read to your child publicly. The form is not important, but the message is. Not only is this another opportunity *to make explicit* what has, in the past, only been implicit, but it is an opportunity to name publicly what you believe is specifically wonderful about your child and how you see him or her developing that wonderfulness in the future. According to child development experts, children become the labels we give them; the bar/bat mitzvah is a unique opportunity for public, positive labeling. No, I'm not saying you should praise your child indiscriminately or insincerely, or for imagined characteristics you *wish* he or she possessed, but rather that this is an opportunity for you to think deeply about what is special about your child and how you think that specialness will grow. One guest at a recent bat mitzvah described the parents' talk as a "reaching for their daughter's soul." This speech is also a way of affording relatives and friends an intimate view of your child that simply isn't possible from their usual distance. It can connect them directly to this person whose growth they've come to celebrate.

On the surface, this new parents' speech is a far cry from the traditional message embedded in the original parents' speech: the father's prayer of riddance. That, you'll recall, was the prayer in which the father thanks God for making him "no longer responsible for the [sinful] deeds of this one." But from a different perspective, that prayer of riddance is also a prayer of pride. "Look, God, we've raised this child to know right from wrong, and now he's capable of being responsible for himself in these matters. We and he—with Your help—have done well."

There is lots that can go into this speech. Some parents talk about how their children have changed, others about how they've remained constant; some talk about how they seem to embody the attributes of their namesakes, others about what those namesakes might have thought about the children had they lived to know them. Some tell funny stories, others recount touching incidents. Many acknowledge rough times, and what it took to persevere. But whatever the approach, the speeches that "work" are those that focus not on the child's accomplishments per se, but on his or her ways of being in the world; on those aspects of the child's "soul" for which the parents are most grateful. This is the speech in which it is okay to break your promise not to embarrass. How many other opportunities, after all, do we get to publicly praise the young person we are launching into the world? My only caution is to keep it short. Parents who talk too long (or too *well*) risk upstaging the child and alienating listeners.

I'll never forget one mother's speech for its aptness.

MIRIAM DRAWS THE LINE

Miriam was an artist known for her skill as a painter, not as an organizer. Planning and arranging Rena's bat mitzvah did not come naturally, she said, as she stood on the bimah facing her daughter who had just chanted her Haftarah flawlessly and had delivered an unbelievably wise and mature d'var Torah.

"Rena," she said, "I could not have done this without you. When I was scattered all over the place, you were the one with the lists, the one who sorted the invitations, the one who collated the booklet. You were there to help plan the menus, to help arrange the party, to figure out who would do what. You were there for everything. But when you came into my study last week and wanted to write this speech for me, I drew the line. This I would do on my own!"

Although Miriam went on to say a few more words, the essence of her daughter and of their relationship had been conveyed perfectly. Everyone, even strangers like myself, got some intimate sense of this child.

Another mother's speech was equally dramatic. Hers directed attention at the audience.

Taking her son by his shoulders, she directed Darren to look out at the faces looking up at them—at the "sea of love." "They are out there for you today in your triumph," she said, "and they will be there for you in your future successes. But more importantly, what I want you to know, is that they will be there for you also when you are *not* experiencing success, when you are *not* flying high. Life for all of us," she explained, "has joys *and* disappointments, moments of pride *and* moments of shame. These are the people who love you and will love you through *all* you experience. Take in their faces and their love. It is your greatest treasure."

Giving Voice to the Pain

The parents' speech is also an opportunity to give voice to the family's pain as well as its pleasures. Often I am asked if and how a particular sadness can be encorporated into the ceremony without allowing it to overtake the joy.

"My father is in the hospital dying," said Marge. "How can I mention it on the bimah? I'll fall apart. But how can I not? It's on everyone's mind."

My response to such questions is always to encourage acknowledgement of the sadness. This acknowledgement is what allows the sadness not only to be honored but to be contained. To the extent that we find ways to give voice to the full range of our experience, we enrich the meaning of the passage and increase its potential to heal. What is dangerous is not what is named, but what remains unspoken. In the silence, feelings intensify, and they become more—not less—likely to usurp the joy. This is not to say that such expression means a big speech. Usually just a brief reference—a few carefully chosen words speak worlds. It not only acknowledges and affirms what everyone is feeling, but it gives permission—indeed, encouragement—for the celebration to proceed. In the face of life's losses, the preciousness of life's blessings becomes even more poignant.

One mother's words epitomize this idea.

Standing on the bimah next to her husband, who was emaciated by the cancer he was battling, Sheila spoke to her son about her pride and her hopes. And she spoke too about what was on everyone's minds, though not their lips. Without actually mentioning the horrifying roller coaster the family had been on since the diagnosis, Sheila brought it out in words that evoked its lessons: "We have no choice," she told Eli, "about the paths we are on. Only about the *way* we will travel them." With this metaphor, Sheila was able to talk about her son's strength, his compassion, his helpfulness, and his capacity to perform even under the most difficult of circumstances. Sheila's words gave inspiration to everyone in the congregation. Her talk was a blessing.

Of course, not all of us have poignant stories to tell, or dramatic ways of conveying a message. And not all of us can or want to make such a speech. There are all kinds of valid reasons for parents not speaking publicly. An alternative is to ask the Rabbi, tutor, some family member, or some close friend to speak on your behalf. What's important is that what gets communicated is that which you—who know this child best—want to highlight as worthy of praise.

THE TRANSMISSION OF PRIDE

One mother, reflecting a few months later on her experience of the speech, talked about how she had emphasized to her daughter the pride her grandfather would have felt had he lived to see her become a Bat Mitzvah. "My daughter was becoming a knowledgeable Jew. She was planning to continue her studies. She was taking this all so much more seriously than I had at her age. And it felt so important to me to be able to say this out loud," she said. "But what touched me even more was what my aunt said to me afterward," she went on. "When I came back to my seat, Aunt Freda leaned forward and whispered into my ear, 'Your father would have been proud of you too!' After all those years of fighting with him, I somehow knew in my heart she was right. It's amazing how connected this all is."

The Power of Participation: Noticing Firsts

In the contemporary bar/bat mitzvah, the child's first aliyah is often not the only first that is happening. In many cases, it's the first time the bar mitzvah child's mother, who never had a bat mitzvah herself, is blessing the Torah. It is almost always, if it is the first grandchild, the first time the grandmother is being called up to the Torah. In many cases there is a widowed aunt being called up for the first time on her own since her husband—with whom she had always shared the honor—had died. These firsts, whether publicly noticed or not, are often moving and important. To the extent that you recognize what's happening, let those involved know that you know. Depending on the situation, this might mean some public comment from the Rabbi, or some private hug from you. Knowing that others are aware of our personal passages eases and enriches those journeys.

One woman, who was talking about her mother's participation in her daughter's bat mitzvah, described it as "a rite of passage for my daughter, and a rite of affirmation for my mother. It was the first time she'd ever blessed the Torah. Women didn't do that in her day, and until her granddaughter's bat mitzvah, she wasn't sure they should! This was my mother's ultimate act of approval. I still haven't recovered."

In one family of recent immigrants from what was then the Soviet Union, the child's bar mitzvah was the occasion in which not only he, but his father, his grandfather, and all of his paternal great-uncles were called to the Torah for the first time in their lives. And it was the child, enrolled by his parents in Jewish day school as soon as they'd landed here five years earlier, who had taught the old men the prayers. Talk about reversals!

Preparing for Firsts

As moving as firsts can be, they can also be uncomfortable, if not embarrassing. Who among us hasn't witnessed the poor uncle or brother-in-law breaking his teeth over the transliteration of the Torah blessings he's attempting to chant for the first time in years while trying to keep his upside-down tallit from slipping off his shoulders, and his ill-fitting yarmulke from falling off his head? It is excruciating and unnecessary. Or what about that story of the great-aunt who was called up for the honor of "dressing" the Torah for the first time in her life? When the Rabbi told her to put on the breastplate, she hung the Torah's ornamental silver piece around her neck!

Should we laugh or cry? No, we should just think ahead. This is one of the easier details we can anticipate and prepare for. It is our responsibility to ensure the comfort and dignity of those we invite to participate in our ceremony. We can't prevent them from being nervous, but we can make sure they know what's expected of them and how to do it. Send them tapes. Explain the procedures. Rehearse them through the sequence. Do whatever it takes to make them comfortable.

This idea of preparing those we invite to participate with us in the ceremony is not simply about perfecting the performance. It is about how we think about others and how we want our children to think about them. Engage the bar/bat mitzvah child in a conversation about helping Aunt Molly with the prayer or demonstrating for cousin Dave the proper way to lift the Torah; these are lessons of thoughtfulness and compassion that have deep roots in our tradition. These may not be examples the Rabbis would have included in their teachings, but they are examples from our contemporary reality.

Inclusion in the Ceremony

With the hope that I haven't made you unnecessarily anxious with all this talk about responsibility, let me emphasize again the value of including as many people as possible in the ceremony. Their participation enhances their engagement, their pleasure, and their connection. Take siblings, for instance. We're all familiar with what younger siblings can do (open the ark, for example, or lead the last prayer), but what about older brothers and sisters, or especially siblings from other marriages, from other religions? Again, within the parameters of your synagogue's guidelines, who can be asked to contribute a poem, a song, a personal prayer? Who can be asked to distribute books, or wine, or yarmulkes? Who can be asked to bake the challah, bless the challah, distribute the challah? You can see what I mean.

Sibling Participation

It's become so routine that younger siblings participate that we often don't notice the power of *their* little dramas. At one recent bat mitzvah, I was struck by a "before and after" demonstration that was vivid. As the Bat Mitzvah's little brother, Toby, rushed up to open the ark, he was practically shaking with terror. Wide-eyed and rigid, he stood like a soldier as the Torah was removed, and then he marched in the processional as if the fate of the entire event depended on his every step. He returned to his seat exhausted. But by the time his sister had completed her Haftarah, and the Torah service was over, and he was sent up to open the ark a second time, Todd practically bounced up to it, all traces of trembling gone. The second procession around the congregation had no resemblance to the first. The little novice had become a pro and his wide, toothless grin was proof of it.

It's less often that we see a special role for the elder siblings. They are usually called up for an aliyah but rarely have any further involvement. On the few occasions where I've heard an older brother or sister speak publicly, it's been quite powerful.

ADAM AND HIS BABY SISTER

Adam's mother had remarried many years after she and his father had divorced. When his mother became pregnant by this new stepfather, Adam wasn't altogether pleased, but their baby soon won his heart. Now Meredith was the Bat Mitzvah, and Adam, an unusually sensitive twenty-three-year-old, wanted to speak. What he talked about was how surprised he was to see what a beautiful and accomplished young woman Meredith had become. "In my mind," he said haltingly, "I keep thinking she's still five. In my heart, she always will be." There was something so poignant about this brother's love. Everyone was in tears.

The bar/bat mitzvah service is a powerful opportunity to reinforce sibling bonds. This is especially useful in remarried and blended families. Think creatively about how siblings, half-siblings, and stepsiblings can make room for and support each other. Help your children talk to you and to each other about what this event brings up and how it can be used for connection rather than conflict.

Chapter 11

The Party: It's Not Just "What Comes Afterward"

The party piece is big. And it's complicated. And no matter how much we are told that it's not what's important, an overwhelming amount of energy and anxiety is often directed toward this part of the experience.

- Will it be too big? Too small?
- Too glitzy? Too down-home?
- Will it be all that my child wants? All that Mother wants?
- At all what we can afford? Maybe we should just chuck the party and take a family vacation instead.
- Or maybe just give the money to charity.

The bar/bat mitzvah party is not just a birthday party for our child, or even just a celebration of his or her accomplishment. It is a celebration of the entire family that has been part of bringing this child to this day and in this way. There are many celebrants involved, many audiences, many agendas, and often many conflicting needs. Even in the most seemingly "uncomplicated" of situations—two happily married Jewish parents, two great kids, and four healthy, supportive grandparents—it's never simple.

In this discussion of bar/bat mitzvah parties, I want to elaborate on three points: one, that the party is mandated; two, that it is, like the rest of the process, a self-portrait; and three, that it is yet another opportunity for magic to happen.

The first thing I want to emphasize is that no matter how secular, no matter how much it has become separated from the ceremony in the synagogue, the party is part of the sacred ritual. It is not simply that which comes afterward.

This might surprise you, but according to tradition, the party is not an option; it is *part of* the celebration. It is the *seudat mitzvah* ("celebratory meal") that not only marks but expands the performance of a mitzvah. The bar mitzvah seudah was prescribed by the Rabbis at least as far back as the sixteenth century. It is traditionally the father's religious obligation to provide such a meal in honor of his son's coming of age. This feast is a joyous way of emphasizing the significance of the mitzvah that is being celebrated.

Judaism Encourages Celebration

Unlike many other traditions, Judaism sanctifies pleasure. Even though at one level the party can be understood as "profane" (from the root *pro fanum*, which means "away from the sanctuary"), at another, it is an extension of the ceremony in the sanctuary and thereby made sacred.

The second thing I want to emphasize is that like the ceremony on the bimah, the party is a direct reflection of who the family is and what it needs. Just look for a moment at the parties of a few of the families in my original study. Start with the first, the divorced and remarried family in which the overriding need was for graciousness and harmony. Theirs was a modest dinner-dance at a local hotel. What was the most difficult of all of the details for this family to tackle? The seating arrangements. They wanted to be sure that people would be happy with their assignments. They wanted to be sure that they wouldn't inadvertently be putting "people who hate each other" together at the same table. The couple was so worried about this detail that they waited until the last possible minute—an hour before the party was to begin— to make the final adjustments. Just watching them wait this long made *me* a nervous wreck. But ultimately, this effort and all of the others paid off. It was an incredibly enjoyable event for everyone, and a real surprise. After such a drawn-out and acrimonious divorce, the couple's determination to make this event a simcha was reflected in every detail and the extended family got the message. Even the ex–in-laws and ex-aunts who had been so polarized by the divisions between the children were infected by the couple's desire for goodwill and graciousness. Seeing everyone dancing the hora together, they said, was the "reward of a lifetime."

In the second family, the one where this was the first bar mitzvah in three generations and where the family seemed most disconnected from ritual and synagogue practice, it was the party more than the ceremony that seemed most "sacred." In fact, this was the one family that did not invite me to the party (a very posh dinner-dance) because, as they put it, they wanted to "keep it private," to "not expose their guests" to anything as profane as research. But in watching the video-tape—which they did share happily—what was most striking was how grown-up the bar mitzvah boy looked. For all the world, it seemed as if he had been transformed. From the little boy who had to have his Haftarah shortened because he felt he couldn't learn it all, to the tuxedoed young man singing with the band's sexy lead singer, he had "grown up overnight." His

parents were thrilled about how socially competent he had become. It was as if in this family—where social skills were valued
more than synagogue skills—it was the party more than the
service that became the vehicle through which the child demonstrated his growth. This is clearly not what the Rabbis had
in mind, but this is how the party functioned for this particular
family.

In the third family's party, where I was one of only three
American guests—the others were all Russian immigrants—
the home-cooked feast in a local social hall could almost
have taken place in Kiev. The toasting, the speeches, the end-
less courses of Russian delicacies—not to mention the
vodka—spoke dramatically of who this family was and from
where it had come. Here the emotional highlight was the uncle's speech. It was about linking the past to the future. With
a glass filled with vodka and eyes filled with tears, Uncle
Boris told little David to "Remember this day forever. All the
love that is gathered around you on this day of your bar
mitzvah and *the bar mitzvah itself* will give you power. Never
forget this day." Uncle Boris was referring to the courage it
took for the family to hold onto its tradition and for what it
will take for the next generation to build on that courage.
This Russian-American party was a direct reflection of where
this family was in its journey and what it needed to propel
that journey forward.

If that party could have taken place in another country, the
last one I studied could have taken place in another century.
This was the Hasidic family's party. With their intense emphasis on living according to the same rules and in the same ways
as their ancestors, this family's party was filled with prayers and
blessings, speeches and more speeches. Here the emotional
highlight came after the meal and after the speeches. It came
during the dancing.

As is customary, the women danced on one side of the

room and the men on the other. The Hasidic rock 'n' roll band was playing an updated *freilach* and the two circles were flying. Suddenly I noticed that many women were gathering by the room divider to watch the men dancing. Curious, I joined them. There, in the middle of the circle of black-suited men with beards and sidelocks and little boys bouncing on their shoulders, was the bar mitzvah boy and his ninety-three-year-old *great*-grandfather. Hands clasped and staring joyfully into each other's eyes, they were twirling around in time to the music. The old man with the long white beard and stooped shoulders was dancing with his rosy-cheeked great-grandson to celebrate the child's coming of age in exactly the way he himself had come of age so long ago. What was most striking, besides the fact that this ancient-looking man could still dance, was the uncanny way in which he and his thirteen-year-old descendant mirrored each other. Dressed identically—black suit, white shirt, black hat—and practically the same height, it was as if the generations that separated them were no separation at all. Aside from the fact that one had a beard and one didn't, they were perfectly in sync with each other.

And this, in fact, is what this family most cherishes. It was a scene straight out of Shalom Aleichem. As the father explained, practically bursting with pride, "Between the generations, there is no gap! What a blessing for the great-grandfather to know that his great-grandchildren are being raised in precisely the same way that he and his father before him and his father before *him* were raised." This party was a dramatic expression of that blessing. So you get my point. *The party is an integral part of the process and the party you plan will be uniquely a part of yours.*

Party as Opportunity

The third idea I want to convey here is probably quite obvious by now: This party is an opportunity. If the party is not a separate event, but an extension of the ceremony, it makes sense to celebrate, and it makes sense to celebrate in ways that reflect whatever is important in your family and your culture. Like all the other details, the party is another opportunity to teach our children what we want them to value. There are no blueprints and no formulas. There is no guarantee that small, informal parties teach our children good values. They can be filled with as much pettiness and acrimony as extravaganzas. Likewise, there is no guarantee that a larger formal party will be cold and meaningless. It can be filled with as much love and goodwill and *yiddishkeit* as the backyard variety. It depends on what values our actions communicate and amplify.

If you were surprised to hear that the Rabbis mandated the party, you probably won't be surprised to hear that very soon afterward they began condemning parents for spending too much on it. Even before Hallmark or the caterers got wind of it, parents were going overboard, and Rabbis in the Middle Ages had to institute "sumptuary taxes" to keep the event from losing its focus or becoming an embarrassment.

These days, I am beginning to detect a growing backlash against excessive consumption. More and more families are actively seeking ways to scale back on the extravagance and find ways of personalizing the event. When parents ask me how to make the bar/bat mitzvah more meaningful or more "spiritual," I think as much about the party as about the service. If Judaism is expressed in all aspects of our lives and not just in what happens in the synagogue, then in what ways can we make the party "Jewish"? In what ways can we blur distinctions between the secular and the sacred? Here are a few suggestions:

Create Ritual Moments

One way is to make opportunities for guests to come together around shared rites throughout the festivities. For example, a *motzi* (blessing over bread) before the formal meal that maybe grandfather recites, a time for toasts and minispeeches from relatives and friends, a speech by the parents or by the child, a special song, a special dance, a story about the family or a favorite family story, a *birkat hamazon* (blessing after the meal). These are moments that encourage active rather than passive participation. They are communal, as opposed to private, experiences that make explicit the implicit reasons for everyone being together. The most famous, if not infamous, of these focusing moments is the candlelighting ceremony.

Happy Birthday to You

Although the candlelighting ceremony has been disparaged by Rabbis and educators as secular fluff and exploited by the media as comedic red meat, I have come over the years to see this detail in a more positive light. Beyond the fact that it is another opportunity for guests to come together as a group to share words, actions, and meanings, it has become, in contemporary Judaism, what sociologist Stuart Schoenfeld explains as a "secular aliyah," another way of elevating those we wish to honor.

Given the limited number of aliyahs at the service and the fact that (in most congregations) only Jews can be called to the Torah, this is an opportunity to bring forward and publicly appreciate many additional people in our lives and in our child's life. It is also an honor that everyone understands—

including those who are not Jewish and those Jews who have become disconnected from what the Torah honor means. Everyone understands the universal symbol of candlelighting. And after all, it's a birthday party, so cake and candles fit.

If we choose, we can build on this custom in ways that enhance Jewish meaning. This is an opportunity for us to say out loud what is special about each of the people we are honoring in this way, *and* also for them to say some of what is important to them on this occasion. Some families make a point of talking ahead of time to those who will be asked to light a candle and inviting them to think about something they would like to say publicly to the bar/bat mitzvah child. They invite them to "bring a blessing," to tell a family story, to sing a special song, or to present some special family or ritual memento. This is a place for the words and actions that couldn't or wouldn't fit on the bimah.

Grandma Kramer chose the candlelighting ceremony as the time for presenting her only granddaughter with the Shabbos candelabra she had brought from Lithuania when she was a girl. In her thick Yiddish-Brooklyn accent she talked about what lighting candles had always symbolized for her and what she hoped they would mean in the future—not only for her granddaughter, but "God willing" for her great-granddaughter as well. In that brief exchange, that connecting of the generations, the flickering birthday candles became imbued with the sanctity of the generations.

In another family, where the grandmother had died many years earlier, the Bat Mitzvah's mother lit the first candle in her memory and read out loud the letter her mother had written shortly after this granddaughter was born. It too talked about future generations and the connections between them. This time too the candles—linking past and future, sadness and joy, loss and promise—became what Judaic studies scholar Jacob Neusner might call "enchanted."

At my cousin Marsha's party for her son's bar mitzvah, the candlelighting took on a different glow. Of all the aunts, Marsha's mother Ethel was the most pious. After everyone else had long gone from the table, she was always still there silently *benching* (praying) from her father's old siddur, the pages practically crumbling in her hands. On top of that, Ethel was the cook at the synagogue's day school. She prepared all of the kosher lunches and organized the annual community seders. Her devotion was renowned.

When Marsha married Ray, a young man who was not Jewish, everyone expected disaster. No one in the entire family had brought parents "such shame." Surely her mother would disown her. Surely the family would dissolve. But neither happened. It was a miracle (made possible, I think, by Uncle Irv's mediation and Ray's goodness—even Ethel couldn't find anything wrong with him). Mother and daughter somehow managed. Despite the tears, and over all the years, they held it together.

Ryan's bar mitzvah was testimonial to that Herculean effort. And Marsha knew it. When it was time to call up the grandparents to light their candles, Marsha called all four of them up together. With tears streaming down her cheeks (it runs in the family), she acknowledged their separate and combined contributions and what all of their love had meant to her and her family. In particular she thanked her in-laws for the wholehearted support they had shown for this bar mitzvah. Ray's parents had arrived a week ahead of time and worked tirelessly in the synagogue's kitchen—helping Marsha and her mother cook all of the food for the huge feast. Thousands, I mean *thousands*, of "Ethel's famous" knishes were produced by this collaborative effort. The unthinkable had indeed come to pass. These birthday candles were about love and about healing, and they couldn't have glowed more brightly.

An Alternative to Candlelighting

Recently I heard of an alternative to the candlelighting ceremony: a tree planting ceremony. It was created by Israela Meyerstein, the same mother who designed "The Last Child's Bar/Bat Mitzvah" described in Chapter 5. Here, instead of calling people up to light a candle, they were called up, presented with a small plastic tree with Velcro backing, and invited to symbolically "plant" it somewhere on the big felt map of Israel that the bar mitzvah boy had designed and decorated with his mother. Each of these plastic trees represented a real tree that he was planting in Israel in honor of the person(s) being called up. He was paying for these trees with some of his gift money.

As each recipient came up, a different Israeli song was played and, as with the candlelighting ceremony, some words were spoken about the people being honored or remembered. I particularly liked his memory of his great aunt and her "juicy kisses." Shaanan explained his decision to do this by talking about the importance of trees (both symbolic and actual) in Judaism: "The Torah is known as the tree of life. It gives us a sense of roots and of always growing. Now I would like to honor some people who helped me and my family grow."

The Party's "Theme"

Another way to make the party Jewish, to integrate the secular and the sacred, is through the party's "theme."

You've heard all of the admonitions against secular themes. The party already has a theme, the Rabbis point out: It is the child's coming of age in the Jewish community. It's the theme of "love, devotion, and commitment," they tell us. No additional theme is necessary. And you've also heard—if an additional theme *is* necessary—about all kinds of Jewish themes that could be used: "Great Jewish Leaders Throughout History" (the Moses table, the Maimonides table, the Ben-Gurion table); "Great Jewish Books" (the Torah table, The Talmud table, the Siddur table); "Great Tzadakah Places" (the survival-center table, the homeless-shelter table, the soup-kitchen table). What you decide to do depends on who you are, who your friends are, where you live, what you want to emphasize. Again, my only advice in this regard is that you talk with each other and with your children about what meanings you want to communicate and how you want to do it.

Family Trees Grow on Tables

While I tend to agree with the Rabbis that additional themes aren't necessary, one family's creative elaboration on the theme of family caught my attention. They made family-tree centerpieces; each table had pictures focusing on a different part and a different era of the family's life. Some tables had pictures of the mother and her family back through the generations, others had pictures of the father and his family. Still others had pictures of the bar mitzvah child and his immediate family—when he was an infant, a toddler, in elementary school, etc. All of the pictures were labeled and dated and their placement was coordinated with the seating arrangements. (For example, at the table where most of the great-aunts and uncles on the father's side were seated, the family tree contained pictures of *their* relatives; at the tables with mostly the mother's family, the trees featured *their* family pictures.) The stories these pictures stimulated kept guests talking all through the meal. And after dinner, they walked around to other tables looking at the pictures there and talking with the relatives who knew *those* stories. It was really an intergenerational feast. People loved it. And the bar mitzvah boy's mother who had put it all together couldn't have been happier: "It was the motivation I had been waiting for for years. I finally had a deadline and a focus for collecting all of those pictures and all of the family history that came with them. I feel I've given everyone, not only my son, a really great present."

Seating: Who Eats with Whom and What Difference Does It Make?

For a seemingly minor detail, this one seems disproportionately charged. But maybe I'm biased because of my history. In my family, it was only my Uncle Bernie who was rich enough to have "sit-down affairs" for his sons' bar mitzvahs. Since he had three sons, there were three big dinner dances in my family and at least three big fights about who sat with whom. I was happy because I got to sit at the teenagers' table next to my cousin Billy's neighbor, Paul. He was gorgeous and my latest heartthrob. But everyone else was up in arms. As usual, my cousin Howard was at the in-between stage (in-between whatever the rest of us were). He was too young to sit at the table with me and Paul and there was no room for him to sit at the table with his parents and the rest of the aunts and uncles. So Bernie and Sarah put Howard at the children's table. When Aunt Edith picked up the little place-card at the entrance to the banquet hall and saw where her son would be sitting, she was furious, and let Sarah and Bernie and all of the other sisters- and brothers-in-law know. Uncle Irv, who'd had a fight with Edith about something similar at the family seder a few months earlier, chastised her for "souring the simcha." She was upsetting her sisters, one of whom was his wife Ethel, who was now defending her husband against my father, who thought Irv should have minded his own business. And so on. The next bar mitzvah was a variation on this theme and the one after that was yet another. These are the stories we cousins—who have by now all been bar and bat mitzvah parents ourselves—tell over and over again with laughter and with tears each time we all get together at another one of our parents' funerals. So you see, I'm not so objective about this particular detail.

Seating by Design

In the family-tree family I described earlier, it seemed simple enough—family segments were seated at separate tables. The mother's side, the father's side, the grandparents' generation, the cousins' generation, and so forth. Maybe there were similar conflicts—probably there were—but I wasn't close enough to see them.

In another family the thinking about seating was entirely different. This was a family in which the divorced parents had each remarried and the four adults were all committed to making this bat mitzvah work. They wanted the event to highlight their goodwill and cooperation. They were determined to use the dinner party as an opportunity for parts of the family who hadn't seen each other for years, such as ex–in-laws and ex-cousins to spend some time together. So the four of them got together and arranged the seating. They worked it out according to whom they knew had liked one another or whom they thought would enjoy meeting each other. What they wanted most of all was to give the bat mitzvah girl the experience of seeing the members of her four extended families "all together as integrated parts of her life" rather than as segmented fragments. It was quite a challenge and they pulled it off.

Doing it "right," as always, depends on what we value and what meaning we want to express.

Focus: The Child, Among Others

Most of the time when people think about the party, they think about how it should be fun for the bar/bat mitzvah child—not just an affair for grown-ups to enjoy. Absolutely. Of course it has to be fun. But when I think about the party and the child, I think also about meaning. Again, what are the messages? What do we want our kids to think about when they think about parties? What do we want them to remember when they think back to this one? Yes, they are the reason for the celebration, but not the only reason. Yes, the party is a kind of reward for all of the hard work and yes, it has to be fun for them and for their friends (and I know that the friends are a very strong influence), but how can we plan it so that it's also fun for Grandma and Uncle Izzy?

Separate or Together?

Foreseeing the challenge of making a party fun for such a wide range of ages and needs, many families gravitate to ways of separating the children's partying from the adults'. The sharpness of the separation ranges from separate tables and separate menus in the same location, to totally separate parties in separate rooms with separate music, separate entertainment, and so on.

When parents ask me ahead of time what I think about parties and generations, my advice most often is about ways of integrating the age-groups and highlighting the connections. On the symbolic level, keeping all of the age-groups together emphasizes the continuity between the world of the elders— the one the child is coming from—and the world of the next generation—the one he or she is going out into. For the parents and grandparents, the pleasure of seeing children running around and having a good time is life affirming. For the children, seeing the adults sitting at the tables creates a subliminal message about safety and protection. The children are not yet ready to be out there on their own, and thankfully they don't have to be.

Sex, Drugs, and Rock 'n' Roll

The party—along with all the other parties happening this year—is also a natural opportunity to talk with our children about social norms and peer pressure. How can we plan it so that the children behave appropriately—civilly and safely? What are the rules about alcohol, smoking, boys and girls alone together? A year full of bar/bat mitzvah parties means a lot of social learning. What lessons does this party provide?

OUT OF THE BABE'S MOUTH

The Weinsteins were worried. Two years ago Ira got a promotion, but it came with a relocation. The family was now living in a very different community, and the social pace—for adults and for children—was a more pressured one than they'd previously known. Ira and Gwen felt they could resist the intensity, but they weren't sure about their daughter Beth. She seemed to be growing up faster than they liked. Here she was "only twelve and a half!" and they were thinking the unthinkable. Their baby and booze? Their child and drugs?

Their sweet little girl and sex? How could they think such things, let alone talk about them? The slew of invitations from her classmates in Hebrew school and the fights about off-the-shoulder party dresses with hems that ended where they used to begin, were more than they could ignore. But, in fact, they did ignore what they were feeling. No one could talk about what was most frightening. The fights became more and more heated but didn't shed any light.

It was planning Beth's own party, however, that made the difference. And it was out of the mouth of the babe that the wisdom came. To their amazement, it was Beth who brought up the worries about drinking, drugs, and boys. It was she, experienced in the ways of such parties, who talked about how to make sure the kids weren't sneaking drinks, smoking in the bathroom, or necking behind the building. It was her talking about these activities that gave Ira and Gwen permission to start the conversation that was long overdue.

Not only did they talk to their daughter about their concerns, but together they decided on a number of strategies for making their party sane and safe: They told other parents what time to come and pick up their children, they told their young guests specifically where they could and could not go in the building, and what kind of behavior was expected. They also asked two slightly older cousins to act as informal chaperones for the teenagers and they instructed the DJ to keep the kids dancing and involved.

By the time their younger child was about to become a Bar Mitzvah, the Weinsteins had organized the bar/bat mitzvah class parents into meeting with the school principal and a local psychologist to discuss norms of adolescent development in their community. This meeting led to several workshops in which parents and children participated in structured opportunities to talk together about these issues.

As difficult as it is, most of us don't need to wait for the bar/bat mitzvah party to begin talking to our children in this way. Most of us don't need to wait for our children to lead in quite the way Beth did. And most of us won't be moved to organize a community response the way the Weinsteins did. But without a doubt, planning the party is an opening for talking with our children about social development and peer expectations. It is an opportunity to make talk possible that had previously been impossible. I encourage you to use it.

Chapter 12

Winding Down: It's Not Over Til It's Over (and Even Then It Doesn't Have to Be)

Like earlier parts of the process, the conclusion of the bar/bat mitzvah weekend is filled with paradox and possibility. Both relieved and saddened, we can't believe that the bar/bat mitzvah is ending. The event we'd spent so long anticipating is about to be history. But its repercussions are just beginning.

The morning after the service and the party is the beginning of the third phase of the ritual process, the phase of incorporation or reintegration. The changes that began so long ago, and that the ceremony and festivities have just celebrated, are now starting to seep in. In this phase we are beginning—both consciously and unconsciously—to absorb what happened and to incorporate its impact into our changing sense of ourselves. Yes, our baby *did* become a Bar/Bat Mitzvah. Yes, it was more powerful than we would ever have imagined, and yes, we really did pull it all off. In addition to this internal reckoning, we are also beginning the process of integrating this changed sense of ourselves into the workaday world we inhabited before we entered the sacred space of bar/bat mitzvah planning. Our special identity as "the bar/bat mitzvah family" will soon be only a memory. There is a lot that is ending and a lot that is beginning in this phase. Much readjusting once again.

With this in mind, we move on to the winding-down period of the bar/bat mitzvah weekend—and the opportunities inherent in what happens here.

Sunday Morning: Bagels, Lox, and Storytelling

The Sunday morning brunch before the out-of-towners leave can be more than just another occasion to feed people. In this more relaxed and informal setting, it can be another opportunity for connections. Take special advantage here of the gathered family's natural tendency to tell stories.

The Hoffmans decided to make the most of this occasion. They labeled the brunch a "storytelling hour" and asked guests to come prepared with old photos and stories. Together with their children, they created a list of questions they wanted answered and a list of topics they wanted to hear about. They also brought along the very incomplete genogram they had begun making as part of Hal's bar mitzvah preparations. They were hoping to gather a lot of missing information as one relative's story invariably jogged the memory of others. A friend of the Hoffmans videotaped this story exchange, and that tape has become a family treasure.

This was especially so as a year later Mrs. Hoffman's mother had a stroke. Although she survived, she never really recovered. The little ones in the family soon began to forget what Grandma had once been like. This video of her telling stories about her childhood in the Ukraine became a window through which they could remember.

Prolonging the Pleasure

Remember the suggestion that you ask friends to help? Here's a favor that can really make a difference: Arrange for others to take guests to the airport for their return flight. This way your celebrating doesn't have to end prematurely because of someone's early departure. Rushing to the airport (or to the train or the bus—or anywhere for that matter) is not the way you want to end this experience.

And speaking of endings, make it gradual. If at all possible, arrange for one or two special guests to stay on a day or so. Their presence will not only help you savor the pleasure and accomplishment of what you've just experienced, but will help ease your return to that routine, "secular" world that is waiting. To the extent that the bar/bat mitzvah weekend is somehow magical, leaving it is a transition from the extraordinary to the ordinary. It can be a letdown.

But many families have found ways to cushion the shift. Here are some examples: One family planned a celebratory dinner out during the week following the bar mitzvah and used it to talk with each other about what was best about the experience and what they could do to hold on to the glow. They also talked about what was worst and what they would do differently for the next child's celebration. One divorced couple planned a post–bar mitzvah family dinner a week after the event to talk about how well it had gone and to savor their pride in themselves and their child.

Another couple decided to give themselves a gift after it was over and planned a weekend away—by themselves. Yet another family began making plans for the bat mitzvah's anniversary. Not only were they going to arrange for their daughter to chant her Haftarah again next year in the synagogue, but they were going to use the occasion as the first gathering of the cousins' club that everyone at the party kept saying should be pulled together.

Even When It's Over, It's Not Over

As much as the post–bar/bat mitzvah time is an ending, it is also a beginning. The impact of all that has preceded is now beginning to reverberate. How do you want to hold onto the treasures you mined, the Jewish connections that got reinforced, the sense of competence and confidence that got amplified, the love that got intensified? How do you want to carry these meanings into the future?

On some very real level, you will be doing this whether you think about it or not. Changes have begun and changes have a life of their own. They will continue to reverberate internally and throughout the family for years to come. But increasingly, families are seeking out deliberate ways of reinforcing those changes that feel most important to them. Here are some strategies I've gleaned:

- Invite local friends and family to have dinner to look at pictures or watch the bar/bat mitzvah video with you— and to talk about what was most significant for them.
- Make the creation of a bar/bat mitzvah album a family event. Even if you've got a professional photographer putting together a formal album, make another with the snapshots you took and the copies people are sending of the ones they took (with their own cameras or with the disposable cameras you'd put out on each table). Do it as a scrapbook including memorabilia—the brochure you created, the notes people sent, a copy of the thank-you letter to the tutor and the Rabbi, copies of the speech, and so on. Label the pictures carefully: who everyone is

and how they're related. Let the children illustrate it, decorate it, and add their own messages to it.

- Send copies of special pictures to grandparents, aunts and uncles, cousins and friends. Talk together as a family about who would enjoy which pictures and why.

- Think about who in the family did *not* rise to the occasion as you would have wished. How might you talk to them about it? Who else might you talk to about it—a thoughtful friend, the Rabbi, a therapist? What other way of understanding what happened is possible and could be helpful? What can you do to de-escalate the tension, to prevent the episode from growing into a major family breach? How can you make "forgiveness" rather than "cutting off" the legacy that gets associated with your child's simcha? What can be learned from the disappointment? How can you use it to avoid similar pain in the future? None of this is easy, and sometimes it's really impossible, but the effort is immeasurably important.

- Make a list of people you're sorry you didn't get enough time with during the weekend. What kinds of trips can be planned during the upcoming year to *make* more time to be with these people? Or, more practically, might it make sense to decide who to call regularly, to write letters, send E-mail?

- Send a copy of the genogram (along with that list of family addresses and phone numbers) to others in the family who expressed interest.

- Review how the mitzvot you began doing regularly prior to the ceremony are continuing. Are there more or others that now seem possible?

- In what ways did the classes you took or the studying you did whet your appetite for more? What are you doing to continue your own Jewish education, and how does your thinking about this reflect on your thinking about your child's continued Jewish education? If in fact your child is planning not to return to Hebrew school, what other vehicles for learning and for staying connected to Judaism might you encourage—Jewish summer camps, youth groups, family study sessions, weekend retreats, or family camps? More and more alternative opportunities are becoming available. Take advantage of whichever you can to reinforce the meaning of what you have just done together. Use the conversational spaces the ritual opened for continued communication about the family's ongoing education. Try to do whatever you can so that your child does not grow up with only a thirteen-year-old's understanding of Judaism.

- What, of all the differences and continuities the bar/bat mitzvah was beginning to highlight—for your child, for you, for your parents—do you want to maintain, to amplify? What can you do to make that happen? You've learned so much during this process. The answers are there and you know how to find them.

Part V

The Big Picture

Chapter 13

From Ritual of Fate to Ritual of Promise: Enacting Our Best Selves

God, I am finally here. The last chapter of this book that I have, without knowing it at first, been working on for almost two decades. Maybe now I can stop processing the journey my family began with Louie's coming of age. Maybe now I can be finished with this bar/bat mitzvah obsession. Or maybe not. We seem to keep on surprising ourselves and each other with our internal discoveries and minitransformations. Just last week, Allen began teaching an adult education course in our synagogue—on Jewish music. What a long way from that conflicted first venture into Jewish ritual and our son's Haftarah chanting. And what an evolution I notice in myself as he changes. But that's another book.

What strikes me here are not the changes, but the constancies. It is amazing to me how much my fascination with bar/bat mitzvah continues. After all these years and all these pages, I am still absorbed by the phenomenon, by all that I understand and by all that remains mysterious.

In this chapter, I want to move beyond the pragmatic details and the specific pieces of advice. I want to explore some larger ideas about the role of this ritual in our contemporary, mostly secular, lives. I want to talk about paradox, performance, and meaning making.

The Paradox of Ritual

Life-cycle rituals are always paradoxical. They celebrate change while simultaneously maintaining the status quo. At their core, they are about both transformation *and* continuity. That's their magic. The well-known structure and shared meanings of the performance provide a way for cultures to maintain order and ward off chaos. They make potentially dangerous transitions safe: The bris allows us to incorporate new members without threat to the tribe; the funeral allows us to lose members with similar protection. Weddings permit individuals to go off together to create new little tribes, but at the same time ensure that those new entities remain part of the old one, not cut away from it. As we have seen throughout this book, the bar/bat mitzvah's central paradox is its ability to encourage our child to grow up and out, while at the same time strengthening the connections that keep us close.

Looking specifically at the contemporary version of this ritual, we see subparadoxes galore. The bar/bat mitzvah is simultaneously sacred and profane: From the Torah on the bimah to the limbo stick on the dance floor, the contradictions are obvious—and all part of the same occasion. The bar/bat mitzvah is both private and public, both an intimate family occasion and at the same time a public event, a cause for community response. It is a very old custom and a modern-day happening. On one hand it is about individual development and on the other about family evolution. It is about joy and about sadness, about belief and action, about the physical and the spiritual. It is both intrinsically meaningful and purposefully useful. It works magically, but it does not work magic. It is a protracted process *and* a Kodak moment. The bar/bat mitzvah—like all life-cycle rituals—is a profoundly complex and compelling phenomenon, its power derived precisely from its ability to contain these multiple contradictions.

But there are other paradoxes associated with bar/bat mitzvah that are unique to this event. The contemporary American bar/bat mitzvah is the most ridiculed of all public Jewish rituals and, at the very same time, the ritual that is most tenaciously retained—even by Jews who perform no other Jewish rituals. It is condemned as hollow show, yet ultimately seen as a loss by Jews who did not have one. It has become a most popular display of family tradition just as the definition of family is undergoing profound transformation. It is both a ritual of fate and a ritual of choice. It is simultaneously a ritual about what we have inherited and a ritual in which the celebrant—the child who is *becoming* a Bar or Bat Mitzvah—is saying, "I 'choose' to accept this inheritance."

The bar/bat mitzvah is about being counted (in the minyan), but it is a life-cycle ritual that doesn't change the count. No member of the community is either added or subtracted. No legal status is changed. The Bar/Bat Mitzvah is now counted in the adult community, but the actual and legal change in census happened with this child's birth. Indeed, any Jew a day older than thirteen is counted in the minyan. No ceremony is necessary. And since nothing legal changes, there are no laws—religious or secular—that regulate the change. The bar/bat mitzvah "certificate," unlike the birth, marriage, or death certificate, or even the high school diploma, is never demanded. No proof of this transition is ever called for, no ceremony marking it ever *required*.

So why do we cling to this ritual that has no legal or religious status, to this ritual that is, in fact, so often—and so understandably—ridiculed: "A trial by decoration"?

> *"We know them by what they celebrate."*
> —Ralph Waldo Emerson

Why has the bar/bat mitzvah become one of the most popular of all Jewish rituals, at a time when we have abandoned most others? I believe the reasons for this go beyond the usual explanations about nostalgia, guilt, and marketplace manipulation. Something authentic is happening on that bimah, and whatever it is—whatever combination of truths—it is that authenticity that keeps the practice of bar/bat mitzvah alive. I have no proof of this, of course, no scientifically verifiable data (but not everything that is important can be measured). All I have are some possible pieces of explanation, some ideas floating around this phenomenon that help me make sense of it:

- It is precisely *because* we have abandoned so many other rituals, so many other connections to our past and our people, that contemporary secular Jews are clinging to the few ritual remnants that *have* survived. For Jews whom sociologists would label "minimally affiliated" or "marginally identified," the bar/bat mitzvah is one of the few remaining means of publicly expressing and connecting with the family's Jewish identity.
- This expression of our identity as Jews meshes with our "postmodern" generation's loss of faith in science and our increasingly respectful attitude toward things spiritual. It fits for us: Boomers facing our parents' death and simultaneously watching our children grow up with so little of the history and tradition that had been such an important part of their grandparents' identities. Ours is

a generation saddened and seeking, a generation marked by desire for new ways of making meaning.

- Because the bar/bat mitzvah is a "folk" custom rather than an edict prescribed by halachic law, it has been able to evolve over the years according to the needs and circumstances of the successive generations. It still "fits," more or less, with most contemporary Jews' sense of themselves. It is both a religious event and a cultural event, an admixture of the sacred and the secular that reduces the distinctions between what sociologists call "folk" and "elite" Judaism. It is a blending of tradition and invention that—as Rabbi Abraham Isaac Kook, first chief Rabbi of Israel, put it many years ago—allows "the old to become new and the new to become holy."

  Since our immigrant days, the bar/bat mitzvah's flexibility has enabled participants to merge Jewish values and American values; it has enabled us to celebrate our children as good Jews *and* as good citizens. With its folk flexibility, the bar/bat mitzvah has been able to accommodate not only the changes in our definition of ritual, but the changes in our definition of ourselves as well.

- The bar/bat mitzvah is a quintessentially Jewish ritual in that it is simultaneously child-centered and family-centered. The focus is on the child, but the child comes into focus as part of the family, the boundaries of each unit are blurred. The bar/bat mitzvah is also a ritual particularly appropriate for our times. It celebrates both the traditional sanctity of the family and the contemporary sacredness of the individual. It is a dramatic expression of what some feminist researchers call "self in relationship."

- No matter what the family's level of religious observance, the bar/bat mitzvah is psychologically useful. To remain healthy, a family with an emerging adolescent needs to accomplish certain developmental tasks. It needs to provide ways to demonstrate the child's increased autonomy (within a consistent connection), to mourn the loss embedded in that autonomy, to deal with the changing needs of elderly parents, and to face the necessary evolution of the couple's relationship. As we have seen throughout this book, the months of preparation surrounding the ceremony, those "hinges of time," are precisely those moments in which relationships are more fluid and all of these transitional tasks become more possible.

• Through the bar/bat mitzvah, the family and the sacred, at some level, merge. Despite the distinction we usually make between the sacred and the secular, between the religious reasons for the bar/bat mitzvah and the family reasons for it, they are obviously not so distinct. The Talmud makes this merging clear. It teaches that "to hear your child's child reading Torah is like hearing the words from Sinai itself." In Judaism, the creation of family is sacred, and the sacred is conveyed *through* the family. The bar/bat mitzvah is a perfect opportunity for remembering our parents' lives in our own lives and in the lives of our children. This, religion professor Arnold Eisen tells us, is not nostalgia for its own sake, but "the nostalgia that moves us to Jewish observance because of our commitment to venerating our ancestors." Dr. Eisen goes so far as to say that for contemporary Jews, nostalgia is itself a mitzvah!

• In our post-Holocaust world, the merging of family and religious sanctity is intensified and important. As Jacob Nuesner eloquently points out in his book, *The Enchantments of Judaism* (Basic Books, 1987), for post-Holocaust Jews, with "no past prior to the immigrant generation, [and] no past outside of America," there is a profound concern with the future and a deep fear of being "the last Jew on earth." For these Jews, "there is a deep sense . . . [that] one's generation marks a turning, either downward or upward toward an open future." And "the choice is made for life every time a bar or bat mitzvah is celebrated." The bar/bat mitzvah becomes "a remedy to that sense of loss and absence. It forms a past and it points toward a future; the newly mature young man or woman is the link."

In this way of thinking, the Torah and bar/bat mitzvah child get connected, and, in effect, transformed. The Torah informs the child and the child gives Torah new life. Symbolically, the Bar/Bat Mitzvah—carrying the Torah through the congregation—momentarily "becomes" the Torah, and the family and relatives crowding to kiss the Torah are simultaneously kissing the child as well.

> *"We become what we display."*
> —Mircea Eliade

Despite all of these elements of explanation, I can still hear the critics: "Yes, the bar/bat mitzvah has gained in importance, but not in significance." It is still "a riteless passage, and a passageless rite." Neither the kid nor the family will be in shul the Saturday following the bar mitzvah. Neither the kid nor the family will be doing anything differently in their daily lives. The only real change is that Hebrew school attendance will no longer be enforced. And the cousins won't be calling again for months. Just like it used to be. The bar/bat mitzvah performance, say these critics, is just that: Performance. Hollow theater.

As you'd expect, I have a different take on the meaning of the performance. It is based not only on what I have observed, but on what experts tell us about the primal function of this kind of enactment. According to Barbara Myerhoff, the anthropologist who wrote *Number Our Days*, a groundbreaking study of an elderly Jewish community in California, "In ritual drama, *we show ourselves to ourselves.*" We show ourselves not only as we are, but "as we might yet become." *The bar/bat mitzvah performance, then, is not a sham, but a wish, a hope, a promise.* Through it we are enacting the story of our "best selves," the selves toward which we are reaching. It is no accident that grammatically the child is not "getting bar/bat mitzvahed," but is *becoming* a Bar or Bat Mitzvah. If what the early anthropologist Mircea Eliade said is true, that "we become what we display," then the bar/bat mitzvah is a performance through which we display our reaching for the most authentic expression of our hopes—not only for our child, but for our parents, ourselves, and our future as a Jewish people.

In ritual performance, says Myerhoff, doing is believing. We are performing an act of imagination, one that has the possibility of transforming what "is" into what yet "could be." Words embedded in symbolic action have magic. The very act of stating that the child and family are changing—emotionally, religiously, developmentally—reinforces those changes that are being celebrated. Rabbi Salkin tells us there are no atheists in the foxhole or on the bimah. Dr. Myerhoff tells us that ritual performance has the capacity "to make the impossible momentarily beyond question." They are saying the same thing.

When the performance is successful, we experience rather than believe. The bar/bat mitzvah is a public enactment of an ongoing process, the evolving story we are telling progeny, parents, and peers. In the liminal, "threshold" space of the ritual act, in that moment when evocative symbols and gathered family interact most intensively, something sacred is happening—even for those who entered the process not expecting it, for those who entered for reasons that critics would call "decorative" rather than authentic.

When the performance is successful, according to Myerhoff, the private is made public and the public (performance) becomes integrated into our private identities. Something *does* change both for the celebrants and for the witnesses. For some, the change is explicit and intentional, for others more implicit and unconscious. For some, the change is immediate, for others, the effect becomes known only far in the future. For some, the consequences of the process can be verbalized, and for others, not. And even for those who think they can describe what happened, the description is necessarily only partial. So much remains unknown and unfolding. What we are left with in ritual (as in life) is interpretation, not fact. What we are left with is the ways we make meaning.

Like all life-cycle rituals, the bar/bat mitzvah is a kind of treasure trove, rich with possibility and potential. Which gems we choose depends on who we are and what we define as valuable. The meanings we make depend on what aspects of the experience we focus on and through which lenses we choose to look. The meanings we make get expressed in our behaviors, our perceptions, our emotions, and our beliefs.

From the ultraorthodox family where the mother watches with joy from behind the traditional divider, to the family who know themselves as Jewish Buddhists and who open the bat mitzvah ceremony with meditation and a quote from the Dalai Lama, the experience is both extraordinarily the same and extraordinarily different.

It is within this sameness and this difference that you are making your meanings and authoring your stories. May you and your child continue to reach high and reach deep. Mazel tov.

Postscript

A Rosh Hashanah Gift and a Thank-You to the Families Whose Stories I've Used

A couple of years ago I was in the synagogue on Rosh Hashanah. Several rows ahead of me and to my left were Margot and her son Jeffrey who had been in my original study in the mid-eighties. As I watched them—the mother as animated as ever, the son now a tall and handsome young man—I kept thinking of their bar mitzvah story, its pain and its beauty. They have no idea how much they are still alive in my head, I thought with a vague sense of guilt. After all these years, I am still using them, first for the dissertation and now for the book.

Walking out of the synagogue at the end of the service, Margot came over to greet me, and then went on to tell me again how much she'd appreciated my work. "You know, sometimes when I'm blue, I reread those pages of your dissertation that I Xeroxed from the library. Ken's mother is in a nursing home now. After the bar mitzvah she said that that would be the last affair she'd ever go to, and from that time on she started going downhill. Now she's so drugged-up that she's hardly alive anymore. But whenever I want to remember her as she used to be, I go back to your description of her. You caught her language and her spirit so well. I always tell Jeffrey that if he wants to remember his grandmother as she used to be, he should read what you wrote."

What a gift Margot gave me.

"Thank you," I said, eyes (for a change) brimming. "You have no idea how much that means to me. You won't believe this, but I'm still thinking about all of you very much. I'm trying to turn what I learned from the dissertation into a book for families. And your stories and your experience are still so vivid and so useful."

"Oh, that would be wonderful. I can't wait to read it."

"I'll send you a copy; we should live so long."

Here it is, Margot. Thank you. And thank you again to all who have shared with me your stories and your lives.

Additional Readings

Diamant, Anita, and Howard Cooper. *Living a Jewish Life: Jewish Traditions, Customs and Values for Today's Families.* New York: Harper Perennial, 1991.

Goldin, Barbara Diamond. *Bat Mitzvah: A Jewish Girl's Coming of Age.* New York: Viking, 1995.

Grishaver, Joel. *Forty Things You Can Do to Save the Jewish People: Some Really Practical Ideas for Parents Who Want to Raise "Good Enough" Jewish Kids to Insure That the Jewish People Last Another Generation.* Los Angeles: Alef Design Group, 1993.

Kimmel, Eric. *Bar Mitzvah: A Jewish Boy's Coming of Age.* New York: Viking, 1995.

Leneman, Helen, editor. *Bar/Bat Mitzvah Basics: A Practical Family Guide to Coming of Age Together.* Woodstock, VT: Jewish Lights Publishing, 1996.

Pipher, Mary. *Reviving Ophelia: Saving the Selves of Adolescent Girls.* New York: Ballantine, 1994.

Pipher, Mary. *The Shelter of Each Other: Rebuilding Our Families*. New York: Ballantine, 1996.

Salkin, Jeffrey. *Putting God on the Guest List: How to Reclaim the Spiritual Meaning of Your Child's Bar or Bat Mitzvah*. Woodstock, VT: Jewish Lights Publishing, 1992.

Strassfeld, Sharon, and Kathy Green. *The Jewish Family Book: A Creative Approach to Raising Kids*. New York: Bantam, 1981.